Wisconsin's Carlisle Indian School Immortals

Native American Sports Heroes Series
Volume II

Wisconsin Indian Reservations

Wisconsin's Carlisle Indian School Immortals

Tom Benjey

Carlisle, Pennsylvania

©2011, 2024 by Tom Benjey
Published by Tuxedo Press
Carlisle, PA 17015
Tuxedo-Press.com

All rights reserved. No part of this publication may be reproduced, stored in a retrieval system, or transmitted, in any form or by any means, electronic, mechanical, photocopying, recording, or otherwise without the permission of Tuxedo Press.

ISBN 978-1-936161-22-5 softcover
ISBN 978-1-936161-21-8 hardback

Cover illustration by Lone Star Dietz for Carlisle Industrial School ephemera, 1910. Frontispiece from American Indian Reservations and Trust Areas, U.S. Department of Commerce, 1996.

Library of Congress Cataloging-in-Publication Data
Benjey, Tom.
    Wisconsin's Carlisle Indian school immortals / Tom Benjey.
         p. cm. -(Native American sports heroes series; v.2)
    Includes bibliographical references and index.
    ISBN 978-1-936161-21-8 - ISBN 978-1-936161-22-51. United States
Indian School (Carlisle, Pa.)-Football. 2. Indian athletes-Pennsylvania-Carlisle-Biography. 3. Football players-Pennsylvania-Carlisle-Biography. I. Title.
    GV958.U33B465 2010
    796.332'630974843-dc22

2010015351

To the late Bob Carroll for his tireless work in preserving football history

Contents

	Contents	vii
	Introduction	1
1	Football Trail of Glory	7
2	Indians Turn Pro	40
3	All-Indian Teams	62
4	Glenn Scobey Warner	70
5	Chauncey Archiquette	86
6	Wilson Charles	102
7	Wallace Denny	116
8	Lone Star Dietz	144
9	Louis Island	164
10	James Johnson	175
11	Frank Lone Star	189
12	Jonas Metoxen	197
13	Thomas St. Germain	211
14	Caleb Sickles	218

15	George Vedernack	234
16	Gus Welch	242
17	Joel and Hugh Wheelock	269
18	Martin Wheelock	281
19	Charles Williams	298
20	William Winneshiek	304
	Appendices	321
	Bibliography	322
	Index	326

Introduction

The on-field accomplishments of Carlisle Indian School football teams have been written about several times and were remarkable. But what these men achieved off-field after leaving Carlisle is equally impressive. Over a quarter century before Indians were granted citizenship and the right to vote, three-quarters of a century before the 1965 Civil Rights Bill, and almost a century before affirmative action laws were introduced, Carlisle Indian School football teams competed toe-to-toe with the best in the land and more than held their own. Some today may consider the Carlisle School to be affirmative action in its purest form because enrollment was limited to students of at least one-quarter Indian blood with tuition, room, board, clothing and health care being paid by the government. Others view Carlisle quite differently. They think Richard Henry Pratt's assimilation policy of maintaining constant contact with the dominant society stripped students of their heritage and alienated them from their families and tribes. Regardless of one's opinion of Pratt, an extraordinary number of the Carlisle football players overcame obstacles placed in their way by prejudice common at that time and accomplished much in life after leaving the school. This book is the story of their triumphs and failures. Unfortunately, only those whose activities were recorded at the time in newspapers or were saved in archives can be written about. There are surely many others whose lives are worthy of inclusion but for whom documentation has not been found.

John S. Steckbeck's 1951 seminal *Fabulous Redmen: the Carlisle Indians and their famous football teams* provided a year-by-year history of the legendary Carlisle Indian Industrial School (CIIS) football program, a variety of statistics about the team, and blurbs about coaches and individual players. Much has been written about mega-star Jim Thorpe and Coach of All Ages Pop Warner. The author recently completed the biography of Lone Star Dietz. These three were not the only Carlisle football stars by any means. They're not even the only Carlisle Indians in the College Football Hall of Fame. Besides Thorpe, five other players were inducted years ago, and Lone Star Dietz is on the ballot for induction as a coach. At least twelve others received All-America mention. Warner is in the Hall in good part due to the work he did coaching the Indians and developing formations that mitigated their weaknesses and exploited their strengths.

Some—many as it turns out—Carlisle players continued their football careers after leaving the school, some as coaches, some as players, and some both as players and coaches. So many of them went into coaching that they helped make the Warner system the dominant offensive scheme during the first half of the 20th century. Some were present at the birth of professional football, while others made the NFL popular when it was in its infancy. Carlisle Indian School footballers played important roles in the development of the sport from the late 1890s through the 20th century up to WWII. Some lived public lives outside of sports and made their mark in other fields after departing from Carlisle. Unfortunately, few people alive today are aware of the Indians' contributions and their names have been largely forgotten. This book attempts to correct that situation. Those who led private lives after leaving Carlisle left behind little documentation of the accomplishments, which makes them difficult to cover. The information that can be found on them is interjected at appropriate places. Because there is no obvious thread among these individuals other than they played football at Carlisle, the book takes the form of a set of mini-biographies.

The first chapter of the book is a brief history of the Carlisle program, from beginning to end. It is intended that this chapter will provide the reader a framework from which to relate the individuals to the team and the phase of the program. The second chapter is a brief history of professional football in America, the early part of which overlaps closely with Carlisle's lifespan. This chapter is necessary because independent or professional football provided opportunities for Carlisle players after their schooling was completed. Indians also played major roles in developing the new game. Two of them, Jim Thorpe and Joe Guyon, are enshrined in the Professional Football Hall of Fame in Canton, Ohio. The third chapter briefly discusses some all-Indian teams on which Carlisle alums played after leaving the school. The fourth chapter covers Glenn S. "Pop" Warner, the coach for the glory days of the football program and a factor in these men's lives. Because Warner is referenced so frequently, it is clearer for the reader unfamiliar with him for his chapter to precede the players' chapters rather than follow them.

The remaining chapters, other than the final one, cover Carlisle players to varying levels of detail, dependent largely on the amount of information that can be found about the person. Their stories are arranged in alphabetical order with brothers sharing chapters. Little further needs to be written about Jim Thorpe or Pop Warner, but some readers may not be familiar with their histories. Therefore, a chapter is dedicated to each to provide a background for the unfamiliar. It is my hope that a previously undiscovered nugget or two about each of them finds its way into the narrative. The amount of space devoted to the others is not intended to be a measure of the significance of their contributions. The amount of information available about them today is the limiting factor. Professional football received little press in its early days, leaving behind fewer accounts of games and meetings than we'd like. Some players and coaches received little press due to their personalities, and others toiled in out-of-the-way places. The last chapter discusses the importance of team captains in the early days of football and recounts a story of courage on the part of several Carlisle captains. The author hopes that people familiar with persons included in this book will share enough tidbits previously unknown about those players to make a second edition necessary. Little is included about the females who attended Carlisle beyond those who married players, not because their stories aren't interesting but because that would require an entire book of its own.

Col. Pratt raised the issue of how football players perform in later life at the 1902 football banquet in his talk titled, "By their fruits you shall know them." Pratt talked about how he came to discuss this topic and then talked about the methodology he used in his "study:"

> I went to the old football pictures, called on the memories of oldest inhabitants and used my own, and succeeded in getting together the names of sixty who have played on our first teams and have gone out from the school. I have put down here and made a mark opposite each one from my memory and the memories of those who know most about it, and from the best information we have I find some very singular results....
>
> Of the list of sixty who played on the first teams (I may not have them all) I have written opposite the names of forty-nine the letters "O. K." You know what that means.
>
> There are only five of the sixty named that we need be ashamed of. There are four about whom I have been unable to get any information. That leaves two. We have been playing football more than twelve years and have sent out from the school at least sixty, as I have said, who played on our first teams, and only two of the sixty have passed away, and that shows that football is a healthy business.

This was the first known attempt to determine how or if football players succeeded after leaving school, but it wouldn't be the last. On at least two other occasions, in 1907 and 1910, and likely others, Superintendents Mercer and Friedman sent questionnaires to former athletes to gather data on their lives after Carlisle. Many of the quotes in this book that the athletes themselves wrote about Carlisle come from those questionnaires that can be found in former student files. It is likely that the superintendents were selective in determining to whom to send questionnaires, more selective in determining which results to keep in the files, and even more selective in choosing responses to print in school publications. So, the results may well have been biased to make the school look good, but the responses that survive were freely given and accurately reflect the thinking of the person writing them.

While researching this book, the author examined a number of census forms and made some observations. Prior to and during their time at Carlisle, students were generally listed on special forms used specifically for populations likely to contain Indians. A section of the form listed the tribes of the person and the person's parents. It also included the fraction of white blood the student was thought to have. The data on these forms was often incorrect because the child did not know the correct information or because the census taker made assumptions and errors. After leaving Carlisle, those who assimilated into the larger society were often classified as white in future censuses, probably because census takers didn't bother to ask. Indians in the population may have been undercounted as a result.

Period illustrations, particularly cartoons, will be included where appropriate to show how the Carlisle team was treated, even by big city newspapers. Today many of these caricatures with oversized noses and other exaggerations would be considered racist. Others make fun of the patricians the Indians so often defeated.

Sit back and enjoy reading about the exploits of Chauncey Archiquette, Lone Star Dietz, Wallace Denny, James Johnson, Caleb Sickles, William Winneshiek, Gus Welch and all the rest. You will surely become acquainted with some interesting individuals you may have never heard of before. Surely some interesting people will be missed, but if information on them surfaces, they will be included in a second edition.

>   Min-ni-wa-ka!
>   Ka-wa-wi!
>   Woop her up!
>   Woop her up!
>   Who are we?
>   Carlisle!
>   Carlisle!!
>   Carlisle!!!

1

Football Trail of Glory

In 1875, Lt. Richard Henry Pratt, after many years of leading Buffalo Soldiers in battle against Kiowa, Cheyenne and Arapaho warriors, was assigned the task of transporting 72 Indian prisoners to St. Augustine, Florida for three years of captivity at Ft. Marion. During the imprisonment, with the influence of Quaker reformers, Pratt evolved the belief that the only hope for Indians to survive in the modern world was to assimilate into the majority culture, much as European immigrants were assimilating. His view was in sharp contrast to that of those who believed that extermination was the only viable option. Gen. Philip Sheridan denied having said, "The only good Indians I ever saw were dead." If he believed it, he was far from alone as that was a very common belief held at the time.

Their confinement over, Lt. Pratt convinced 17 of his former prisoners to pursue further education at Hampton Institute (now Hampton University). The Hampton, Virginia school had been founded a decade earlier by Gen. Samuel Chapman Armstrong as a boarding school to educate recently freed slaves by training "the head, the hand, and the heart." Educating African-Americans and American Indians in the same facility, although segregated from each other, was controversial to some in those times of racial segregation as many thought that blacks and Indians were not educable. However, the experiment was successful enough that Hampton Institute continued its Indian division until 1923.

Richard Pratt, son of a singing Methodist, summarized his philosophy as, "Kill the Indian, save the man." He formulated a model similar to that being used at Hampton and successfully lobbied the government to set up a school just for Indians at an unused Army post. On October 6, 1879, Lt. Pratt, considered by some to be "an honest lunatic," and the first contingent of students, largely sons of Lakota chiefs (boys had little economic value when confined to reservations because they could no longer hunt buffalo or make war, but families could still receive a bride price for girls), arrived at the Carlisle Indian Industrial School located in Carlisle Barracks, adjacent to Carlisle, Pennsylvania. America's second oldest military facility—the one that housed the Hessian troops captured at Trenton by Gen. George Washington after crossing the Delaware—was not being used and thus made available for the Indian boarding school.

Students divided their days between academic studies and vocational training. They dressed in military uniforms and lived regimented lives. Free-time activities included music, athletics and literary or debating societies. Although Carlisle Indian Industrial School was essentially a trade school coupled to elementary and high school academics, Pratt envisioned some of his students advancing to college and professional schools. Extracurricular activities, particularly the literary and debating societies, helped prepare higher level students for further

Richard Henry
Pratt, Susan &
Mary Longstreth,
Spotted Tail,
Rebecca Haines
*U. S. Army
Military History
Institute*

academic work as well as to think more critically and to communicate more clearly, skills that would serve future leaders well. Although Pratt desired that his former students assimilate into the dominant culture, many returned to their tribes and used the skills learned at Carlisle to become effective tribal leaders.

By the early 1900s, the girls and boys each had two societies from which to select: the Susan Longstreth Literary Society, the Mercer Literary Society, the Standard Literary Society and the Invincible Debating Society, respectively. Susan Longstreth, a Quaker educator who operated a school in Philadelphia for young ladies for 50 years, was a long-time supporter of Pratt's experiment. Major Mercer was the superintendent of the school after Pratt departed. These societies were much more than what their names imply as some of them formed bands, played sports, held dances and put on plays. They also had their own colors and elected officers as did the Freshman, Sophomore, Junior and Senior classes. Besides the usual officers, all of these groups elected a Critic, whose function may not be obvious to modern readers. The author found a definition in the *1918 Quittapahilla,* Lebanon Valley College's yearbook: "Over each meeting presides the Critic and he, by mode of criticism, points out the strength and weakness of the respective numbers with special reference to errors in style, English grammar, elocution, logic, literary structure and the speakers' manner on the floor." While some of the details may vary between schools and organizations, the description will hold in the main.

Rather than returning to their reservations during school breaks, students received practical experience in their "outing" periods working off-campus at farms and businesses to further expose them to the dominant culture. In order to "kill the Indian," Pratt kept his charges away from their families and tribes three, four or five years at a time, depending on their period of enrollment. In 1883, explaining his philosophy, he wrote, "In Indian civilization I am a Baptist, because I believe in immersing the Indians in our civilization and when we get them under holding them there until they are thoroughly soaked."

Part of Carlisle's curriculum included off-campus work and study with white families in the East. The government saved money by not having to house and feed the children during the outings. Students had the opportunity to earn money of their own and were forced to save a significant portion of it. As the school's superintendent, Pratt constantly battled Congress for funding and did not fare very well. He was not shy about publicly criticizing the government's stinginess and other shortcomings, particularly those in the Bureau of Indian Affairs.

The outing period was essential to keep costs within budget. However, some other funding sources would emerge.

One day in 1893, Superintendent Pratt was sitting in his office attending to administrative trivia when he heard a knock. He opened the door to see forty of the school's finest athletes standing outside with something on their minds. Pratt invited them into his office and the school's best orator stepped forward. The boy presented his case so eloquently that, although so personally opposed to football that he had banned its play because serious injuries had occurred in some games played in 1890, Pratt agreed to reinstate inter-school contests. However, he had two conditions:

1894 Carlisle Indians; *Cumberland County Historical Society, Carlisle, PA*

1. You must never slug. Because if you slug another player, the people who are watching the game will say that you are just savages.
2. In two, three or four years, the Carlisle football team will whip the biggest team in the country.

Thus, inter-collegiate football was born at Carlisle. Actually the Carlisle Indian Industrial School was never a college, but its opponents included the most famous institutions of higher learning. Soon, the school newspaper would report on "football hair" sprouting on campus each September.

In keeping with Pratt's admonition, the Carlisle team scheduled Yale and Penn, two of the "Big Four," (Harvard, Yale, Princeton and Penn) in just their second full season of play and still posted a 4-4-0 record! The next year, 1896, Carlisle played and lost to all of the "Big Four" in successive weeks as well as to Brown, but they won the rest of their games to avoid a losing season. The Harvard and Yale games were close enough that the Indians could have at least tied either of them. The father of American football, Walter Camp, said, "The team must have put up a capital game with Harvard, and their work this season certainly shows that they are in the first class." Frank Cayou scored the first points scored against Yale that season when he raced 75 yards for a touchdown. Several writers considered the calling back of Jake Jamison's touchdown in the same game to be a major officiating blunder that cost the Indians a tie with the Eli. *The New York Sun* was favorably impressed by their play against Yale: "Never was a team seen on the football field who fought harder, fairer and with so little unnecessary rough play." *The Sun* also thought the game should have been a tie were it not for an official's blunder. The *Rochester Advertiser* echoed that sentiment in a caustic tone: "Now, if we have a right to rob the Indian anywhere we certainly have a right to cheat him out of football games." Not only did the team survive the suicidal schedule, but they also convinced the experts that they were first rate. Newspapers alternated between romanticizing the Indians, praising them for their stoicism or clean play, and belittling them, claiming that they could not rebound from adversity while ignoring the evidence to the contrary. Headline writers and cartoonists were often not very charitable. Indians were often said to ambush their opponents or massacre unwary teams. Players were often depicted as sneaky, skulking marauders or as caricatures with large noses and buck teeth. Scalping knives and tomahawks were often shown as being at the ready.

At the end of the 1896 season, Carlisle started what became near-traditions: Thanksgiving and post-season games. The Indians lost to Brown University 24–12 on Thanksgiving Day, and a post-season game against Wisconsin in Chicago was added. The Indians defeated the Champions of the West 18–8 indoors under the lights in the Chicago Coliseum. This was the Indians' first trip out of the East. Many more would follow.

The November issue of Carlisle Indian Industrial School's newspaper, *The Red Man,* was subtitled "Games With The Big 4," and its eight pages contained reprints of articles from

Skulking Indian; *New York Journal* 10-24-1897

newspapers around the country. Typical was the editorial from the *Boston Herald:*

> The statement in our account of the football game on Saturday between the teams of the Carlisle school of Indians and Harvard, that, if the men making up the former had scientific training added to the strength, quickness and endurance which they now possess, no college team in the country could stand against them, is a conclusion endorsed by most of the college graduates and undergraduates who are experts in football and who witnessed the game.

That scientific training wouldn't arrive for a few more years, but Carlisle competed while waiting.

The Indians sported a new look for 1897: uniforms in their school colors. A committee headed by former student then vocal teacher, Mary Bailey, researched the issue of school colors over the summer of 1896 and students voted to accept the committee's recommendation at the first Saturday evening meeting of the 1896–97 school year. It was too late to obtain football uniforms in school colors for the season about to start, so 1897 was the first year the Indian first team was clad in Red and Old Gold. Not too late for 1896 was "Carlisle Indian School March," composed by former student and then current bandmaster, Dennison Wheelock. It was played at football games and other events. Carlisle was also honored with another march that year. Celebrated pianist Robert Tempest of Philadelphia, who had recently visited the school, wrote "Roosters of Carlisle," borrowing an Indian melody that had been printed in the school paper for the refrain.

The football program was generating considerable revenue for the school by this time. *The Indian Helper* of April 17, 1896 reported on one use of the proceeds: "The 28 shower baths in the gymnasium are well patronized. These are not to take the place of the tub bath, but are in addition to the weekly scrub all hands are required to take."

Carlisle played, and lost, to three of the Big Four in 1897 by respectable scores, ending up at 6–4–0 in its first winning season. Carlisle once again suffered four losses in 1898, coming up short against three of the Big Four for another 6–4–0 record. However, the team took another post-season road trip, beating Illinois, Cincinnati and The Ohio State University Medical College in just seven days. In five short years, Carlisle had established itself as one of the better teams in the country just below the Big Four. The Indians were very close to achieving what Pratt had directed them to do.

1899 was a pivotal year for Carlisle football because Pratt's first choice for head coach, Glenn S. "Pop" Warner, finally became available. Pratt, not knowledgeable about football himself, had asked Walter Camp, the country's foremost authority, to recommend a coach. Camp suggested a young, innovative coach by the name of Glenn Scobey Warner, better known as Pop. However, Warner was not available until internal politics convinced him to leave his alma mater, Cornell. When Warner asked for $1,200 for the season plus expenses, Pratt didn't blink. After some minor negotiations, they shook hands and a new era started. The football world would be forever changed when "The Old Fox" took the coaching reins of this up-and-coming team of undersized footballers and embarked on a grueling schedule. Carlisle players gained their first victory over one of the Big Four when they defeated the Penn Quakers 16–5 in Philadelphia. *The Red Man* was so proud of that victory that it put "WON" in all capital letters by the score for that game. Carlisle students, led by their band, began a tradition of parading through town in their nightshirts after important victories.

They lost to two of the Big Four that year, Harvard and Princeton. The 22–10 loss to Harvard happened without the services of team captain and star player Martin Wheelock, who was too ill to play. The players were treated to a post-season rail trip to San Francisco (they always traveled first class) where they defeated the University of California 2–0 on Christmas Day. This road trip may have been the longest taken by a football team up to that time. The Warner era at Carlisle had begun with a 9–2–0 season, their best so far, a victory over one of the Big Four and capped with a win over previously unbeaten Cal. On the way back, Warner agreed to play an exhibition game with the Phoenix Indian School team that was coached by a Harvard alum. Because Harvard had switched to leather uniforms that year, so had the Phoenix coach. The players roasted in the leather suits and were soon exhausted. The Carlisle team stayed on for a few days and shared pigskin tricks with the locals. At season's end, Isaac Seneca was named

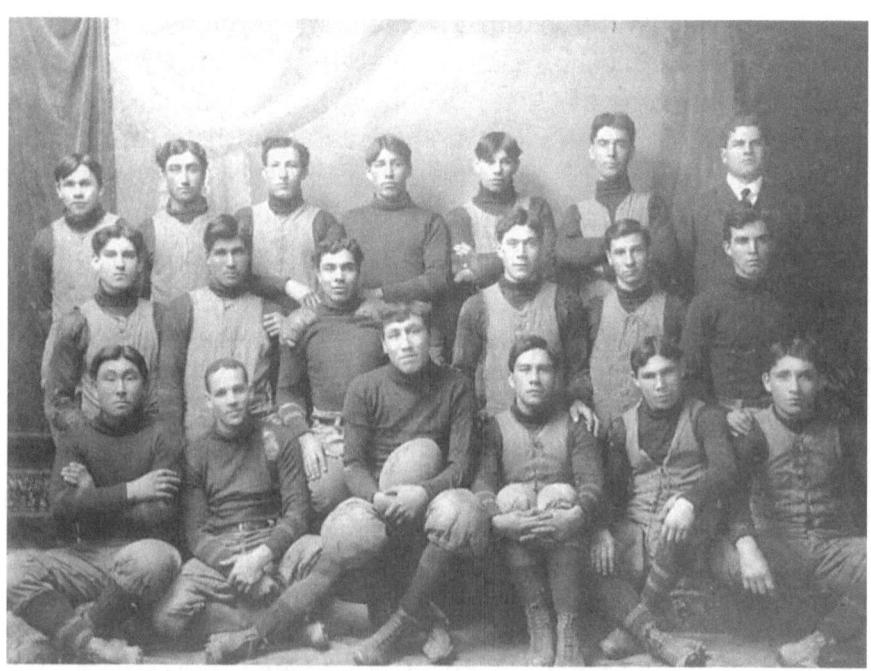

1902 Carlisle Indian School Football team
Cumberland County Historical Society, Carlisle, PA

to Walter Camp's All-America team, the first Indian to receive the honor and one of the few players outside the Big Four to be selected.

The 6–4–1 1900 season was a bit of a letdown for the Red and Old Gold, with losses to the three of the Big Four they played and, for the first time since 1895, there was no postseason road trip. The undersized 1901 team lost a close one to Penn 16–14 and, crippled by injuries, was beaten by Harvard 29–0. However, Carlisle did not have another losing season for over a decade.

Carlisle returned to winning ways in 1902 with an 8–3–0 season, splitting with the Big Four by losing to Harvard and beating Penn for the second time. The *Philadelphia Press* summed it up, "There was no doubt about the victory as the Red Man outplayed his palefaced foe at all points of the game and tied the second Red and Blue scalp firmly to his belt by the decisive score of 5–0." On defense much of the game, Carlisle scored a touchdown early in the second half, missed the extra point and played field position the rest of the way in an extremely hard-fought game with the improving Quakers.

The 1903 squad led by All-America quarterback James Johnson was probably the best Carlisle squad to date. The Indians lost to Princeton and Harvard but beat Penn again 16–6. The one-point 12–11 Harvard loss was a heartbreaker for the players, coming oh so close but still losing. It was also the game in which big Charles Dillon, a Carlisle guard, scored the touchdown using the famous "hidden ball" play. Mose Blumenthal has often been given credit for sewing a piece of elastic in the hem of Dillon's jersey to keep the ball from coming out, but Freddy Wardecker, owner of Blumenthal's former menswear store, does not believes that Mose did the actual sewing. Although Blumenthal's store, also known as "The Capital," had sewing machines, the proprietor did not know how to operate them. He probably supervised the project. Quarterback James Johnson received the kickoff and placed the ball under Dillon's jersey while the team huddled. The Carlisle backs faked having the ball and then raced downfield to retrieve the ball from under the back of Dillon's jersey to touch the ball down for the score. Pop Warner later wrote that he was glad that Harvard outscored Carlisle that day because he didn't like to win on a fluke. The *Boston Sunday Post* had this to say about the game: "With a team outweighed nearly forty pounds to the man, crippled, bruised and battered from other contests, and on a foreign field, the Indians gave an exhibition of football that has no parallel in the annals of Harvard football."

After finishing the season 11–2–1, Pop Warner returned to his alma mater, Cornell, to coach the 1904–6 seasons. Richard Henry Pratt, then a colonel, was relieved of his command because of his most recent negative comments regarding the Bureau of Indian Affairs. Major William A. Mercer, a cavalry officer, was selected to replace him as superintendent of Carlisle. Former Carlisle stars Bemus Pierce and future hall-of-famer Edward Rogers were brought back to coach the 1904 Indian team. Their only losses in this 9–2–0 season were shutouts by two of the Big Four, Harvard and Penn.

Likely because of the turmoil surrounding Pratt's departure, Carlisle did not participate in the St. Louis World's Fair. The band did play there, however, as part of the Pennsylvania exhibit. In the fall, the school got a second chance. Promoters were unable to get the Army-Navy game relocated to the Fair to coincide with President Roosevelt's visit, but they were able to arrange a Carlisle-Haskell Institute game on the Saturday after Thanksgiving. A Thanksgiving Day game previously arranged with Ohio State became a warm-up on the trip to St. Louis. The Indians' second team beat the Buckeyes 23–0 two short days and a few hundred miles away before overwhelming Haskell 38–4. President Roosevelt didn't see the game but a large crowd of the curious did. Eight Haskell players were so impressed with the Carlisle program that they later enrolled there.

1905 saw Carlisle coached by committee. George Woodruff, the renowned former Penn coach, was advisor to the coaching team of Bemus Pierce, Siceni Nori, Frank Hudson and Ralph Kinney. The Indians again lost to Penn and Harvard in back-to-back games but did beat a team that gave them much satisfaction, the "soldiers" at West Point. In an 11-day period, with permission from the War Department, the Indians beat Army 6–5, then demolished Cincinnati 34–5 and lost games to two semi-professional teams, Canton A. C. and Massillon A. C., 8–0 and 8–4, respectively. A decade later the Canton-Massillon rivalry would be the stuff of legends and would provide a place for Carlisle stars to continue their football careers and change football history.

The Carlisle Indians had gained a national reputation for excellence in football, and athletically-inclined boys on the reservation were becoming increasingly aware of it. Some boys aspired to attend Carlisle to play football with this heroic bunch. Other boys dreamed of playing in the Carlisle band. Still other boys, and some girls, too, wanted to attend Carlisle because of the educational opportunities. While no one would confuse the education that was provided at Carlisle Indian Industrial School with that of an Ivy League college, Carlisle provided opportunities that were not otherwise available to most boys and girls on the reservation. Students returning from Carlisle used their educations to move into leadership positions, a fact that did not go unnoticed by children on the reservation.

Before the 1906 season started, Pop Warner tutored Carlisle coaches, former stars Bemus Pierce and Frank Hudson, in the new rules instituted to keep President Roosevelt from banning the game. The neutral zone was established, the distance needed to make a first down was increased from five to ten yards, and the forward pass was legalized. The rule changes eliminated some of the disadvantages Carlisle teams had faced previously, including lack of size, and allowed them to capitalize on their strengths—speed, agility and conditioning.

Warner developed a new offensive scheme to exploit Carlisle's strengths, speed and deception, and offset their weaknesses, size and depth. Warner's system, known to us as the single-wing, revolutionized football.

The two Indian coaches led their charges to a 24-6 victory over Penn but were outplayed by the Crimson in a 5-0 loss at Harvard. They unexpectedly lost to Penn State on a field goal, the only score in the game. Not reported by The *Arrow* (Carlisle's school paper changed its name in 1904) or Steckbeck was a Thanksgiving game hastily arranged with Vanderbilt while the team was on the road for games with Minnesota, Cincinnati and Virginia. The Champions of the South wanted a crack at the slayers of the Champions of the West and beat the Indians 4-0. Three victories against one defeat in 12 days isn't bad. Neither was a 9-3-0 season with a tough schedule.

On September 21, 1906, *The Arrow* reported, "Carlisle Indian football management decided to have its eleven directly coached by full-blooded redskins of intelligence. This was done largely because the Indian will work harder for an Indian coach

Onondagas Will See the Game; *The Syracuse Herald* 11-21-1911

than for the average college expert trainer. Coach Glenn S. Warner is undoubtedly the only white man who has ever been able to hold fast the attention of the redskinned footballist and teach him better things." At the end of the season, the *New York World* opined, "Bemus Pierce by skillful handling of the Indians has placed them in the front rank of the college world...Carlisle has done so well that the team is rated as one of the high class organizations of the year." The December 21 *Arrow* announced that Warner would return as athletic director in charge of coaching all sports. Bemus Pierce and Frank Hudson were praised but were not available year round. It was probably not coincidental that Mrs. Warner visited Superintendent and Mrs. Mercer over Thanksgiving.

1907 was Carlisle's strongest team to that time and, in Pop Warner's opinion, one of their best teams ever. The high points of the 10–1–0 season were another victory over Big Four foe Penn and their first ever over Harvard. Frank Mt. Pleasant, whom Walter Camp later snubbed by naming him only to the Honorable Mention All-America team due to a perceived lack of ruggedness, led the Indians to victory with his passing and a 75-yard touchdown run in the 23–15 triumph. A parade of students in their nightshirts greeted the team upon their return to Carlisle. Hundreds of townspeople turned out with them to welcome the victors. Warner savored the 18–4 victory over Chicago and their coach, Amos Alonzo Stagg, considering it one of the high points of his career. The only loss in the otherwise perfect season was a 16–0 shutout in a downpour of rain by Big Four nemesis Princeton. Little Boy, one of Carlisle's best linemen, explained why the Indians usually did poorly in inclement weather, saying, "Football no good fun in mud and snow." Jim Thorpe sat frustrated on the bench his first year on the team as Mt. Pleasant punted and threw 50-yard spirals, the first person Warner saw do this.

Mt. Pleasant's snubbing by Walter Camp was not an isolated incident. Writers not infrequently found ways to disparage the Indians' successes by focusing on their infrequent losses. Detractors portrayed Carlisle's defeats as character flaws held by people of the Indian race. Reasons given included lack of discipline, disinterest in training, and being too close to their aboriginal state. These writers' theories conflicted with Warner's observations. Furthermore, they would soon have an Indian to both deify and denounce.

Jim Thorpe vaulted to the position of starting left halfback in 1908. In his first year as a starter, Carlisle lost only to Harvard and Minnesota and tied Penn. Carlisle won the other ten. The Indians either lost to or tied the national champions, depending whether one thinks Harvard or Penn best that year. Jim Thorpe had a good year showing much promise, so much that Walter Camp ranked him a third team All-American. The following summer, Thorpe left school to play minor league baseball. Pennsylvania was the only Big Four team scheduled for 1909. That game accounted for one of Carlisle's losses, the first one in four years to the Quakers, in this 8–3–1 Thorpe-less season.

Moses Friedman, a civilian educator, replaced Major Mercer as Carlisle superintendent in 1908, but little changed with regard to the athletic program. Penn and Princeton were the Big Four teams Pop Warner scheduled for 1910. For reasons unknown, Harvard Law School replaced Harvard on the 15-game schedule. Western Maryland College mercifully canceled their game; otherwise the Indians would have had to play 3 games in seven days. A combination of injuries and bad luck resulted in a disappointing season with no Big Four victories and an 8–6–0 season.

Jim Thorpe, no longer a skinny kid, returned for the 1911 season. Pop Warner viewed this team as his greatest at Carlisle as it began the best three-year run in Carlisle's Football Trail of Glory. Gus Welch, Alex Arcasa and Lone Star Dietz all scored touchdowns in the win over Penn while Thorpe nursed an injury on the bench. Thorpe used his heavily bandaged leg to kick a field goal in each quarter for the victory over Harvard. This 11–1–0 season was their second and last campaign with two wins over "Big Four" opponents. The Indians picked up where they left off in 1912 but let up in their loss to Penn, the only member of the Big Four on that year's schedule. The scoreless tie was to a very good Washington and Jefferson team. However, it was not the one that was rewarded with the honor of being the Eastern representative in the New Year's Day game in Pasadena, California as has been reported elsewhere. It was in the much-written-about game against West Point that Pop used the double-wingback offense to thwart the Soldiers 27–6. Trouncing Brown 32–0 on Thanksgiving Day was a fitting capstone to Thorpe's career at Carlisle and the 12–1–1 season. Again in 1913, Penn was the only one of the Big Four on the schedule, but this time it was a 7–7 tie. The other blemish to their 10–1–1 record was a 12–6 upset by Pitt. Carlisle completed a three-year run of 33 wins, 3 losses and 2 ties against the toughest teams with only ten home games, and those were the warm-up games.

Carlisle Indian School teams were so well-known and respected that youth teams sometimes named themselves in their honor, much as kids' teams are called the Yankees or White Sox today. For example, a Syracuse, New York YMCA league named their basketball teams Syracuse, Harvard, Rutgers and Carlisle.

Some think that the Indians were pliable and easily bent to Warner's will, but that wasn't true in all cases. In a 1933 interview with Alan Gould of the Associated Press, Gus Welch recalled a headstrong player named Asa Sweetcorn who, as a running guard, felt that his contributions were being disregarded in Warner's newspaper columns. He reacted by drawing attention to himself. Instead of running plays as his coach diagrammed, Sweetcorn "...would go ripping around an end, legs and arms flying, making gestures at everybody but taking out nobody. I took him aside to find out what was going on. Slyly he wispered to me: 'Gus, that's psychology. I keep 'em all worried and guessing and then they say, My what a great running guard this Sweetcorn is.'" Reporters rewarded him with positive mention in their columns and opposing teams started to take notice of him. Navy concentrated much of their effort against Sweetcorn to his detriment. Soon he was groggy and bloody. At half-time, Pop suggested that a substitute be sent in for him. Welch responded, "No, this Sweetcorn is just faking. Let him stay in." After taking terrible beatings game after game, Asa began to wise up a bit but not completely. When he had about reached the limit of punishment he could withstand, he said something to Welch about needing a "medicine man" but Welch disagreed, "Never Mind medicine man; send for a priest."

Some think that the vaunted Carlisle Indian School football program ended in August 1918 when the school closed, because Carlisle Barracks, its home, was to be used as a hospital to treat soldiers wounded in The Great War. While it is true that the Red Peril of the East would take the field no more, Carlisle's competitive football ended before that. In his seminal work on Carlisle Indian School football, *Fabulous Redmen*, John S. Steckbeck places the end of Carlisle's football trail of glory at February 25, 1915, the date of Pop Warner's farewell dinner. I mark the end a year earlier. On February 6, 7, 8 and March 25, 1914, a joint commission of Congress under the direction of Inspector E. B. Linnen conducted an investigation of the Carlisle Indian School. The changes brought about by the commission led to the demise of the Carlisle football program. Although the U.S. Army technically brought the program to an end when it took back Carlisle Barracks in 1918, the football program was already dead, though still staggering from 1914 to its official demise.

FULL OF PERSONAL LIBERTY

Drawn by
Lone Star Dietz
for
The Carlisle Arrow
11-20-1914

Judge Cato Sells, new Commissioner of Indian Affairs, apparently at the urging of the Indian Rights Association and a student petition, began an investigation of Superintendent Moses Friedman's management of the Carlisle Indian Industrial School in January 1914. It seems that Cumberland County Judge Sadler (it is not clear whether it was Wilbur, the father, or Sylvester, the son, because the hereditary judgeship was transferred from father to son in that year) meted out a 60-day jail sentence, possibly at Friedman's urging, to an Indian girl and boy for an infraction punishable only by a fine under Pennsylvania law. The infraction was not stated but debauchery is a definite possibility. This did not sit well with the Philadelphia-based Indian Rights Association. There were also accounts of arrests of Indian boys found drinking alcohol in the town of Carlisle. According to Indian School staff and other students, "negro bootleggers" were to blame, not tavern owners. The timing could not have been worse for Carlisle as the walrus-mustachioed Judge Sells was on a rampage to stop the scourge of alcohol on his wards while trying to clean up the corrupt government agency.

On Friday, February 6, 1914, a joint commission of Congress arrived unannounced in Carlisle to interview staff and students at Carlisle in an attempt to get to the bottom of the situation. It was not a pretty sight. Superintendent Friedman made an unauthorized trip to Washington to plead his case, blaming Gen. Richard Pratt, founder of the Carlisle Indian School, with meddling but was told to get back to his post. Local newspapers ran editorials supportive of Friedman but several students and faculty members criticized his leadership. Meanwhile Inspector J. Linnen interviewed witnesses.

Rosa B. LaFlesch, outing manager, testified that discipline: "...is better now than when I first came here, although it is lax yet." She went on to say, "They [students] have no respect for him [Supt. Friedman]." Wallace Denny, assistant disciplinarian (and Pop Warner's long-time trainer) gave four reasons or causes for student dissatisfaction:

1. Superintendent Friedman reduced the number of receptions and sociables per month to one each.
2. Students were given more difficult [academic] work.
3. Food was of a poor quality.
4. Employees did not work in harmony with Superintendent Friedman.

John Whitwell, principal teacher, reported that Mr. David H. Dickey, outing agent, found Pop Warner drunk with Gus Welch. Whitwell also claimed that students wrote "the Jew" and other such things on a blackboard in reference to Moses

Friedman. He accused Friedman of carrying almost 200 students who were no longer at the school on the roll. Angel DeCora, native art teacher, presented the commission with a list of twenty-eight girls who had been "ruined" and sent home. Band director Claude M. Stauffer was accused of beating a 17-year-old female student, Julia Hardin, at the insistence of Hannah H. Ridenour, a matron.

Pop Warner was accused of mishandling athletic funds. One of the charges was that the athletic association paid Hugh Miller, sports editor for the Carlisle Sentinel, and E. L. Martin to publicize the Carlisle team in the cities in which they played. The fact that hundreds paid out for PR resulted in thousands in gate receipts seemed to escape the commission. Or, it appeared unseemly to the senators and congressmen for the school to pay for publicity when they had franking privileges and reporters constantly asked them for stories. Warner was found to have kept scrupulous records but was criticized for how some of the money was spent. He argued that he was getting the best value for the school when he purchased canned goods from his family's Springfield Canning Company. The coach also mentioned disbursing some of the money to the players. "At the close of the season the boys are given a $25 suit of clothes and a $25 overcoat; that is, the first team. And the first team also gets a souvenir of some kind." This explains some of the $25 and $50 chits at Wardecker's Men's Wear (formerly Blumenthal's). Warner was also criticized for recruiting star athletes from reservations, something he adamantly denied. He countered that many of his best players had never seen a football before arriving at Carlisle.

Commissioner Sells dismissed Friedman and Stauffer, bringing charges against Friedman for theft of funds. Oscar Lipps was brought in as acting superintendent. During his trial, Friedman claimed it was Chief Clerk Siceni J. Nori who embezzled the money and destroyed the records. State charges against Friedman were then dropped and moved to federal court when it was learned that Nori needed the money to make support payments for his estranged wife and children. Friedman was acquitted, resigned, and took a job that paid $3,000 a year. A cook was suspended for taking an Indian boy into a saloon and buying him liquor. That infraction was worth a fine and imprisonment for the cook. Pop Warner was allowed to stay on as athletic director.

A result of the Congressional Investigation was a change in the curriculum and stricter requirements for admission. A number of the faculty changed and many students did not return in the fall. The investigation brought out the fact that, although Angel DeCora and her husband, Lone Star Dietz, had not been teaching native arts for about two years due to curriculum changes, Superintendent Friedman had kept them on because he thought they were assets to the school. Dietz was teaching mechanical drawing but DeCora had no specific duties. The commission apparently agreed with Friedman and did not recommend their dismissal. Complaints of students loitering in the former Native Art Department led to the Leupp Art Building being reassigned to the new alumni association. Students would no longer make or decorate things to be sold by the school. Resale items were to be purchased in New York.

At the beginning of the 1914 football season, an article, probably written by Hugh Miller or E. L. Martin, titled, "Carlisle Indian Stars Are Teaching the Palefaces How to Play Football Game," was printed in newspapers around the country. Bemus Pierce, Albert Exendine, Frank Mt. Pleasant, Frank Cayou, Wiliam Gardner, Wilson Charles, William Garlow, Emil Hauser (better known as Wauseka), Pete Hauser, Charles Guyon (also known as Wahoo), Fritz Hendricks, Ed Smith, Antonio Lubo, Joseph Schoulder and Thomas St. Germain were or had been coaching football at colleges and high schools around the country. Jimmie Johnson, Gus Welch, Lone Star Dietz and several others had or were assisting in Carlisle by 1914.

After the great 1911–1913 run, things changed drastically football-wise in 1914 and not for the better. Pop Warner described the 5-9-1 1914 season as disastrous. Some excellent players, Gus Welch and Pete Calac for example, were back, but the team lacked the depth of talent it had enjoyed in former years. The season started off with the usual victories in three warm-up games, but the margins of victory were smaller than the previous year. The next four games were played against tougher opponents. All four were lost. In 1913, the Indians went 2-1-1 against the same four teams: Lehigh, Cornell, Pitt and Penn. Next they were pummeled by Syracuse, a team they had beaten the previous year, by a score of 24-3. They then played to a scoreless tie with Holy Cross, an opponent Carlisle defeated the only other time they played. The big game of the year was against the Fighting Irish of Notre Dame at White Sox Park in Chicago. Carlisle put up a good fight until Gus Welch was injured making a tackle. Notre Dame swamped Warner's charges 48-6 in the only time the teams from the two legendary programs met.

Carlisle easily handled cross-town rival Dickinson College 34-0 without Gus Welch, who stayed behind in Chicago's Mercy Hospital, but the annual Thanksgiving opponent, Brown, was a tougher match. Carlisle outplayed and outgained the Bears 3 to 1 but fumbled away a 20-14 loss. Three post-season games were arranged this year. The first was a charity game for the Children's Charitable Hospital of Marblehead, Massachusetts just two days after the Brown game. The opposition was an all-star team composed primarily of former Harvard players. The All-Stars prevailed 13-6. A week later, the Indians were in Birmingham, Alabama where they beat the University of Alabama 20-3. *The Carlisle Arrow* mentioned that a third postseason game, a game against the University of Georgia, was to be played in Atlanta the following Wednesday but did not report on the game. However, contemporary newspaper accounts show that Carlisle played Auburn in Atlanta and lost

7–0. This game has not been forgotten by the Auburn faithful because it figures prominently in their folklore regarding the origins of the "War Eagle" battle cry. Auburn supporters recalled the game this way:

> The 1914 contest with the Carlisle Indians provides another story. The toughest player on the Indians' team was a tackle named Bald Eagle. Trying to tire the big man, Auburn began to run play after play at his position. Without even huddling, the Auburn quarterback would yell "Bald Eagle," letting the rest of the team know that the play would be run at the imposing defensive man. Spectators, however, thought the quarterback was saying "War Eagle" and, in unison, they began to chant the resounding cry.

The only problem is that the Carlisle roster included neither a Bald Eagle nor a War Eagle. However, it did include a Hawk Eagle—the star right guard. Given that Hawk Eagle sounds more like War Eagle than does Bald Eagle and Hawk Eagle was a very good player, the essence of the story may well be true. It's just the details that are muddled.

The National Archives' file for Charles Guyon contains a footnote to the Carlisle-Auburn game. Apparently Wahoo underwrote that game and, due to Carlisle having an off season and a short time to effectively promote it, lost $2,897.75. His lawyer requested that Oscar Lipps return half of the loss. Lipps blamed the season's results on Carlisle having an "off" year and predicted that, after all accounts were finalized, Carlisle would show a small loss for the season. So, Guyon was out the money.

Even though the congressional investigator had wrested control of the athletic funds from Warner, many things continued to operate pretty much as they had. But now it was Superintendent Lipps sending chits to Blumenthal's to pay for the players' citizen clothing.

The Auburn game was the last one Pop Warner and Lone Star Dietz coached for Carlisle. After their game with the Indians, University of Pittsburgh officials began discussions with Pop Warner to head their football program. At season's end, with negotiations concluded, Warner was feted at a farewell banquet attended by former Carlisle lettermen and friends. The death of Carlisle football formally honored, all that remained was for the corpse to die.

The University of Pittsburgh offered Warner, and he accepted, a salary of $4,500 which was very good money in 1915. However, one of the most ardent supporters of amateur athletics and outspoken critics of professionalism in sports, tenured Amos Alonzo Stagg, was paid $6,000 by the University of Chicago in 1905, a full decade earlier. It is no wonder that Carlisle's 1907 thumping of Chicago was one of the victories Warner savored most.

Carlisle needed a new football coach. As soon as Warner's impending departure was made public, speculation ran rampant in newspapers across the country. First, Al Exendine was to take Warner's place if he could be released from his contract with Georgetown. Next it was Frank Mt. Pleasant, who chose the University of Buffalo instead. Pop's protégé, Lone Star Dietz, was an obvious choice, but he opted to leave the Indian Service and took his first head coaching job at Washington State College, establishing the Carlisle-Washington State connection. Gus Welch was at least one writer's choice if Dietz wasn't available. Several former players, including Charles Guyon, Bemus Pierce, Frank Hudson and Frank Cayou, applied for the job. But none of the Carlisle stars was chosen or would accept the job, probably the latter in most cases. In March, newspapers reported that well-known Indian lawyer and former Texas A & M quarterback, Victor M. "Choctaw" Kelley (often spelled Kelly) had been selected for the job. Before leaving for Pullman, Dietz predicted that Kelley would not be successful as the new Carlisle head coach. Gus Welch later charged that Kelley's hiring had been a political decision. The fact that Kelley's appointment was made by the Commissioner of Indian Affairs, Cato Sells, supports Welch's contention.

Leaving his former job at Southeastern State Normal School in Durant, Oklahoma, Coach Kelley arrived in late August to take the reins of the Carlisle football team. Gus Welch, who had had a successful year of coaching at Conway Hall, a preparatory school in Carlisle, agreed to assist Kelley with the varsity. Although stars like Welch were gone, the season started encouragingly enough with a 21–6 defeat of Albright College. But the scoreless tie the next week with Lebanon Valley College, a team that had not scored on them in their 14 meetings, threw cold water on Carlisle's dreams of mediocrity. The following week at Lehigh the competition improved, and Carlisle doomed its fate by making errors, losing 14–0. Rousing speeches by "Choc" Kelley and former Carlisle great Al Exendine may have boosted the Indians' performance against Harvard but mistakes, such as penalties, destined their defeat, even though they outgained the Crimson 275 yards to 175. Harvard prevailed 29–7.

Next up was Pop Warner's new and undefeated team, the University of Pittsburgh. Pittsburgh, considered by some to be the best team in the country, pounded Carlisle to the tune of 45–0, their worst defeat of the year. The next week neither team played well when the Carlisle-Bucknell contest ended in a scoreless tie, Carlisle's second of the year. Unable to move the ball inside the opponent's 20 or defend the forward pass, Carlisle lost to a West Virginia Wesleyan team that it had hoped to beat. A week later, looking like the Carlisle of old, the Indians scored 23 points in the first half, but the breaks went Holy Cross's way in the second half. Carlisle had to hang on for a 2-point victory. Dickinson College was ready for the Indians this year and fought hard to the end. But the Indians fought back and pulled out a 20–14 triumph on Dickinson's home field. Two Carlisle fumbles spelled defeat in their 14–10 loss to Fordham. A fumbled punt on Fordham's 15 was returned 85 yards for a touchdown, and a fumble at Fordham's 3 near the end of the game sealed the Indians' fate. Last up on the schedule was the annual Thanksgiving game in Providence, Rhode Island against Brown.

What happened off the field was, perhaps, more interesting than what happened in the 39–3 shellacking at the hands of a strong Brown team featuring Fritz Pollard. One of Lone Star Dietz's friends at Carlisle informed him that, to get back at Dietz for the statement he had made about Victor Kelley, Kelley had given a copy of Carlisle's playbook to Brown. Brown had been invited to Pasadena, California to play an East vs. West game on New Year's Day against Dietz's team after the town's little floral parade was over. An editorial in *The Providence Journal* considered the statement to be absurd, saying that Brown coach Robinson had played Carlisle so often that he

The Providence Journal 11-28-1915

knew their plays better than Kelley and needed no assistance from him. Besides that, it asserted, when Brown played Carlisle it thought it was going to be playing against the University of Washington, not Washington State. Someone in Providence had confused the schools.

The Thanksgiving game was such a resounding defeat for Carlisle that *The Providence Journal* ran a cartoon depicting the then current state of Carlisle's program as having seen better days. A week later *The Journal* ran two articles about Carlisle on the same page. In one article, Gus Welch blamed Victor Kelley for the poor season, saying, "There was a meeting three weeks before Thanksgiving at which Superintendent Lipps, Manager Meyer, Kelley, Capt. Calac and myself were present. It was decided then that Kelley was to be dismissed as head coach. Now they want to make me the goat of the whole affair. I want the public to know the facts." This chaos was a far cry from Carlisle during its glory years. The other article reported a decision made in Washington, DC that would subordinate football at Carlisle to the point at which the team would not be competitive.

Rumors circulated in newspapers across the country that intercollegiate football at Carlisle was to end. Carlisle's team was not disbanded but came close. The 1916 schedule wasn't in place until late October because football wasn't allowed on campus for a month. When the schedule finally came out, it had only five games on it and those were not with top caliber teams. Physical education instructor M. L. Clevett took over the coaching duties. The first game was against Conway Hall with the Indians winning 26–0. Susquehanna University, a team for whom 24–0 was the closest they could get in eight previous tries, was the next opponent. The 12–0 loss to Susquehanna was a blow to the Indians' ego because they knew they had lost to a weak team. Carlisle then traveled to Conshohocken to play their Athletic Association. Tied at 6–6, Coach Clevett withdrew his team at halftime due to the brutal treatment his team was receiving. Clevett was thrown into jail for refusing to return half the guarantee money. Eventually the money was returned and Clevett was released, but the game was never finished. Two weeks later former Carlislians Joel Wheelock and William Winneshiek helped Lebanon Valley College defeat the dejected Indians 20–6 for the Dutchmen's first victory in the long series. Carlisle closed the 1–3–1 season with a 27–17 loss to Alfred University in New York City.

Leo F. "Deed" Harris, Carlisle High School alum and former Warner scout, took the coaching reins for the 1917 season. He tried to prepare the team for a nine-game schedule similar to those Carlisle was accustomed to playing. Unfortunately, Carlisle's players were young and small. Also, a quarantine to prevent the spread of an epidemic on the school's grounds forced the team to relocate to one of the school's farms for much of the season, preventing organized practice. Carlisle started the season like Carlisle of old with 59–0 and 63–0 shellackings of Albright and Franklin and Marshall, respectively. Things went downhill quickly with seven successive losses, including the worst defeat in Carlisle's proud history at the hands of Joe Guyon's then current team, Georgia Tech, in Atlanta, 98–0. Their last game both of the season and ever was a 26–0 loss to Penn, bringing the in-state rivalry and Carlisle Indian School football to a close.

When the United States entered the First World War in 1917, allowing or encouraging students to enlist became a topic of discussion among school superintendents. Hervey B. Peairs of Haskell Institute in Lawrence, Kansas and John Francis of Carlisle discussed the ways they were dealing with the issue in their correspondence in April, 1917 concerning Gus Welch's application for the athletic director position at Haskell. Peairs began the discussion with a question:

> What policy are you adopting with reference to the enlistment of boys in the army? There is quite a demand

here among the boys to be allowed to enlist, but at least 50% of the parents object. Probably about 50% are very willing to have their sons enlist and do their part. I have felt that I ought not to allow any of the boys or young men to leave the school and enlist in the army without the consent of the parents, even though the boys are of the age when they can lawfully enlist without such consent.

Francis responded:

With reference to the enlistment of boys here that are over 21, I have permitted them to go without the consent of the parents; under that age I required them to obtain the consent of their parents. I have also tried to avoid anything like a wave of wild excitement sweeping through the school, but on the other hand I have let them understand that where, after careful consideration, they felt they wished to enlist in the Army or Navy the school was proud to have them go and would do everything possible to help them go, and those of our boys who have enlisted have gone in this spirit.

Several former Carlisle football players were quick to join up. *The Carlisle Arrow* and *Red Man* issues of that time contained lists of former students and, if known, where they were stationed. Those who had attended college after leaving Carlisle were often commissioned as officers. Because of their athletic prowess, some were given the opportunity to represent their units in athletic competitions. *The Carlisle Arrow* and *Red Man* also included a former student's recollection of being treated as an oddity:

An Indian officer writes: "In the army one has splendid opportunities to make acquaintances, and being the only Redskin officer in camp, people want to meet me just for curiosity's sake."

The U.S. Army prevented further embarrassment to the once-proud school by taking the facility back to be used as a hospital to treat soldiers wounded in World War I. The mantle for Indian athletics was passed to Haskell Institute in Lawrence, Kansas, where football again flourished before Depression-era government funding cuts ended the Indian football trail of glory forever. In 1920, after the war was over, Society of American Indians passed a resolution demanding that the government reopen Carlisle or that another, comparable facility be established. Carlisle Barracks was instead used for the Medical Field Service School.

In 1931, Pop Warner planned a reunion of Carlisle Indian School football players at the 1932 Summer Olympics held in Los Angeles. He wanted to have a scrimmage with former stars, but it was necessary for Jim Thorpe and other Carlisle luminaries to attend for it to be successful. Jim Thorpe, then strapped for cash, did attend the Olympics courtesy of Vice-President Charles Curtis and was seated in the Presidential box. He received a standing ovation from the 105,000 present for the opening ceremonies in the Los Angeles Coliseum when his name was announced. The Federation of American Indians also proposed that a reunion of former Carlisle students be held, presumably in Carlisle. It is not known if either of those reunions materialized, but the one proposed by former player Isaac Lyon did, at the New York State Fair in Syracuse in 1941. Pop Warner attended, along with a large number of former students. Attendance at the fair jumped largely due to interest in seeing the Carlisle Indians.

In early 1937, a newspaper article datelined Philadelphia discussed the unusual accents of many former Carlisle students:

> American Indians with a Pennsylvania Dutch dialect may confuse visitors to western reservations, but William "Lone Star" Dietz, assistant coach of the Temple University football team, can explain it.... "For years

hundreds of Indian boys and girls were brought from the reservations to Carlisle, and after they had become oriented to the institutional surroundings, they were sent to farms in Dauphin, Lancaster, Lebanon and other predominantly Dutch counties. There they were reared with the farmers' children, went to their schools and learned the topsy-turvey Pennsylvania Dutch dialect. They naturally acquired the accent and never lost it."

Thorpe and Warner died in the 1950s and were soon followed by many others. The last of the great football players died in the 1970s. The last surviving Carlisle student died a few years ago, but memories of the school linger on.

In 1910, Superintendent Friedman mailed a questionnaire to former football players no longer at Carlisle, as Pratt and Mercer had done before him, apparently to refute the widely held belief that athletes "never amount to much after leaving school" was a myth. Who received the questionnaires is unknown as is who returned them. What is known is some players returned them, and some of these responses still exist in student files. The results found comprise no scientific study but do represent the thinking of some individuals. Charles Guyon responded, "I owe my success to the training I have received in the two schools I have attended, and to make it short—I am working for something higher—to the highest goal." Caleb Sickles frankly stated, "From my own experience I think that the pupil who has attended Carlisle should never go back to the reservation to live. If he has holdings I would advise him to sell them, put the money in the bank and seek employment or attend a school and obtain a professional or technical education." Ed Rogers answered, "What little degree of success I have attained I attribute entirely to my early training at Carlisle" and offered, "I might add although the subject is not mentioned nor no opinion is requested that to abolish non-reservation schools is a mistake and would be a serious detriment to the progress and welfare of the future young Indians."

The next chapter discusses what several of the players did immediately after or, in a few cases, while attending Carlisle. Carlisle Indians played significant roles in the development of the early professional game. This book tells their stories along with numerous others.

Celebrating an early Carlisle victory; *Pennsylvania Engraving Company*

2

Indians Turn Pro

Professional football took a very different developmental path than did baseball. Football in America evolved much like rugby had in England in that both games were born at the elite schools in their respective home countries and grew to become interscholastic sports. American inter-scholastic sports began when Harvard and Yale, modeling themselves after what they viewed as their British counterparts, Oxford and Cambridge, competed in rowing. It was natural that the elite schools would be among the first to compete against each other in football (soccer and rugby) in this country. In the 1880s, Yale's Walter Camp, "Father of American Football," instituted the rule changes that differentiated American football from its English cousins when he was a student playing the game. Camp continued his involvement with football long after graduation and dominated the rules committee until 1905.

In the earliest days of American football, players were amateurs associated with the colleges they attended. Soon graduates played. It wasn't long before gypsy players matriculated at a school just long enough to play in an important game. Some were never students of the institutions they represented or, in at least one case, were students at other or both institutions. Ruling elites such as Theodore Roosevelt promoted sports to young men of his class as a means of preparing them for leadership. It was not for money that these amateur athletes were to compete, but for roles in leading the country. The brutal contests of strength, speed and wit helped determine who would later be making the major decisions for the nation. Requiring that college sports be amateur events for the most part restricted participation in them to the scions of the wealthy and powerful because few others could afford the luxury of paying college tuition while making no income.

Charges of professionalism started early on when players for other schools, of course, were paid outright, with free clothing, or for jobs which required little work. Professional (paid) coaching was soundly criticized as well. William Rainey Harper, President of the fledgling University of Chicago, set a precedent in 1893 when he offered, and Amos Alonzo Stagg accepted, a tenured position as associate professor in charge of the Athletic Department for $2,500 per year. Stagg had a good salary and a job for life, or at least until mandatory retirement age. The often sainted Stagg was an ardent supporter of amateurism and a constant critic of professionalism in athletics.

In those days, college athletics were seldom under the control of college administrators. Student and athletic organizations generally raised the money to field a team and pay the coach. Football also generated profits that the associations could use to support other athletics at the school. Walter Camp, who also espoused the merits of amateurism, accumulated $100,000 for Yale's athletic fund over a ten-year period even while using some of the money to pay athletic tutors.

Camp, however, was not paid for his efforts as he had a good-paying job as an executive of the New Haven Clock Company. But then, he was merely an advisor and not the coach.

Athletes were not to be paid, and this restriction was not just for playing football. Scholarships and part-time jobs were considered to be marks of professionalism. However, student-athletes from humble backgrounds, if they were good enough athletes and businessmen, sometimes found ways to afford playing college amateur sports. Some found paying jobs with alumni or supporters of the school's teams. Ace Clark, captain of the Washington State College 1916 Rose Bowl team, took entire years off to work at manual labor to save up enough to pay his way through school. In 1900, Penn State became one of the first colleges to officially authorize athletic scholarships to cover tuition, room and board. There were no set eligibility standards. It was not uncommon for the managements of two squads about to play a game to negotiate player eligibility in the week leading up to a game. There weren't even set rules regarding professionalism. Some schools allowed their athletes to play professional or semi-pro baseball over the summer. As a practical matter, it would have been difficult policing hundreds of baseball teams across the country, especially considering that players often played under assumed names.

Carlisle Indian School, being a government facility with students who were wards of the government, had an unusual situation. Neither its academics nor its economics resembled those of a prestigious university; nor did the views of its faculty and administration. Providing ways for students to earn money was an important issue for school administrators. Pratt instituted outings as a central part of his system, in part because they gave students the opportunity to make and save some money of their own. Later, the Native Art Department provided a venue to sell the objects that students created in the classroom. Even after Warner's departure, Superintendent Oscar Lipps signed chits for athletes to redeem for clothing at Blumenthal's Men's

Wear. So, even though Carlisle's athletes were at least the equal of their counterparts at elite institutions, their financial status was definitely not. Few Carlisle students had affluent parents, whereas college students of the day largely came from the upper classes. While some, such as Jim Thorpe, received modest incomes from their allotments of tribal lands, many did not. Even if they had money in an account at the reservation, getting the Indian agent to release it was a challenge.

High schools also picked up the game and played according to college rules, but those students not wealthy enough or so inclined to attend college found their playing days ending at graduation. Soon town, neighborhood or company teams gave ordinary people with athletic ability an opportunity to play football as young adults, sometimes longer. Because they were not affiliated with schools, these teams were dubbed independents. For some reason, independents sprang up in the Great Lakes region in mill towns from New York to Wisconsin. Mill workers did not attend college and often worked at least part of Saturday, making it impossible for most to attend college games, assuming they had the money or interest in doing so. Sunday was when the working class could play or watch football, and that is when they did it. Cities often had blue laws that prevented games being played on Sundays, so the city teams that existed had to play mostly road games.

Independent games were often hardfought with neighboring towns over bragging rights for the superiority of one locale over another. Partisans bet on their teams, often in large amounts. Team managers brought in ringers to ensure their teams' success and to protect their wagers. On November 12, 1892, the Allegheny Athletic Association of Pittsburgh (AAA) paid former Yale All-American William "Pudge" Hefflefinger $500 to play guard against Pittsburgh Athletic Club (PAC) in what is acknowledged as the game involving the first professional player. It is not unlikely that other players were paid prior to this, but AAA's financial records documented the fact that

Hefflefinger had been paid to play. In 1895, David Berry, manager of the Latrobe YMCA team and editor of the Latrobe Clipper, paid John Braillier $10 more than expenses to play quarterback for his club. Braillier used the money to purchase a pair of pants that he wore proudly at Washington and Jefferson College, where the future dentist also played football. Braillier is the first known college player to also be playing on Sundays for pay. Independent football had become semi-pro as teams began paying a star or handful of stars to augment their local boys who played for the fun of it.

Complaints of professionalism of college players were widespread, but Carlisle probably had fewer instances, or at least reports, of its players playing on Sundays than did many football powers, due to logistics if nothing else. Because Carlisle played most of its games on the road, nearly all after the early season warm-ups, players were generally at distant cities on Saturdays, returning home late Saturday night or heading off to another city for a midweek game. This made travel from Carlisle to another city for a Sunday game difficult. Also, Carlisle players were under closer watch by their coaching staff and administration than were college students. Carlisle officials had tighter control and would not have been pleased to have their stars injured in a Sunday game and unable to play the next Saturday. However, under certain circumstances it appears to have happened. Keith McClellan, author of *The Sunday Game,* discovered that Frank Mt. Pleasant, played for the Altoona Indians in 1905 and recruited some of his teammates. Warner, wasn't at Carlisle in 1905. It seems unlikely that Pop would have allowed his players to risk injury playing for another team—at least during the season. Gus Welch related a story much later about having played for a professional team in Pottstown, Pennsylvania and having recruited some teammates to join him. However, a decade later Carlisle and Notre Dame were reputed to have more former or current players involved in the professional game than any other schools.

Indians Turn Pro

Caught along the sidelines in Philadelphia-Homestead game
Philadelphia Inquirer 11-24-1901

Western Pennsylvania was an early hotbed of independent football. Going into the 1900 season, the Duquesne Country and Athletic Club (DC&AC) was the dominant team but was burdened with a bloated (for its day) payroll. The Homestead Library Athletic Club (HLAC), supported by Carnegie Steel money, was on the ascendancy. HLAC hired Bill Church away from Georgetown University and loaded up on stars, including former Carlisle star Bemus Pierce and several DC&AC players. Historians disagree on the details of what happened in this time period. The NFL position is that William Chase Temple became the first owner of a professional team by taking over the DC&AC in 1900. Another historian believes that Temple left DC&AC between the 1899 and 1900 seasons and joined HLAC as its football chairman. Greensburg and Latrobe also expected to contend in 1900. The Greenies, financed by local stockholders, brought onboard Carlisle All-American Isaac Seneca and some other stars.

The 1900 season proved to be a financial disaster for the western Pennsylvania powers. The DC&AC and Greensburg teams folded. Latrobe returned to being a town team. HLAC was the only one of these teams to return the next year at full strength. That year it played several college teams and a few independents. Hawley Pierce, Bemus's brother, was on the roster of this undefeated team. Unfortunately, rain fell on almost all of its games, dampening enthusiasm and creating box office losses. William Temple had had enough of football. He later moved to Florida where he was credited with developing the Temple orange.

In 1902, baseball's upstart American League was plucking stars from the National League, creating a bidding war for players, with perhaps the most intense competition being found in Philadelphia between the Athletics and Phillies. Phillies owner Col. John I. Rogers responded to this threat by forming a football team. Athletics owner Ben Shibe followed suit and put his baseball manager, Connie Mack, in charge of the new football team. Rogers and Shibe felt that winning the football championship of Philadelphia would help their baseball teams. And if one of them beat Pittsburgh, that team could claim the world's championship. So, they contacted Dave Berry who agreed to reassemble the old Homestead team, thus forming the National Football League. The two Philadelphia owners so distrusted each other that they made Berry president of their new league. They contacted New York and Chicago about joining the league but were unsuccessful.

David Berry recruited a number of the best players available for his team including Artie Miller, a former Carlisle star, who spent his summer working as a lumberjack in Wisconsin. Berry had recruited so many stars that he called his team the Pittsburgh Stars. The Philadelphia As roster included wacky lefthander Rube Waddell, who had just finished his first season with the club, going 24–7 after joining the club on July 1. Manager Connie Mack found it necessary to dispatch two Pinkerton agents to the West Coast to accompany the "sousepaw" to Philadelphia. He had been pitching quite well for the Los Angeles Loo Loos. Waddell was a great talent but his eccentric habits made it necessary for Mack to keep him close during the off-season. Connie did not risk injuring Waddell by playing him in a football game, but he might have been an asset to the team as he had played rugby in the off season for several years. The new league's teams played several excellent games, but much money was lost in this inaugural year of the NFL. The league standings were so muddled that it was difficult to determine which, if any, had a legitimate claim to the championship. Enter Tom O'Rourke, manager of Madison Square Garden, in need of a New Year's event.

Needing to fill the Garden, O'Rouke came up with a grandiose idea about holding a World Series of Football. Unfortunately for him, the college teams weren't interested, so, he turned to the independents. The four best independents that year were the three NFL clubs and the Watertown, New York Red and Blacks. The Red and Blacks had already claimed the World Championship of football in spite of having lost to the Athletics, at home no less. O'Rourke invited three of the four teams, figuring that New York fans wouldn't be interested in watching a team from Pittsburgh. Watertown refused to risk its self-proclaimed championship and the Philadelphia teams weren't coming, at least not as the Phillies or Athletics.

The clever O'Rourke put together a five-team tournament: the New York team, an amalgam of the best of the Phillies and Athletics players; the New York Knickerbockers; the Orange, New Jersey Athletic Club; the Warlow Athletic Club; and the Syracuse Athletic Club, rechristened the All-Syracuse team, with the addition of the Pierce and Warner brothers plus the

Watertown backfield. O'Rourke optimized the schedule to promote the greatest interest (read box office). New York was supposed to easily dispense with All-Syracuse in the first night's contest, but O'Rourke was unaware that Syracuse had loaded up his team. Pop Warner later wrote that his brother, Bill, talked him into playing this game, the only pro game he ever played. Warner's head injury probably caused him to miss an extra point and three field goals. Syracuse won anyway. Two nights later they defeated the Knickerbockers 36–0, without the elder Warner, to win the first World Series of Football.

The NFL disbanded after the season was over. In 1903, the Franklin team in Venango County, Pennsylvania loaded up with every talented player it could find and there was no real competition to test them. O'Rourke invited Franklin to the second World Series of Football at Madison Square Garden, and the team accepted. This time Watertown agreed to come but was pummeled by Franklin in a game most notable as the one in which the officials were in full evening dress, including top hats and white gloves. Some opined that they were officiating a funeral. In a way they were because this was football's last World Series. The Franklin team was disbanded after the game and other Pennsylvania teams didn't pick up their high-priced players.

As Western Pennsylvania football declined, Ohio football ascended in places like Canton, Akron, Shelby and Massillon. However, this ascendancy moved forward, and sometimes backwards, in fits and starts. Carlisle played the vast majority of its games against college teams but did occasionally play athletic clubs. Because athletic clubs and other independent teams did not have the opportunity to practice as often as college teams, they were viewed as being a notch below them. In 1905 for some strange reason—most likely for money—Carlisle scheduled both Canton and Massillon clubs as part of a 6-games-in-19-days suicidal road trip. The Indians beat the four college teams but lost to the much heavier Canton and Massillon

Donshey's sidelights of the Indian-Tiger battle in the mud.
The Plain Dealer 11-16-1905

squads by respectable scores. Playing, and beating, Carlisle improved the stature of these rivals.

In 1906, as interest and support in the game was increasing, an event happened that set the professional game back for almost a decade. The problem started to brew when Canton lured several players away from rival Massillon for higher pay. Rumblings about crooked work during the game erupted after the Massillon newspaper, *The Independent,* accused Canton coach and captain, Blondy Wallace, of having someone on his team throw the game. Wallace sued for libel but withdrew the suit, most likely because *The Independent* had enough evidence to prove its claim. Tensions ran high because a lot of money had been bet on the game. A brawl at the Courtland Hotel Bar erupted among Canton followers that put an end to pro football in Canton and Massillon—at least for a while. Ohio football descended into what historian Milt Roberts called the "Unglamorous Years." Football continued but without the high pay and fanfare of the preceding years.

As Carlisle Indian School football improved to a high level in 1907, critics complained of professionalism at the school. Pop Warner responded with a letter he circulated to newspapers and college football programs. He claimed that 52 of the 54 players on the 1907 roster were regularly enrolled students; the other two were employees. However, some students were enrolled at places like Conway Hall, Dickinson College or Dickinson School of Law. Warner accepted that allowing students to play on the varsity more than four years and allowing employees to play might not be cricket. So, he announced that, in the future, Carlisle would only allow students to play and for a maximum of four years.

Something neither Warner nor his critics mentioned is that Carlisle stars sometimes played for college teams after having played for Carlisle. Jim Thorpe did mention being approached by a number of schools who wanted him to play for them. James Johnson, Ed Rogers, Frank Cayou, Joe Guyon, Mike Balenti, Thomas St. Germain and Frank Mt. Pleasant, for instance, played for Northwestern, Minnesota, Illinois, Georgia Tech, Texas A & M, Yale and Dickinson College, respectively, after finishing their studies at Carlisle. Lehigh University raised concerns about the eligibility of these players in 1908 when that school refused to play Dickinson College if Mt. Pleasant was on the squad. No other complaints have been found for Carlisle Indians playing for more than four years, when the surplus was for a college or university. There were some complaints about players shifting to Haskell Institute, though. Some of these men were named to All-America teams at the schools where they played after leaving Carlisle.

Professionalism with regard to baseball had been an ongoing problem for Carlisle for a number of years when Pop Warner eliminated it as an intercollegiate sport in 1910. The Indians, of course, excelled at its replacement, lacrosse, and produced All-Americans in that sport, but providing Carlisle students the opportunity to compete in a truly American sport

Indians Turn Pro

was not the reason for the shift. Star athletes, many of whom were football players or track stars, would leave school to play baseball for pay. Carlisle student files contain several entries for students leaving to play baseball. Some did not come back and others' eligibility to play intercollegiate sports became an issue. At that time hundreds, if not thousands, of minor league and semi-professional baseball teams needed players. Although the pay was low, it was attractive to young men who loved to play the game and who had little money. That former Carlisle student, Albert "Chief" Bender, had been a huge success in major league baseball surely encouraged others to aim for the big leagues even if they didn't have Bender's talent.

Jack Cusack considered 1912 the Renaissance year for professional football because so many teams began to blossom that interest in the game increased dramatically in a large part of Ohio. A Canton team was organized that year as the Professionals to distance itself from the 1906 Bulldogs scandal. Cusack, then 21, took the job as team secretary-treasurer as a favor to team captain Roscoe Oberlin. He did the job for free. The alternative was to take a share of the profits—should there be any. After some internal squabbling and tactical maneuvering on the part of Cusack, he took over as manager.

After a 6–3 season, Jack Cusack felt he needed to attract more former college players to compete, and to do that he needed to pay them. He switched his players from a profit-split basis to salaries. Cusack and Oberlin backed the team financially as partners. Even with several of the college men on the 1913 roster, Canton still lost to Akron, its then arch rival. Cusack believed that, if football were to become profitable, it had to live down the 1906 scandal and regain the public's trust. A major obstacle, Cusack thought, was the constant jumping from team to team by players wanting to make a little more money. He approached the owners and managers of the other Ohio teams who agreed verbally to treat players who had signed with another team as that team's property until the other team released him. This collusion resulted in increased respectability and lower player salaries. Even with that agreement, Canton still lacked something—a strong rival in neighboring Massillon.

Canton-Massillon contests had been quite popular earlier, but Massillon dropped its team after the 1906 scandal. In 1914, the Massillon Chamber of Commerce invited Cusack to a meeting, during which they proposed to start a team by enticing away the Akron Indians' best players. When Cusack refused to play the team if it were formed that way, the backers decided against it. Canton sorely needed a rival in Massillon to be financially stable. In 1915, a group of Massillon businessmen, led by Jack Whalen and Jack Donohue, formed a team. Knowing that he would have to upgrade his team to compete, Cusack contacted every All-American he could think of and landed some of them. However, many would only play under assumed names to protect their primary employment. Coaches in particular were in jeopardy of losing their jobs because colleges and sportswriters were generally opposed to professional football. One of his best catches was the former Carlisle star, Bill Gardner, who soon figured in an historic event.

Canton, then known as the Bulldogs again, opened the 1915 season with a 75-0 shellacking of the Wheeling Athletic Club, followed by a hard-fought 7-0 victory over the always tough Nesser brothers' Columbus Panhandles. A 9-3 road loss to the Detroit Heralds, a team they had beaten the previous two years, was followed by a 41-12 win over the Cincinnati Colts, a team that was better than the score indicated. The Bulldogs then easily dispensed with the "Champions of Pennsylvania," the Altoona Indians, that included Carlisle players Alex Arcasa, Joe Bender, Joe Bergie, H. Brennan, Furrier, Fritz Henderson, Hoffman,Ted Pratt, Stilwell Saunooke, Shipp, George Vedernack, Hugh Wheelock, Joel Wheelock, Bill Winneshiek and Woodring. (First names of some of these players are unknown.) Several of these names never appeared in accounts of Carlisle games, so it is likely they never started for the varsity or got enough playing time to mention. Also, some may have been playing under assumed names. For instance, Stilwell Saunooke had last played on the varsity in 1903, making it questionable that he could still play competitive football. Current players may have taken others' names to mask the fact that they were playing on Sundays.

Next up on the schedule were the Massillon Tigers. Cusack didn't know exactly who was on that team because so many played under assumed names. One who played under his own name was Notre Dame star end, Knute Rockne. Notre Dame quarterback Gus Dorais was Rockne's passing partner on both teams. Through painstaking research, Keith McClellan, has determined who were most of the players on the Massillon roster, and the team was loaded with talent. Cusack knew he was up against a very tough team and needed to do something. Anyone who read the papers knew that Jim Thorpe was assisting Indiana University that fall. Some may have even known that he was playing on Sundays for the Pine Village Athletic Club. Cusack dispatched Bill Gardner to Bloomington to talk with his old teammate. Gardner returned with a signed contract under which Thorpe would play for Canton for $250 a game.

Jack Cusack's financial advisors thought he would put the Bulldogs into receivership by committing to the unheard of sum of $250 a game. Sure, a few players had been paid even more than this for the odd game, but never had anyone made a commitment to pay this much game after game. Cusack estimated that attendance at his team's games had averaged about 1,200 people up to that point in the season. The peak was the game at Detroit which drew 2,900. Home games against Columbus and Altoona drew 2,500 and 2,400, respectively. 6,000 attended the Canton-Massillon game at Massillon, and 8,500 turned out for the standing-room-only rematch in Canton. Cusack's gamble paid off in spades. Thorpe's hiring was a watershed event for professional football. His ability to attract large, for that time, crowds made football an economically viable business, even if paying stars handsomely. And two Carlisle stars had played prominent roles in making this happen.

Canton and Massillon split with each other and tied for the Ohio championship in 1915, but Canton was a stronger team in 1916. Cusack added three more Carlisle Indians: Pete Calac, William Garlow and Gus Welch. Jack added additional All-Americans to his roster as the schedule toughened. Thorpe returned to captain the team when the baseball season ended. At times Canton had four or five All-Americans warming the bench; the team was that strong. In 1968 Cusack stated that he felt his 1916 Canton Bulldogs could stand up against any of the pro teams of the current era. The Bulldogs went 9–0–1, giving up a single score all season and that one on a blocked punt. Canton was "Champion of the World" again. 1917 was a similar story. With Thorpe and Calac leading the way, Canton finished 9–1, splitting with Massillon. By this time, the U.S. had entered WWI and professional football was stopped until after the Armistice.

Jack Cusack took a job in the Oklahoma oil fields during the war and wasn't around when it was time to restart the team. A friend of Cusack and Thorpe, Ralph Hay, offered to take over the Bulldogs and Cusack let him. Jim Thorpe, team captain, told a reporter that he intended to field an all-Indian backfield for 1919 by recruiting Joe Guyon and Gus Welch to play alongside him and Pete Calac. Instead, Welch accepted the Washington State coaching job made available by Lone Star Dietz's firing. Hay basically reassembled the 1916–17 Bulldogs for 1919 and signed former Carlisle Indian and Rambling Wreck, Joe Guyon, who some thought was better than Thorpe. Given the age difference, he may well have been at that time. However, when the chips were down, Big Jim carried the Bulldogs on his back to important victories. Canton won the championship again in 1919 but struggled financially. The Black Sox baseball scandal that year cast a pall on all sports, but professional football was hurt more than the others.

Red ink, team-jumping by players, skyrocketing salaries, fickle fans and the Black Sox scandal haunted the professional teams. Something had to be done, and a regular league sounded just like the ticket. On the evening of August 20, 1920, Ralph Hay held a meeting of team owners and two players, Jim Thorpe and Stanley Cofall, in the office of his Hupmobile dealership in Canton. This meeting gave birth to the American Professional Football Conference (APFC). Membership rules that first year were so vague that no one is certain exactly which teams were in the league and which weren't. The league did have some rules, or at least understandings. Members voted not to recruit undergraduate college students, not to lure away other teams' players with offers of higher salaries, to cooperate in making up schedules and, most importantly, to put a cap on player salaries. Unfortunately, only four teams were represented at the meeting: Canton, Akron, Dayton and Cleveland. Three other teams had written to Hay before the meeting, most likely to arrange games with Canton. Hay chose to include these teams as league members. However, exactly which teams wrote him is murky.

On September 17, a second meeting was held. In addition to the four original members, six other teams were represented: Rochester Jeffersons, Hammond Pros, Decatur Staleys, Rock Island Independents, Muncie Flyers and Racine (Chicago) Cardinals. Due to the heat, the meeting was held in the showroom and then-illegal cold beer was distributed to the owners, who sat on running boards of new Hupmobiles. New members were accepted and the league name was changed to the American Professional Football Association (APFA). Jim Thorpe was named President, more likely for name recognition than any presumed executive skills. Missing was one key component: a viable Massillon team for a rivalry with Canton. Membership fees were set at $100, but there is no record of any team actually paying it. Rules were not discussed, so they defaulted to the college rules then in force. Three more teams joined the league in 1920: the Detroit Heralds, Columbus Panhandles, and Chicago Tigers, none of whom were required to pay the $100 fee.

Teams played warm-up games in September against non-league teams and began their league schedules, such as they were, in October. A retired Jim Thorpe played only when it was necessary for the Bulldogs to win or tie. The league finished its first season unable to name a champion or to keep all of its teams. A league meeting was held in Akron on April 30, 1921. By a vote, the undefeated Akron Pros were awarded the "World's Professional Football Championship." Joe Carr of the Columbus Panhandles was elected President, a move that turned out to be an inspired choice.

Twenty-one teams were listed as being in the APFA in September; only 13 were listed in the final standings, largely due to having played too few league opponents. Thorpe, Guyon and Calac were in Cleveland's backfield that year and, after playing two games, the Decatur Staleys moved to Cubs Park in Chicago. At year's end, both Chicago and Buffalo, who had a slightly better record, claimed the league championship. After George Halas and Dutch Sternaman were awarded the Chicago franchise—well, not the only Chicago franchise as the Cardinals also had one—Halas was given a seat on the league's executive council. A council meeting naturally awarded the 1921 championship to the Staleys. Halas wanted to name the team the Cubs because they were playing in what folks today call Wrigley Field, but cubs are cuddly creatures, not exactly the image of a ferocious football team. So, Halas picked the grown up version of the animal for the team we know as the Bears.

The day before the January 1922 league meeting, nine University of Illinois players were banned from college athletics for having played for Taylorville, Illinois in a game against Carlinville, whose management had hired Notre Dame ringers. Headlines demanded action by the pro teams to end the practice of enticing college players to play for pay. The pros needed a scapegoat but not one who would cost the other teams the loss of a large gate. The Green Bay Packers fit that bill perfectly and agreed to withdraw from the league and be refunded their $50 franchise fee. The team owners then discussed, but did not pass, a salary cap. Two days later the fledgling football association got the most publicity it had to date when the *Chicago Herald and Examiner* headline blared across eight columns, "Stagg Says Conference Will Break Professional Football Menace." Knute Rockne announced that Notre Dame would treat harshly any of its players who had played for Carlinville. The Associated Press said Rockne had "...long been known as a staunch enemy of professional football." That is, since he had last played for Massillon. Eventually eight players were dropped by the Irish, necessitating that four sophomores, Stuhldreher, Miller, Crowley and Layden, start in the backfield the next year.

At the June meeting, owners felt they needed a grander name to reflect their grandiose ideas and renamed themselves the National Football League, even though they had no team on the Atlantic seaboard and the westernmost team was on the east bank of the Mississippi. Among the teams that were added—teams came and went so fast in those days that the league had trouble keeping up with them—were teams from Green Bay, Wisconsin and LaRue, Ohio. The Green Bay Blues, coached by former Irish backup Earl "Curley" Lambeau, were soon redubbed the Packers by the press. The LaRue team, the Oorang Indians, featuring Thorpe, Guyon and Calac, is worthy of a chapter of its own.

In the off-season, league President Joe Carr borrowed the reserve clause from baseball. Players who played for a team one year were reserved for it for the next year. This kept players from jumping from team to team for better offers. Carr also had 15% of players' salaries withheld until the end of the season. That also caused players to stay put, especially later in the season.

After winning the 1922 championship, Canton Bulldogs' owner Ralph Hay, the man most responsible for establishing the NFL, wasn't selling enough Hupmobiles to offset the Bulldogs' financial losses and sold the team to a group of local businessmen. The Bulldogs continued their championship ways under the new ownership but also continued to hemorrhage money. After winning another championship while losing $13,000 in 1923, the new owners of the Bulldogs had had enough and sold the franchise, players and all, to Sam Deutsch, owner of the Cleveland Indians franchise. Had Deutsch decided to field both teams, the league would have had problems. Instead, he merged the two franchises into the Cleveland Bulldogs to represent both the team's location and its players. The Bulldogs won the 1924 championship, despite a 23–0 December loss to the Bears, because of a league rule sponsored by George Halas; the rule allowed only those games played between NFL teams before November 30 to count toward championship consideration. So, Halas's rule cost him a championship. The 1925 season was extended to December 20.

Chicago won the league championship in 1925 but this time it was the Cardinals, not the Bears. However, the Bears won something more important near the end of the season. On the Monday before Thanksgiving, Harold "Red" Grange signed a contract with the Bears two days after finishing his college career with the University of Illinois by gaining 192 yards against the Buckeyes of Ohio State. During his college career, Grange set records not yet equaled. The "Wheaton Iceman's" performance against the previously unbeaten Michigan Wolverines in 1924 is the stuff of legends. All he did was to return the opening kickoff 95 yards for a touchdown, then race through the Michigan defense for three more long touchdowns in the first twelve minutes of play. "The Galloping Ghost" returned briefly in the second half to run for one touchdown and throw for another.

A *Chicago News* reporter, apparently no fan of professional football, wrote, "He is a living legend now. Why sully it?" University of Michigan coach Fielding Yost said, "I'd be glad to see Grange do anything else except play professional football." Grange's college coach, Bob Zuppke, was opposed to professionalism and told him, "Football just isn't a game to be played for money." Recognizing the hypocrisy, Grange replied, "You get paid for coaching, Zup. Why should it be wrong for me to get paid for playing?"

Grange's business manager, C. C. ("Cash and Carry" to some) Pyle, arranged a 10-game-18-day exhibition tour for the Bears and their new star. The tour was to open on Thanksgiving Day as a home game against the cross-town rival Cardinals. 36,000 people, by far the largest crowd to attend a professional football game to that time, packed Wrigley Field in spite of a snowstorm that hit that day. It was still snowing on Sunday when 28,000 showed up to see Grange and the Bears host Columbus. Only 8,000 hearty souls turned out in St. Louis the following Wednesday, due to a continuing snowstorm and 12 degree temperature. The following Saturday a rainstorm

Oorang Indians coming to town; *Baltimore News* 12-6-1922

didn't discourage 35,000 from attending a game in Philadelphia. The next day 65,000 paid plus an estimated 8,000 gate-crashers watched Grange and the Bears play the New York Giants at the Polo Grounds. That game turned around the Giants' season financially, turning a loser into a winner. This game was one of the most important games in the history of pro football, not because of what happened on the field but because so many fans were in the stands and because it was New York. Professional football was now important.

The next game was in Washington, DC, where President Calvin Coolidge, not a sports fan, when introduced to Grange and Halas of the Bears, said, "Glad to meet you young gentlemen. I always did like animal acts." 25,000 Bostonians watched the Bears play the Providence Steamrollers on Wednesday. The next day in Pittsburgh, Grange suffered a blood clot as a result of a torn muscle caused by being kicked in the arm. 20,000 Detroit fans requested refunds because he was unable to play and 18,000 cheered him in a token appearance in a home game against the Giants to end the tour. He was beaten up and worn out but $150,000 richer. They started a second tour of nine games on Christmas Day in Coral Gables, Florida, playing games in other Florida cities, New Orleans and up the West Coast from San Diego to Seattle, all to large crowds. Attendance and money had reached new levels in the NFL. Jim Thorpe raised semi-pro football to a professional level in 1915 and Red Grange took it a step higher in 1925.

When asked about his contributions to pro football in later life, Indian Joe Guyon responded:

> Take like when I went to the New York Giants in '27. I must have been about thirty-five then. But I spearheaded the Giants to their first world championship. Spearheaded them, yeh. Did everything. I kicked kickoffs clear through the uprights. I could still outrun those

pro ballplayers. That was my last year of pro football, because that baseball injury ruined everything, but gosh-darn, I enjoyed New York.

Thorpe, Guyon and Calac completed their professional playing careers before the end of the decade, but Carlisle's participation in the NFL was not over. Lone Star Dietz was hired to coach the Boston Braves in 1933. A controversy over the team's name change to the Redskins to honor Dietz continues long after his departure after the 1934 season. The importance of Carlisle players to the birth of professional football was not forgotten by Jack Cusack, one of the midwives. In a 1968 interview, he told Bob Curran, "Consider such giants of the game as Big Jim Thorpe, Doc Spears, Milton Ghee, Carp Julian, Bill Gardner, Pete Calac, Dr. Hube Wagner, Robert Butler, Howard (Cub) Buck, Greasy Neale, Fred Sefton, P. C. Crisp, Bill Garlow, Costello, and Ernie Soucy; if they were not real 'professionals'—well, what were they?"

3
All-Indian Teams

After finishing at Carlisle, many of the football players wanted to continue their on-field participation. Relatively few athletes of any era are good enough at their sport to support themselves playing a boy's game. This was especially true in the years during and immediately following Carlisle's all-too-brief foray into the world of big-time college athletics. However, some of the Indians, as discussed in previous chapters, were talented enough to support themselves by working as athletes. Many who were top-notch athletes and still wanted to play couldn't make enough money at it to consistently put bread on the table for their families. So, some Carlisle alums started teams of their own to give themselves and their former teammates further opportunities to play and, if lucky, to make a few bucks. This chapter covers Carlisle Indian School football players who later played on teams that were comprised of all Indian players, or at least advertised to be so. But first a little background about those teams is needed. The earliest All-Indian team which was formed to provide a place for former Carlisle students to play was the Detroit Carlisle Indians, or ex-Carlisles or Braves as they were often called. However, the 1915 Altoona Indians and 1916 Pitcairn Quakers could both boast of having many former Carlisle players, the exact number of which may never be known due to the practice of using assumed names, sometimes multiple names, when playing professionally. Current and former Carlisle students working for the Ford Motor Company created the Detroit team in 1916 to give themselves an opportunity to play football on their day off work. Creating an alumni team may not have been an original idea: also operating in Detroit around that time was a team of Harvard alums who, not surprisingly, called itself the Harvards. The Altoona and Pitcairn teams were sponsored by the respective Pennsylvania Railroad operations where many of the players worked during the week. The Detroit, Altoona and Pitcairn teams played many of the professional teams that later formed the National Football League (NFL). However, not all former Carlisle players still active in professional football played for All-Indian teams. Some, such as Jim Thorpe, Pete Calac and Joe Guyon, played for the Canton Bulldogs alongside All Americans from major universities.

In 1922, an all-Indian NFL team, the Oorang Indians, was formed. Although it listed a number of excellent players on its roster, its primary purpose was to promote and sell Oorang Airedales, a breed of dog sold nationwide by owner Walter Lingo who operated out of that football capital, La Rue, Ohio, the smallest town to ever have an NFL franchise. Lingo loved his dogs more than anything. However, American Indian lore fascinated him. As the story goes, in the winter of 1921, he, Jim Thorpe and Pete Calac were possum hunting on Lingo's expansive farm when the idea struck him to sponsor a professional football team to promote his enterprise. Speculation has it that alcoholic beverages may have played a part in the decision.

It is accurate that Thorpe was an avid sportsman who loved to hunt and fish and kept hunting dogs throughout most of his adult life. It is also accurate that Lingo was a tireless promoter of his Oorang Airedales and often took famous people hunting as a way of getting publicity. It is likely true that he took Thorpe hunting. However, it is unlikely that the team was born at the end of a day's hunting near La Rue, Ohio.

On February 16, 1922, a report came out of Milwaukee that Joe Plunkett and Ambrose Clark of Chicago had acquired an NFL franchise to replace the one in Green Bay that had recently been dropped from the league. Jim Thorpe was reported both to have signed with the team and to have recruited such

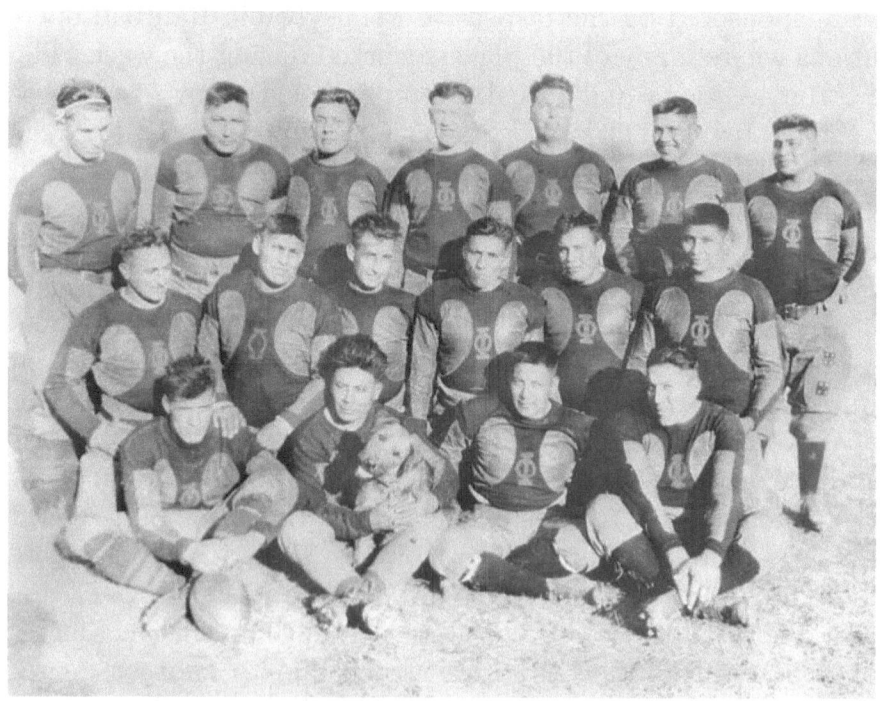

1922 Oorang Indians NFL team included several former Carlisle Indians: Leon Boutwell, Joe Guyon, Stilwell Saunooke, Bill Winneshiek, Bemus Pierce, Nick Lassaw, Elmer Busch, Jim Thorpe, Thomas St. Germain & Pete Calac. *Cumberland County Historical Society, Carlisle, PA*

luminaries as Al Nesser of the Akron Pros, Ed Conley of Valparaiso University, and several players from Notre Dame.

A week or two later, Jim Thorpe announced that he was retiring from football: "I've sung my swan song in football. I have laid aside a tidy sum and feel that it is about time I retired from active football playing. My decision is not influenced by a desire to avoid the hard knocks of the game, for I love it above all others, and am confident I could continue in the game for five years longer without appreciable letdown in my play. It is simply that I feel that I have played long enough and mean to turn my attention to hunting and fishing and less strenuous sports." That didn't sound like a man who had agreed to form a team earlier that winter. Maybe he had something up his sleeve.

On March 18, Walter Lingo and Jim Thorpe announced the formation of a new NFL franchise called Jim Thorpe's Indians of Marion, Ohio, better known as the Oorang Indians, from Thorpe's home in Yale, Oklahoma. Lingo put up the $100 franchise fee which was less than the price of one of his Airedales. Thorpe, as well as a number of other sportsmen, was a shareholder in the Oorang Kennels Company. The primary purpose of the team was to promote Oorang Airedales, not necessarily to win football championships, but a few wins would be nice. And, by the way, almost all the games would be played on the road, a situation Carlisle and Haskell players would find familiar. The team was to be composed entirely of Indians because Lingo had somehow convinced himself that a supernatural bond existed between Airedales and Indians. So Thorpe and Lingo set about recruiting former Carlisle and Haskell stars as well as some others.

The roster included names like: White Cloud, Lone Wolf, Hill, Winneshiek, Busch, Long Time Sleep, Calac, Boutwell, Guyon, Attache, Eagle Feather, Fred & Henry Broker, Saunooke, St. Germain, Downwind, Running Deer, Strong Wind, Thunder, Big Bear, War Eagle and Earth. Some of these names

OORANG INDIANS

No.	Name	Pos.	College	Tribe	Wgt.
30	WHITE CLOUD	L. E.	CARLISLE	TUSCARORA	175
22	LONE WOLF	L. T.	CARLISLE	CHIPPEWAY	190
7	HILL	L. G.	CARLISLE	IROQUOIS	200
3	WINNESHEIK	C.	CARLISLE	TUSCARORA	185
20	BUSCH	R. G.	CARLISLE	MISSION	220
14	LONG TIME SLEEP	R. T.	CARLISLE	FLATHEAD	195
4	COLAC	R. E.	W. VIRGINIA	MISSION	195
8	BONTWELL	Q. B.	CARLISLE	CHIPPEWAY	188
10	GUYON (Capt.)	L. H.	GEORGIA TECH	CHIPPEWAY	190
6	ATTACHE	R. H.	SHERMAN	MISSION	185
32	EAGLE FEATHER	F. B.	CARLISLE	MOHICAN	215
9	F. BROKER	FULLBACK	CARLISLE	CHIPPEWAY	190
11	H. BROKER	QUARTERBACK	CARLISLE	CHIPPEWAY	175
12	SANOOK	END	CARLISLE	CHEROKEE	180
26	WAR EAGLE	GUARD	FLANDEAU	CHIPPEWAY	210
5	EARTH	HALFBACK	CARLISLE	MISSION	180
2	J. THORPE	HALFBACK	CARLISLE	SAC & FOX	190

	1st	2nd	3rd	4th
CHICAGO				
OORANG INDIANS				

CHICAGO VS.
ROCK ISLAND
SUNDAY, NOV. 19TH AT 2:15 P. M.

should be familiar from earlier chapters, but others were coined by Walter Lingo to give the players what he thought were more Indian-sounding names. Attache and War Eagle were listed as having attended Sherman Institute and Flandreau Indian School, respectively. The rest were supposed to have attended Carlisle. It's hard to tell exactly who all of these guys were.

Jim Thorpe was paid well—$500 a week to be exact—but his duties were not confined to football. Besides practicing during the week, he and the rest of the team were involved in the daily operations of the kennel. They also had to practice their pre-game stunts. The team required three special train cars to travel to games because they took dogs with them to show off for the crowds. Some credit Walter Lingo with having invented the half-time show. And the dogs didn't perform by themselves; the players were an integral part of the entertainment. Skits included Airedales retrieving targets that Indian marksmen had shot; dogs trailing and treeing a bear; Indian dances; tomahawk, knife and lariat throwing; and Indian scouts demonstrating their wartime exploits with Airedales in WWI, including war veterans delivering first aid in no man's land. Sometimes before a game Nick Lassaw, dubbed Long Time Sleep by his teammates due to the difficulty in getting him up in the morning, wrestled a bear.

The other teams—their owners at least—liked the Oorang Indians because they filled stadiums. Their on-field performance was, unfortunately, not as good as their theatrics. Most likely they were too tired to play well. Chicago Bears' tackle Ed Healey thought Thorpe was a poor coach, especially with discipline. He also thought the players were rough. "I have a vivid recollection of how they used the 'points.' By that I mean the elbows, knees and feet in their blocking and tackling. They'd give you those bones and it hurt. They were tough S. O. B.s but good guys off the field."

However, their off-field antics are the stuff of legends. In one story, a bartender in Chicago wanted to close up shop but some Indians put him in a phone booth and turned it upside down so they could drink until morning. Of course, the Bears disemboweled the Indians on the field later that day. In St. Louis, several players left a bar one night to find their trolley going in the opposite direction. Not wanting to wait forever or walk back to the hotel, they picked up the trolley and turned it around to head in the direction they desired. Sometime quarterback Leon Boutwell put it into perspective: "White people had this misconception about Indians. They thought we were all wild men, even though almost all of us had been to college and were generally more civilized than they were. Well, it was a dandy excuse to raise hell and get away with it when the mood struck us. Since we were Indians we could get away with things the whites couldn't. Don't think we didn't take advantage of it."

After two years of seeing his team play uninspired football and coping with shrinking crowds due to having already seen the dog stunts, Walter Lingo mercifully pulled the plug on the Oorang Indians' football team. But he wasn't done with using

Bears vs Indians
November 12, 1922

Indian athletes to promote his dogs. The 1926 Oorang Indians baseball team, featuring Jim Thorpe, Pete Calac and several of the same players who had formerly played on the football team, barnstormed around Ohio. Although the all-Indian NFL franchise was gone, the concept of all-Indian football teams did not end with the demise of the Oorang Indians.

In the early 1920s, former Carlisle great Pete Hauser coached the Hominy Indians. Based in Hominy, Oklahoma, the Indians criss-crossed the country playing, and beating, most that dared to book a game against them. After two successful years, Hauser stepped down. Former Haskell great John Levi took over as player-coach and the team continued to win. The team reached its zenith on the day after Christmas in 1927 in Pawhuska, Oklahoma, the capital of the oil-rich Osage tribe. Their opponents were the new NFL champion New York Giants who featured former Carlisle and Oorang star, Joe Guyon, but it's not clear if he and the Giants' other stars made the trip. The Indians won 13–6 and again defeated the Giants two weeks later in San Antonio, Texas. Few Carlislians would have been young enough to have played for Hominy, so it was largely a Haskell outfit. (An early Hominy star was a John Martin who, better known as the Gashouse Gang baseball player Pepper Martin, was eventually discouraged from playing by the St. Louis Cardinal management.) The Great Depression took its toll on such luxuries as barnstorming Indian football teams, causing Hominy to fold its tent in the early 1930s.

All-Indian Teams

Histories of these all-Indian teams are sketchy but Robert L. Whitman wrote a book about the Oorang Indians. One of the biggest problems facing researchers, like Whitman and the author of this book, is determining exactly who played for these teams due to the use of fake names either to disguise players' involvement or to make them sound more colorful. Those players who have been determined to have strong ties to Oklahoma are included in this book. Surely, some will be overlooked for various reasons, the inability to find information on them being the greatest. The author hopes enough information surfaces after publication of this book to expand this chapter greatly.

1922 Oorang Indians NFL team, manager, owner, Mrs. Nick Lassaw & Mrs. Thomas St. Germain *Cumberland County Historical Society, Carlisle, PA*

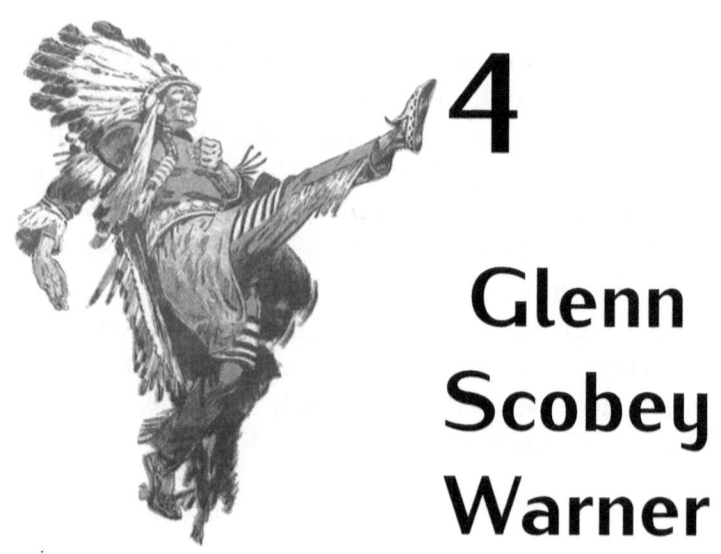

4

Glenn Scobey Warner

Pop Warner, the Carlisle Indians' coach and athletic director in their glory years, was not an Indian and never claimed to be one. The closest Warner would ever get to being an Indian was when he was made an honorary Sac and Fox. It is necessary to know a little about Warner because he was an integral part of the team and of the players' lives in Carlisle and, in some cases, in later life. This chapter is intentionally short; readers wanting to know more about "the Old

Name: Glenn Scobey Warner Nickname: Pop, The Old Fox
DOB: 4/5/1871 Height: 6'0"
Weight: 205 Age:
Tribe: N/A Home: Springville, NY
Parents: William H. Warner, Adaline Scobey
Early Schooling: Griffith Institute
Later Schooling: Cornell University
Honors: College Football Hall of Fame, Charter Member, 1951
Helm's Athletic Foundation Hall of Fame, 1951
Stanford Athletic Hall of Fame
Greater Buffalo Hall of Fame, 2001

Fox" can read the biographies already written about him. The purpose of this chapter is to provide the reader unfamiliar with Warner a brief overview of his life with an emphasis on his time at Carlisle. It might even include a nugget or two rescued from the dustbin of history unknown even to those knowledgeable about Warner.

Glenn Scobey Warner was born on April 5, 1871, on a farm near Springville, New York, the first-born son of William H. and Adaline Scobey Warner. The family moved into town when Glenn was 10, a relocation that made playing baseball on a daily basis more practical. He also played what passed for football at the time, but baseball was his game. He was a fireball pitcher and could hit the long ball. After he completed high school, he moved with his family to Wichita Falls, Texas, to work on their wheat farm and cattle ranch. After a year of working on the ranch, he spent two more years in Texas learning the tinsmith trade and making some money. However, his 1892 vacation in his old hometown changed the direction of his life.

At 21 years of age, he returned to Springville just in time to play baseball for the town team in a series of games against the hated rival town's team. Both teams hired ringers and he established a friendship with one of his town's ringers, John McGraw, that paid off in later life. After some success betting on harness races, he convinced himself that he was an expert and followed the Grand Circuit the rest of the summer. He lost $150, all he had previously won plus everything else he had except his return trainfare, on the first day. Broke and not desiring to explain to his father what had happened to his money, Warner considered pursuing the course his father had wanted him to follow from the start. His father wired him the $100 necessary to enroll in law school at Cornell.

Money in hand, he caught the day train to Ithaca and, on the ride, made the acquaintance of football captain Carl Johanson who, upon seeing Warner's size (200 pounds), ordered

Warner coaching; *U. S. Army Military History Institute*

him to attend football practice that afternoon. Despite having little experience, having missed the two previous weeks of practice, and having to play in a game the next day, Warner was made starting left guard. He did not relinquish that position during his playing career at Cornell. However, he was still more interested in baseball. On the first day of spring practice, Glenn tried to impress the coach even though he had been told to take it easy, and he developed a sore arm. The next day, in spite of the pain, he threw at full speed again, ruining his arm forever. His baseball career over, he dabbled a bit with boxing and track but found that his best opportunities were then in football.

Shortly after arriving at Cornell, he acquired the nickname "Pop" because he was three years older than his classmates. The name stuck to him like glue the rest of his life. Pop played football and studied law for two years, then graduated. He was elected captain for the following year but, since he had completed his law degree, he had to take some graduate level courses to be on the field. His father couldn't be expected to pay, so Warner solved that problem by selling watercolor landscapes he painted.

Some consider Glenn Warner to have been Cornell's greatest guard ever. However, after starring for three years, his playing days were essentially over. He passed the bar examination and was ready to litigate at season's end. After finding a law firm in Buffalo that was willing to accept him, he went to work in January 1895. Before his slim body of clients could grow to provide him a decent income, an opportunity to supplement his income by coaching football appeared. While pondering the idea of making $25 a week in the fall, he got another offer for $35. Not wanting to let an opportunity escape, Warner negotiated with Iowa Agricultural College (today's Iowa State) to prepare its team for the season by working with it for five weeks at $25 a week. His assistant worked with the team the rest of the season while Warner coached the University of Georgia for $35 a week for the whole season. So, in Pop's first year as a head coach, he mentored two college teams, a feat that has seldom been duplicated. It should be noted that Warner lost the entire $125 salary from Iowa State in a wager on their first game. This two-team scheme worked well enough that Warner prepared the Iowa State team for five seasons running while coaching elsewhere during the season. After two successful years at Georgia, Warner's alma mater beckoned. He also had on-field success in his two years at Cornell, but internal politics made staying there unwise if not impossible.

The Carlisle Indian School football team had been described by sportswriters as a fine set of athletes sorely in need of first-class coaching. Superintendent Pratt took that to heart and looked for the best coach he could find. Walter Camp recommended Warner, thinking that this innovative young coach would be a good fit with the Indians. Warner asked for a salary of $1,200 plus expenses and Pratt didn't blink. So, when Pratt offered him the job, he jumped at it.

The 1899 Carlisle team, Warner's first at the Indian school, was loaded with fine players, several of whom may have already been first team All Americans had they played for one of the Big Four. Warner soon found that the methods he had used previously, and those under which he had played, would not work with the Indians. Pushing players hard and swearing at them was the norm for coaches at that time, but the Indians did not respond well to what they considered abuse. He recalled that a near mutiny resulted and several good players stopped coming to practice because of his tactics. Pop observed that they were not used to being sworn or cussed at and found the experience to be humiliating. Ives Goddard, a noted language expert, offers this opinion:

> For one, Indian languages do not have the equivalent of using the name of deities in legal or religious oaths and hence do not have the use of 'God' etc. in what is called profanity in the narrow sense, taking the name of God 'in vain.' Secondly, they typically do not have slang words for sexual and other intimate functions and body parts, so there can be no equivalent of using 'four-letter words' in English. (Some speakers of some languages may avoid some words or use jokey substitutes, though.) Probably all languages have offensive ways of talking about people or cussing people out, considered serious or even 'fighting words.' In general, however, there are unfortunately few details available about the specific usages in these areas in various languages.
>
> My guess would be that the Carlisle students who objected to swearing did so because of Christian upbringing in Protestant churches whose missionaries condemned such language in English.

Warner called a team meeting for all the players, including the ones who had stopped coming to practice. He explained that his verbal outbursts were meant to emphasize points and were not intended to demean players. He promised to tone down his language and asked them to come back to practice. "The next day, the Indians returned to practice and I went on to coach without using a lot of profanity to motivate my team. I soon found out that I would get better results from them by this method. Once this problem was settled, the Carlisle team began to concentrate on football. And the results were impressive."

The 1899 team with Warner at the helm was Carlisle's best to date. It was the first Indian team to beat one of the Big Four, Penn. The only losses were to that year's national co-champions, Harvard and Princeton. The Indians also defeated that year's West Coast power, California, on Christmas Day. For the first time ever, Walter Camp named an Indian, Isaac Seneca, to his All America first team at halfback. He also named Martin Wheelock to his second team at tackle and Frank Hudson to the third team at quarterback. Hudson was also the preeminent kicker of his day and others on the team, including Wheelock, were pretty darn good. It was reported in the press that, "Warner, the Carlisle coach, attributes the skill of the redskins in kicking to the fact that the lower part of the leg is hung straight from the knee, instead of slightly curving, as is the case of Caucasians."

Major Pratt allowed the long football trips because the travel was educational for the players. That the school usually made a good bit of money couldn't have hurt. It was upon the team's return from the California trip that Major Pratt made Warner an offer to be the school's athletic director. The $2,500 salary was an offer he couldn't refuse. Because he then had a full-time position at Carlisle, Pop closed out his off-season law practice. However, he occasionally used his knowledge of the law to draft a contract for a player who was turning pro. Because the athletic director was responsible for all sports, Warner had to bone up on track, something he had never coached. Gaining a rudimentary knowledge of coaching track from books and conversations with experts, Warner inaugurated Carlisle's first ever track team in 1900. The track on which the Carlisle teams raced still circumnavigates Indian Field, the site of the Indians' football battles on Carlisle Barracks, current home of the U. S. Army War College.

Glenn made an interesting observation regarding his athletes: "And it was a noticeable fact that the Indian football players were often the brightest students at Carlisle and their teachers frequently remarked on how much quicker they were to learn than the other students."

Warner's 1900 team went 6–4–1 against a tougher schedule than was played the previous year. The 1901 team was weak overall, causing it to be one of the few losing seasons Warner experienced at the Indian school. Wanting to rest his first-string halfbacks for the upcoming game with Penn, Warner left them home when the team went to Michigan to play Fielding Yost's point-a-minute team. The backups, Louis Leroy and Edward DeMarr, decided Detroit was close to home and ran away, leaving Carlisle without running backs for the game. Their absence didn't materially affect the outcome of a game Warner had little hope of winning.

A junior player on that year's squad was a young man by the name of Charles Albert Bender. He would likely have turned into a good football player if he had persisted, but Connie Mack, manager of the Philadelphia Athletics from 1901 to 1950, beckoned. The young Chippewa left Carlisle to play in the big leagues where the future Hall-of-Fame pitcher was often called "Chief."

Things improved football-wise in 1902 when, by beating Penn again and losing only to Bucknell, Harvard, and Virginia, the Indians again had a winning record. After the season, Pop's younger brother and sometime assistant, Bill, talked him into agreeing to take what turned out to be the princely sum of $23 to play for a professional team in the World Series of professional football held at Madison Square Garden over the New Year. The Warner brothers held up one side of the line at guard and tackle. Carlisle Indians Bemus and Hawley Pierce held up the other side of the same line. In the first game, Pop received a bad cut on his head but didn't leave the game. After the injury, he missed a kick after touchdown and three field goals in a winning effort. As he told it, "The next morning—following the game—I awoke feeling very stiff and could only move my tired body with great difficulty. I even had to call upon my brother, Bill, to help me get dressed that morning because of the tremendous pain that I was suffering. After that single game, I decided to retire from my career in professional football."

The team improved considerably in 1903, having its best team yet, beating Penn again and losing only to Princeton and Harvard. The single-point loss to Harvard featured the much-written-about hidden ball or hunchback play that gave the Indians a lead. Warner later wrote, "In a way, I'm glad that Harvard was able to come back to win because I never liked to win a game on a fluke, although the hidden ball play was within the rules at that time."

Cornell alumni were upset over their football team's performance in the last four games of the 1903 season. The coach with whom they were dissatisfied was one William Warner, Pop's younger brother. After being approached by a Cornell faculty committee, the elder Warner agreed to return to coach his alma mater in 1904. Knowing that Superintendent Pratt would likely be forced out of his position at Carlisle, due to public statements he had made which would make conditions at Carlisle uncertain, surely made Pop's decision to leave easier. His results in 1904 and 1905 at Cornell were slightly better than his brother's had been, from a won-lost perspective. 1906 was much better but he was involved in a campus controversy.

In early 1907 after an 8-1-2 season, Warner resigned to make peace at the school. He had found it necessary to drop a star player from the squad. "But my disciplining of this player nearly caused a campus riot. The player was a hero among the school's student body, and naturally my action created an uproar with them and caused a lot of trouble and unrest.... I had felt in my heart and mind that I was right in regards to my handling of the matter, because I had done what any coach would have done if he has any backbone to him."

Pop Warner apparently didn't sever all his ties to Carlisle when he departed for Cornell. In 1906 Carlisle's new superintendent, Major Mercer, invited Warner to help prepare the Indians for the upcoming season. Radically new rules had been adopted after the outcry over the large number of deaths of football players experienced in 1905. The new rules shifted the advantage from bulk to speed and deception as well as legalization of the forward pass. Warner spent a week coaching Carlisle's coaches with his new innovations. One of the things Warner imparted to Bemus Pierce and Frank Hudson, former players then coaching the Indians, was the earliest incarnation of his new formation. He later wrote to football historian Col. Alexander M. Weyand,

> As to the single wing formation I started using this in 1906. That was the year the rules were radically changed making it necessary to have seven men on the line of scrimmage and making it illegal to help the ball carrier by pushing or pulling. Walter Camp in his writings often referred to it as the Carlisle formation. I do not remember what team it was first used against. I also originated the double wing formation but I believe I used it before the Dartmouth game of 1912 [Carlisle only played Dartmouth one time. That game was played in 1913]. Although it sure worked havoc on Dartmouth I think I used it two or three years before 1912.

Perhaps it was seeing Frank Mt. Pleasant throw 40-yard spiral passes or it was seeing how well the Indians ran his offense under the Indian coaches, but Warner agreed to come back to Carlisle for the 1907 season. He later recalled:

> Carlisle played good football from the first, but it was in 1907 that the Indians rounded into true championship form., downing Pennsylvania by a score of 26 to 5, Minnesota by 12 to 0, Harvard by 23 to 15 and Chicago by 18 to 4. With the exception of the unbeaten Pitt team of 1916, it was about as perfect a football machine as I ever sent on the field. Typically Indian, too, for among the first-string men were Little Old Man, Afraid of a Bear, Lubo the Wolf, Little Boy, Wauseka, [Frank] Mount Pleasant and [Mike] Balenti. The boys clicked into shape early in the season, and the very first game convinced me that a big year was ahead....
>
> The Carlisle eleven of 1907 was nearly perfect. Jim Thorpe, by the way, made his first appearance that year, subbing now and then for [Fritz] Hendricks. The forward pass had just been permitted by the new rules and we were about the first to see its value and develop its possibilities to the limit. How the Indians did take to it! Light on their feet as professional dancers, and every one

Emil Hauser, James Johnson, Al Exendine, Pop Warner
Cumberland County Historical Society, Carlisle, PA

amazingly skillful with his hands, the redskins pirouetted in and out until the receiver was well down the field, and then they shot the ball like a bullet. Poor Pennsylvania, among the first to experience Carlisle's aerial attack, finally reached a point where the players ran in circles, emitting wild yawps. The one defeat of the 1907 season was handed to us by Princeton....

Few things have ever given me greater satisfaction than that Chicago victory. Stagg's team up to then, was laying claim to the championship and sports writers refused to concede that poor Lo had a chance. The game, in fact, was to be a field day for the great [Chicago quarterback Wally] Steffen, famous for his twisting, dodging runs and educated toe...Steffen did kick one field goal but that was his only pretense to glory. [William] Gardner and [Albert] Exendine were on him every time he tried to run back a kick.... I remember that Carlisle's share of the gate was $17,000, an almost incredible sum in those days....

Our ends that year were Gardner, a Sioux [sic], and Exendine, an Arapahoe [sic], and I still maintain that they have never been surpassed for sheer brilliance. Pete Hauser, who did the kicking for us, was a big Cheyenne with a powerful toe, his punts averaging 60 yards, and under instructions he always raised them sky high. Gardner and Exendine were off at the swing of his leg, and it was rarely that they failed to keep up with the ball. In the game with Chicago they made life miserable for Wally Steffen, invariably nailing him in his tracks, although [Chicago coach Amos Alonzo] Stagg finally assigned three men to block each end.

1907 was not the end of a team's great runs; it was just the continuation of what Warner started in 1899 and continued for some years. Warner observed that some of the tougher teams became reluctant to schedule Carlisle now that they were often beating Penn and had defeated Harvard. Never again would they be able to schedule three or four games against the Big Four; even scheduling two Big Four opponents became less common. The undersized Indians and Warner's offenses that capitalized on speed and deception were a perfect match. The combination was so effective that other coaches copied it. Warner started marketing a correspondence course on the rudiments of football in 1908. Soon the Warner system dominated American football.

Carlisle peaked with three straight one-loss seasons in 1911, 1912 and 1913. Warner considered the 1911 team as the best, having defeated both Penn and Harvard. It should be noted that Jim Thorpe had departed before the 1913 season, so Carlisle wasn't a one-player team as some have suggested. The outcome of the government investigation into improprieties at the Indian school in early 1914 made it impossible to field a competitive team, so Warner left.

Reno Gazette 12-9-1915

Much has been written about Warner's role in the stripping of Jim Thorpe's medals, so that needs no repeating. However, what may be new information is that student records from the Carlisle Indian School contain numerous mentions of students leaving to play summer baseball. Even the school newspaper mentioned individuals and their teams. No mention was made of pay, but it was common knowledge which teams were professionals. It is highly unlikely that Superintendent Friedman and Coach Warner were unaware of this. They probably knew Thorpe left to play minor league baseball but didn't expect to see him return and, if they did, they certainly did not expect him to become the physical specimen who did return.

The most famous football referee of the period, Mike Thompson, officiated many Carlisle games and said this about Warner:

> I first saw the Indians in 1902, when I refereed their game against Cornell. Bill Warner, Pop's brother, was captain of the Cornell team that year, as Pop had been in 1894...Pop knew his Indians. He walked and acted like one, and came to be a man of few words, mostly grunt, until his boys really believed that he had Indian blood. He knew an Indian's strength and limitations, capitalized on the former and avoided the latter. Warner showed each man his job individually, demonstrating it, not talking it. Perhaps he gave his quarter a little theory, but for the most part he depended upon their native cunning, skill and love of the game to do the rest. The Indians loved trick plays. Pop gave them plenty and knew just when to pull his tricks. I doubt that any other coach could have approximated his success at Carlisle...

Warner himself learned that coaching the Indians required a different approach than coaching white players. "While at Carlisle, I had developed a theory that the Indian boys had been trained by their forefathers to be keen observers. Often when the Indian boys were exposed to a new sport or game they would usually refuse to participate. Instead, they would stand and watch the older, more experienced Indian boys, who were participating in the new sport or game, demonstrate how it was to be played. Then after having studied the play or actions, or motions of their elders, they would attempt to mimic those same actions, or motions, and would usually be almost as accomplished as those who they had just observed."

Warner shared some other insights into his Carlisle players in a 1933 interview. "Carlisle was a school where the Indian would come as a mere boy and stay there a number of years obtaining his education. I had a chance to develop him from the ground up and to use his ability during his best athletic years.... Some of my boys came to Carlisle entirely uneducated and it took them years to get through, meaning I had them on my teams when they were more mature." When asked what the optimum age for a football player was, Warner responded, "It is hard to lay down a general rule because one man may be at his best at 27 and another at 20. On the whole, however, I would say that 23 is a fine age for a football player. He is old enough to know some of the tricks of the trade and young enough to have plenty of speed and fire."

Decades later, a Carlisle substitute, John Russeau (Chippewa), remembered Warner as "...a strict disciplinarian who would take no excuses for 'holding back' by his players, and who enforced rigorous training by the whole team. His favorite penalty for rule infractions was a long cross-country run with the player in full football uniform. 'Pop' made sure the delinquent did not lag in his run–from one to five or ten miles–by following along on horseback."

After leaving Carlisle, Warner went on to coach at Pitt, Stanford and Temple, to win national championships and to win the Rose Bowl but he always loved the Indians:

Great teams, those Carlisle elevens that I coached, and what was even finer, sportsmen all. There wasn't an Indian of the lot who didn't love to win and hate to lose, but to a man they were modest in victory and resolute in defeat. They never gloated, they never whined, and no matter how bitter the contest, they played cheerfully, squarely and cleanly. Whenever I see one of those all-America teams, I cannot help but think what an eleven could have been selected from those real Americans who blazed such a trail of glory across the football fields of the country from 1899 to 1914. One might go a long way before he found a better line-up than this:

Exendine	right end
Wauseka	right tackle
Bemus Pierce	right guard
Lone Wolf Hunt	center
Martin Wheelock	left guard
Hawley Pierce	left tackle
Ed Rogers	left end
James Johnson	quarterback
James Thorpe	right halfback
Joe Guyon	left halfback
Pete Hauser	fullback

And for substitutes, if substitutes were ever needed for these iron men, how about such players as Bill Gardner, Lone Star Dietz, [Antonio] Lubo, Afraid of a Bear, Little Boy, [Isaac] Seneca, [Jonas] Metoxen, [Pete] Calac, [Frank] Hudson, [Frank] Mount Pleasant and Gus Welch?

As great a coach as Warner was, he was no better at predicting the future than anyone else. In an article for *Baseball*

Magazine, Pop looked into his crystal ball and saw a limited future for football:

> Football will never be a great national game, for a variety of reasons. The season is shorter, not so many games are possible as in baseball, for instance; and the game is not so open or spectacular. But, in my opinion, one of the main reasons why it will never be a popular sport, is the fact that it depends too much on careful coaching.
>
> Glenn Warner

Charleston Daily Mail 11-4-1933

5

Chauncey Archiquette

T he Marquis de Lafayette had a clerk named Otsiquette during the Revolutionary War. Otsiquette had two sons with an Oneida woman named Sarah Hanyost and then returned to France. After the Treaty of Fort Stanwix in 1784, which formally ended the war between the Iroquois and the Americans, Lafayette requested that the boys, Peter and Edward, better known as Neddy, be sent to France. Peter went and received a classical education. He returned to America in 1792 and died almost immediately of pleurisy. Neddy rebelled and hid in the woods so he could stay behind. He continued living with the Oneidas and raised a family. At some point his family name morphed into Archiquette. In 1823, he led an early

Name: Chauncey Edward Archiquette   Nickname:
   DOB: 11/17/1877   Height: 5'7"
Weight: 158   Age: 21
   Tribe: Oneida   Home: Green Bay, WI
Parents: John Archiquette & Elizabeth Smith Archiquette
Later Schooling: Haskell Institute Commercial Course

From Left to right: Chauncey Archiquette, Capt. Charles
Roy & Charles Guyon (Wahoo) on 1906 CIIS baseball team
Cecilia Balenti-Moddelmog

group of migrants from New York to lands along Duck Creek near present-day Green Bay, Wisconsin. During the Civil War, his grandson, John Archiquette, left his farm to enlist in the 14th Wisconsin Volunteer Infantry Company F. After the war, he returned to his farm and to serve on the Indian police force, where he held the title of Captain. He soon married Elizabeth Smith and started a family. At the time of Elizabeth's death in 1888, Capt. John Archiquette had eight children: Joel, Martin, Christine, Melinda (better known as Belinda), Josiah (Joshua), Chauncey, Robert and Irene. The six older children attended Carlisle Indian School and the youngest two went to Hampton Institute. He remarried in 1890 to Sophia Doxtator, with whom he had four children. One of them, Oscar, would document his father's life.

Chauncey Edward Archiquette arrived in Carlisle on September 21, 1890 at 12 years of age to begin a five-year term of enrollment. That week's edition of *The Indian Helper* announced his arrival: "Peter Powlas brought with him from Oneida Wisconsin: Lucinda Kick, Melinda Metoxen, Lydia Powlas, Melissa Green, Ophelia King, Alice Powlas, Moses King, Isaac Metoxen, Martin Wheelock, Taylor Smith, Whitney Powlas, John Powlas, Chauncey Archiquette, Brigman Cornelius, and Isaac John." Due to having neighbors and siblings at the school, he most certainly would not have been lonely. He went out on two outings during his first enrollment, one of which was quite lengthy as it lasted almost 17 months. He received little other mention during that time, but that wouldn't last forever.

After his term was up in June 1895, he returned home just for the summer. In the fall, he enrolled for another five-year term. Now that Chauncey was a large boy, he became more active in extra-curricular activities and thus received more mention in school publications. In April 1896, he became an officer of the Invincible Debating Society by serving as sergeant-at-arms. That month he also became the starting left fielder for the varsity baseball team. That fall, he played football but didn't get into any varsity games. Prior to 1896, he probably played on his shop team and moved up to the junior varsity or the second team. However, almost no records exist for those teams and their games. The May 28, 1897 issue of *The Indian Helper* included a little riddle: "Why should Archiquette be called 'Flour and Eggs?' Because he makes a good batter." That riddle immediately followed the write-up of a game with Gettysburg College that the Indians won 27–1. Unfortunately, no box score was included. However, the riddle implies that Chauncey had a good day. Sports weren't allowed to occupy all of his time.

Archiquette spent half his days in the harnessmaking shop, learning that trade. The other half of his school day was spent in academic classes. The fall of 1897 was his break-out year in football. He played right end on a team that went 6–4, losing to Princeton, Yale, Penn and Brown, scoring on all but Princeton.

The next summer he played baseball again. In August, 1898, the all-seeing "Man-on-the-band-stand" noticed his baseball playing and wrote, "Ah, Chauncey Archiquette is making a home-run, and another, see? He is the star catcher in the field, too."

That fall, Chauncey was a member of the Senior Class and played right end again on the football team. The 1898 team, the last one before Pop Warner was first hired, went 5–4, losing to three of the Big Four, again, and Cornell, scoring in all of their losses. He graduated in February and returned home in March but didn't stay there long. Chauncey then enrolled at Haskell Institute, in the commercial program most likely, and also played sports. He also played baseball in the summer, probably for Haskell. At summer's end, it was back to school for Chauncey. He found himself in a familiar position that fall—at the right end of the Haskell Indians' line. His first mention for his football playing at that school was a dubious one: he was ejected from the first game against Fielding Yost's team, cross-town rival Kansas, for slugging. Apparently, these games were grudge matches because the Indians walked off the field early in the second half of the rematch in mid-season. Although Haskell was shut out in both games, by scores of 12–0 and 18–0, respectively, they held the 10–0–0 Jayhawkers to their lowest scores of the season. Haskell, ended up at 4–5–0 but Archiquette apparently impressed his new teammates because they elected him captain of the 1900 team. They made a good choice.

Haskell started their season with a 28–0 defeat of Kansas State Normal College of Emporia, Kansas. Their next opponent, the University of Missouri, was waiting for them. *The Lincoln Evening News,* in a demonstration of objectivity, observed, "The Missourians had been expecting so much from their pets, too, that the result was heart rending. They started the season with a hurrah and a bluff that they could lick all opponents. Three coaches were hired, a mass meeting of students was called, subscriptions for the support of the team poured in, and all was roseate and promising. But now a dark cloud overhangs the future.... Tigers repeatedly dropped the ball, especially in trying to catch punts, and one of those bobbles by Hogan gave Haskell a touchdown. Captain Archiquette got the ball, and with a clean field, sprinted across the goal line." Haskell shut out Mizzou 11–0. They would go on to a 9–1–0 season, losing their last game to Washburn College, a team they had beaten the first time they met earlier in the season. Only four of their opponents scored on them—three actually because Washburn scored in both of its games. Chauncey played basketball in the winter and baseball in spring and summer before football season rolled around again.

Haskell's 1901 season started off with three easy victories over weak opponents. On November 4, they met the University of Minnesota in what was described beforehand as the biggest game Haskell had ever played. The *Lincoln Evening News* reported, "The Haskell men are confident of winning from Minnesota. They recognize the fact that the Gophers play a great deal stronger game than any other team Haskell has ever met, but they are prepared to put up the game of their lives." Sportswriters found that several former Carlisle players would be in the game. They couldn't have known that some future ones were there as well. Captain Archiquette—he was elected again—played opposite Ed Rogers, last year's Carlisle captain but that year a Gopher. Thaddeus Red Water, Haskell's left guard, had also played for Carlisle the year before. Left tackle William Baine was at Carlisle the previous year and Charlie Guyon, who was not at Haskell that year, met up with the team in Minneapolis to play left end. Newspapers hyped the impending battle between Archiquette and Rogers, "The struggle of these two men alone will be well worth seeing, as the Haskell captain is said to be one of the fastest Indian players in football this fall." The Indians' hopes were dashed in a 28–0 loss. Five days later, they rebounded and beat John Outland's Kansas team 18–5. Next they beat Missouri and two smaller schools. Their 7–2–0 season ended with an 18–10 Thanksgiving Day loss to Nebraska. In his two years as captain, Archiquette was 16–3–0. Not bad at all.

A summer of playing first base for the Haskell team followed a winter of basketball for Archiquette. And some winter it was! Haskell claimed the national championship after defeating the M. W. A. team of Independence, Missouri, previous claimants to the title. The win was by way of forfeit when, early in the second half, with Haskell leading 17–15, the Missourians left the court, complaining of unfair treatment even though two of the three officials were from Missouri. Their victims included teams from the Universities of Nebraska and Kansas.

Chauncey was no longer a student after graduating from the Commercial Department in the spring. He was then hired as Assistant Disciplinarian at the school. In what seemed to be an annual coaching change, John Outland took the reins as head coach of the 1902 squad. Fallis was team captain and Chauncey played right halfback. In addition to the new coach, the team was also greeted by another upgraded schedule. Even with that, the Indians finished 9–4–1 with losses to Illinois, Nebraska, Bethany College and Kansas State. Their wins included victories over Kansas State, Missouri, Texas and Kansas. The Kansas game, in which he scored two touchdowns, was a personal highlight for Chauncey.

In January 1903, *The Lincoln Evening News* contradicted *The Indian Leader* by stating that the Haskell Indians had won the basketball championship of the West the previous year (instead of the National Championship), but expected them to repeat after a 35–18 defeat of Dr. James Naismith's Kansas University team. They didn't repeat but had a good season that included a tour east of the Mississippi. That summer, Chauncey played first base and batted clean-up for the Nebraska Indians. He was also team captain. A new man seldom gets those honors, so he may have played for them in earlier seasons. The Nebraska Indians were a barnstorming team that traveled across the Midwest and even crossed the Mississippi on occasion. They had a phenomenally high won-loss record, but often competed against teams whose players had day jobs.

The Indians' players devoted their summers to baseball and became very good at it.

The 1903 football season started promisingly with a 45–0 thrashing of Colorado College and a 6–0 win over Texas. Next up on the schedule were the always-tough Nebraskans whose Coach "Bummy" Booth threatened to take Haskell off his schedule because of their lax eligibility rules. Martin Wheelock's recent transfer to Haskell from Carlisle prompted his outburst. The game start was delayed over an hour in a dispute over using an old Kansas man named Tucker as an official. Eventually Booth allowed Tucker to be used. The Indians lost 16–0 but bounced back with wins over Kansas and Missouri. Next up was a big game with Amos Alonzo Stagg's Chicago team. The Indians played the Maroons to a standstill but scored fewer points. They then ran off three straight wins before losing badly to Kansas State to end the season. 7–3–0 under a first-year coach wasn't bad. In fact, their play prompted promotion of a post-season game between Carlisle and Haskell. But that was not to be—not yet, anyway. Charles Guyon, who had returned to Haskell, was elected captain for 1904.

In the middle of another fine basketball campaign, reports stating that Chauncey might be turning pro hit the papers:

> Archiquette, the Indian who played on Haskell football team for the past three years as quarter and end, is to be given a try-out with the Kansas City Blues at center field. He is a fast and heady player, and those who have seen him play will agree that he stands a good chance. He is an artist at unhooking the long ones, and a hard hitter. He uses a bat about four inches longer than the limit and when he lands it is all over. He has played with the Haskell Indian baseball team around the state for several years.

> A wire service article elaborated a bit:

This new Blue is a graduate of Haskell and is one of the best-known athletes of the West. He has made his name famous as a football player, and has added further laurels to his athletic prowess as being equally good at baseball. Those who have seen him play say that he is lightning on his feet and is a sure fielder. He will prove a drawing card, if he does not find the company too fast.

He must not have made the team or his over-sized bat was not allowed because, in the fall, he was back out on the gridiron in a Haskell uniform. The 1904 season started auspiciously with ecumenical thrashings of the Quakers of Friends University and the Baptists of Ottawa University. The Indians' first real test was their cross-town rival, Kansas University, whom they beat convincingly, 23–6. They dispatched Missouri by a wider margin, 39–0. They found the lot at Austin much tougher and were stalemated until Pete Hauser kicked a 45-yard field goal, the game's only score, one that barely cleared the crossbar. After Ottawa canceled a rematch, all that stood between them and the Missouri Valley Championship was their nemesis, Nebraska. Cornhusker coach Bummy Booth didn't show the Indians much respect:

> This is the fourth year we have played the Indians, and every year we have counted on a hard game and found a comparatively easy one. We don't like this game, but we have to play it, and that means that we are going to play it hard and give these people all they want this year. The players, with the exception of Captain Benedict, are in good shape, and they ought to be able to play as well Saturday as any time this year. Benedict will be able to get in the game, I think, and we can put up as good a front against them as we did against Minnesota. I know these Indians, nearly every one of them, and I know just what they can do. So when I say that we are going to win from them by at least fifty points, I ought to have a

little idea of what I am talking about The Nebraskans are getting into the game well in the past few days and they are going to play against those Indians as hard or harder, if possible than they did against the Gophers.

On November 10, under the headline,"Booth Predicts Score of Sixty to Nothing," *The Lincoln Evening News* doubted that the game would be played:

> There is still a possibility, even at this late date, that the Haskell-Nebraska game, scheduled for Kansas City Saturday will be called off. Manager Davis has received a telegram from Coach John Outland of Washburn who had been selected for referee, declaring that under no consideration will he officiate at the game. This announcement took the local authorities off their feet, as they had thought the official question settled when Hoagland and Outland had been decided on a week ago. The question of choosing a referee will now take up the time until the game, and it may prove an insurmountable obstruction. The Haskell management announced some time ago that it would consider no Nebraska man as an official, and Manager Davis said this morning that he was stumped as to a man to suggest. Haskell evidently thinks they will get the worst of the deal, and they seem to be looking for a man who will help them out in doubtful situations.

The article brought up the fact that officials were not the only controversy:

> Coach Herrnstein, of the Haskell Indian team, insists that [John] Warren, the big Indian guard, who will probably go into the game against Nebraska, is not in any sense a "ringer," and was not brought to Haskell especially for this game."The idea that Warren is there solely to play football is a mistake," he said, speaking

about the matter while in Kansas City Sunday night. "He is taking regular work there, and is right in line for a good position in the school. He is an expert harness-maker, and if the superintendent of the harness shops resigns, as is now his intention, Warren will probably succeed him in that position. He had been planning for some time to come to Haskell, and hastened his coming a little in order to join our party as we were coming back from the Texas trip." [yes] "I have been opposed all along to the mystery which has been thrown around his identity and did not give him the name of 'Big Chief' or 'Big Brave.' That was started by some Lawrence correspondents, and some of the people at the school thought that it might increase the interest in the team to let it go on that way."

In spite of everything, Nebraska kicked off on time at 2:35 p.m. with John Outland as referee, Ralph Hoagland as umpire, and Lt. Cosad as head linesman. Pete Hauser kicked a field goal to complete Haskell's first possession. Nebraska was stopped on downs and was forced to punt. After a 15-yard return, a 15-yard off-side penalty against Nebraska, and a 40-yard run by Moore to the 5-yard line, Porter carried the ball over for a touchdown. By making the kick after touchdown, the score was Haskell 10, Nebraska 0. After Nebraska got the ball, they were unable to make a first down and punted the ball back. Pete Hauser immediately kicked a 40-yard field goal. Haskell 14, Nebraska 0. Haskell got the ball back after a fumble on Nebraska's 35. Archiquette carried the ball around his left end for a 15-yard gain but fumbled it away. The half ended with no further scoring. The only scoring in the second half was Bender's 23-yard field goal and a safety. That made the final score Haskell 14, Nebraska 6.

In the middle of the following week, Coach Herrnstein observed:

Elation over winning from Nebraska has not yet died down at Haskell institute. Emil Houser is the only man in, bad shape. His face was trampled on and is badly lacerated. Fallis, Dubois, and Oliver are limping, but they will be all right in a few days. Archiquette, the star halfback, does not remember a play made in the second half. He does not know that he fumbled two punts and he asked the score three or four times while changing clothes before he could remember it. He stopped calling signals early in the second half. He could think of noplays but those numbered five and he threw the team into confusion by continually calling thirty-five, forty-five and fifty-five plays that had no place in that part of the game. Fallis, and afterward, Moore, called the signals during the last of the game. When Emil Hauser went back to punt just before Nebraska made her-safety, it was Fallis' place to kick instead of Hauser's. Hauser had one eye shut and misjudged the distance as he stepped back. Standing so close to the center the ball naturally reached him high and hard.

About this time, they announced that Haskell would play a game against Carlisle at the St. Louis World's Fair the Saturday after Thanksgiving to coincide with President Roosevelt's visit. Haskell was scheduled to play Washington University of St. Louis at the Fair on Thanksgiving Day. The Indians annihilated the Crepe and Myrtle 42–0 or 47–0 (accounts vary), hardly breaking a sweat. Meanwhile, the Carlisle second team smashed the Ohio State eleven 23–0. Neither Indian team risked its best players in these warmup games. The main even came two days later. Although President Theodore Roosevelt didn't attend the game, the stadium was packed. Haskell moved the ball well early in a drive that was capped by a Pete Hauser field goal. That was all they would get. Carlisle prevailed 38–4. However, Haskell accomplished something

Carlisle never did; they went undefeated through the regular season. Their sole loss this year was in the post-season. Carlisle's losses in the one-loss seasons were regular season games. Soon, Chauncey would be back at Carlisle and would be followed by some of his teammates. But there's more to the story as Jim Thorpe's biographer, Robert W. Wheeler, found out when he interviewed Thorpe's Haskell classmate and friend, George Washington.

If not the biggest, Chauncey Archiquette was one of the biggest men on campus. So big that younger boys tried to emulate him. One of them was a scrawny little boy named Jim Thorpe. After practice was over, the lad would run back and forth across the field in his best imitation of his idol. One day Chauncey noticed what the lad was up to and had a chat with him. Seeing that Jim was serious about wanting to play football, he put his Carlisle training to use and made the boy a football out of leather and stuffed it with rags. Now that he had a ball to play with, Jim organized games with other boys and improved so much that he started to compete with older boys in some athletic contests. Archiquette left something of himself behind when he left Haskell.

Chauncey returned to Carlisle in September 1905 after another summer of baseball, most likely. This time he wasn't a student but was putting what he learned in the Commercial Course at Haskell to work in his position as assistant clerk. The 1905 edition of the Carlisle Indians was a good one and portended the future greatness. Haskellites Charles Guyon, who was then going by the name of Wahoo, Alfred Dubois, and Scott Porter (Little Boy) also transferred to Carlisle that year. Others would follow in future years. George Woodruff, Hall of Fame Coach most closely associated with Penn was advisory coach that year. He was assisted by Ralph Kinney, a first team All-American fresh from Yale, as well as two former Carlisle stars, Bemus Pierce and Frank Hudson.

Chauncey continued to play right halfback as he had in his later years at Haskell. The first three games were won by an average margin of 51 points. Players were substituted early and often to give the backups some playing time. Things started getting serious in the fourth game, an 11–0 win over Penn State. Virginia was taken down by a 12–0 score. Dickinson College was walloped in Harrisburg 36–0 in the first meeting between the teams in four years. Some bad blood had developed when Warner was coaching the Indians, but that seemed to be behind them at this point. Fumbles doomed the Indians to a 6–0 defeat at the hands of Penn. That game was followed by a 23–11 loss to Harvard in the mud. The following Saturday, the Indians bet the Cadets at West Point 6–5 in an historic game made possible only by permission of the War Department. This was the first time the Indians met "the soldiers" on an athletic field and they prevailed. This game, the ninth of the year, must have been considered the last regular season game because Coach Woodruff left the team at that time. He did not accompany them on their extended trip to Ohio, Western Pennsylvania and Washington, DC. Carlisle played five games in fifteen days against three college teams and two independent teams. They lost to the independents, Canton and Massillon, and beat Cincinnati, Washington and Jefferson, and Georgetown. After the Georgetown game, Chauncey's college playing days were over. He was a varsity starter from 1897 through 1905. Few other players could make such a claim. He was also one of the few Carlisle stars to never play for or assist Pop Warner. Warner arrived during his first year at Haskell, returned to Cornell after the 1903 season, and didn't return to Carlisle until 1907.

Barely two weeks after the end of football season, a basketball team was organized to represent the school and Archiquette was elected team captain. This was Carlisle's first formal attempt to officially field a team for the new sport. Previously, basketball had just been played regularly on campus and irregularly off-campus. Chauncey's return must have had something to do with this move; it's not clear if he coached the team or was just its captain. Physical Director Alfred Venne was in charge of the gymnasium and, in this capacity, may have served as coach. When James Naismith wrote, in *Basketball: Its Origins and Development*, "Carlisle was the first Indian school to play basketball...," he surely meant as an intra-mural sport. He also had an explanation why they took to it so well:

> I have talked to several coaches of Indian teams and have found that coaching a team of Indian boys presents several problems that are not found among white boys. One coach told me that he had several good players who would not take part in the sport for fear of ridicule, and that some of the boys felt it inexcusable to make a mistake. They would not run this chance before a group of people. Besides, the Indian teams are usually made up of comparatively small men. This fact is a distinct handicap to them; but their ability to move quickly and their art of deception overcome the disadvantage of their height, so that wherever these teams play they are assured of a large crowd of spectators.

Shortly after Christmas, a series of intra-mural basketball games were played between the classes: Seniors vs. Juniors and Sophomores vs. Freshmen. The Senior girls played a game against the Junior girls. The girls were more enthusiastic toward the game when women's rules were followed. Part of the New Year's festivities was a game between the varsity and the Sophomore boys. That two Junior boys were first string varsity players likely influenced the choice of opponents.

Carlisle's first, official intercollegiate basketball game was played at Lehigh University on January 20, 1906 with a large crowd present due to the fact that all Carlisle's players were well known football players. Frank Mt. Pleasant. was surely a drawing card. The Indians lost 32–19 due to a lack of teamwork. The next week's practices were devoted to improving teamwork. A week later, when they hosted Muhlenburg College, Charlie Wahoo was on the floor. Carlisle prevailed 105–4. Their tight defense allowed the visitors to take few shots. The season ended on March 6 with a victory over Susquehanna University. The varsity basketball team went 7–6; not bad for a new team.

That spring, like most springs, found Chauncey on the baseball diamond, but this year he was in a Carlisle uniform. His surroundings weren't too strange because some of his fellow football and basketball teammates were also on that team.

Immediately after graduation, Wilson Charles got married in a most elaborate affair. Chauncey served as one of the groomsmen. Instead of competing in Annual Class Contest on April 30, as members of the staff, he and Siceni Nori judged the field events. After spending much of the summer as an outfielder for the school's baseball team, in August he departed for Pawhuska in the brand new state of Oklahoma, where he had a position as clerk at the Osage Agency.

There is no record of his returning to Carlisle but he kept in touch for a while. School records show that he responded to questionnaires in 1907, 1909, 1910 and 1911, but only copies of his 1907 and 1909 responses still exist. From these responses, we can learn a few things. He was promoted to Stenographer around August 1906 and was making $900 a year in 1909. In addition, he was provided furnished quarters at the Osage Agency and still owned his allotment back in Wisconsin. His answer to Question 11; Have you done anything for the betterment of your people?; was revealing. "I have not been among my people for eighteen years, and for a few days visit each time. Therefore I could not do them any good nor any harm."

He was still single, living in Pawhuska and working at the Osage Agency in 1915 when he registered for the draft. The 1920 census lists his parents and him as having been born in

New York rather than Wisconsin, but that doesn't seem likely. The 1924 Oneida census lists him as married but doesn't list his wife, probably because she wasn't a member of the tribe. The 1930 census listed his father as mixed blood and his mother as Oneida. Chauncey was listed as having been born in Wisconsin. This census is probably accurate. It also listed him as being married to a woman named Rhoda who was his age, 51, and who had a son, Scott, about 23. Mother and son were both born in Tennessee as were her parents and his father. USGenWeb archives for the Pawhuska Cemetery include both Chauncey and Rhoda Sweeney Archiquette, but no others of that family name. According to the cemetery, Rhoda died in late 1930. A 1926 newspaper article titled "Vanishing Americans Fade Out of Sport" said that Chauncey "has not been heard from, or of, for lo, these many, many moons. Like Metoxen, his famed teammate, he left without leaving a forwarding address." That wasn't exactly true. He left a forwarding address but the school where he left it was closed in 1918.

Chauncey likely stayed active in sports after moving to Pawhuska but his best days were surely behind him or were after being there a few years. He was too old to play on the Oorang Indians and probably for the Hominy Indians, but may have assisted with coaching that team when his friend, Pete Hauser, coached them. But there is no evidence to support that.

He lived in Pawhuska until his death in 1949. For a time Pete Hauser lived with Rhoda and him, and they remained friends until Hauser's untimely death in an automobile accident at which Chauncey was present.

6

Wilson Charles

The details of Wilson Charles's early life are somewhat vague. The first record of his existence that could be found was the 1885 census of the Oneida Agency which listed him as being six years of age. His father, Julius Charles, may have been of mixed blood and, according to Susan G. Daniel's research, died in 1884. His mother, Sophia Metoxen Charles, was a 23-year-old widow with three children. Besides Wilson, there was 5-year-old Elias and 3-year-old Josephine. These ages are approximations at best because birthdates for people of that period are questionable. Most of the censuses

> Name: Wilson Beleves Charles
> DOB: 3/10/1879
> Weight: 150
> Tribe: Oneida
> Parents: Julius Charles & Sophia Metoxen Charles
> Early Schooling: Episcopal Day School, possibly Oneida Indian School
> Honors: American Indian Athletic Hall of Fame, 1971
> Nickname: Chicken Legs
> Height: 5'9"
> Age: 20
> Home: Brown County, WI

put Wilson's year of birth at 1879. However, when he registered for the World War I draft, he wrote March 10, 1881 as his date of birth. That date is possible but squeezes the births of the three Charles children into four years. On the other hand, he may have shaved off a couple of years to make himself eligible for the draft. The family disappeared from the rolls after the 1885 entry. Perhaps censuses were not taken in those years. Wilson showed up next on the 1892 roll listed with Hulda Doxtator Wheelock Charles, his paternal grandmother and the grandmother of Dennison and James Wheelock, the famous Carlisle bandmasters, through a previous marriage. His grandfather, David Charles, appears to have died sometime after the 1885 census and before 1892. Wilson's siblings were listed with their maternal grandparents, Abram and Jerusha Metoxen, on the 1892 roll. Josephine Charles's relationship was listed as adopted and Elias Metoxen as a son. The 1902 census implies that both may have been considered Metoxens and may have been adopted. Wilson and Huldah were listed together for several years. Around the turn of the twentieth century, they were listed as living at the Oneida Indian Boarding School. However, it is unlikely that he attended that school or, if he did, not for long because he was soon at Carlisle. One newspaper account stated that he attended Haskell Institute before entering Carlisle.

The July 12, 1901 issue of *The Red Man and Helper* listed Wilson Charles among those who had gone home recently. Because students were not usually allowed to return home before the end of an enrollment and that enrollments at that time were generally for five years, he probably first enrolled at Carlisle around 1896. He was old enough to have enrolled much earlier and very well could have. Unfortunately, both his Carlisle student file and those of his siblings have been lost. Without them, we can't know for sure when they enrolled. Because they were orphans, it is reasonable to assume that they were enrolled when young. The lack of records makes it necessary to surmise their activities from later statements. In September, at the end of his summer at home, he returned to Carlisle for another enrollment, this time as a Freshman.

Wilson Charles
Cumberland County Historical Society Carlisle, PA

Wilson's name showed up a bit more often in the school newspaper in 1901 when he vied for the fullback position on the varsity football team: "Charles is rather light, but he is a good punter and the best dropkicker on the field." He made the team but not the first team. He spent the season on the bench until the last quarter of the last game—a trouncing by Columbia University at the Polo Grounds in New York. With the Indians losing 40–0, Wilson finally got to play and made the most of it. In addition to making good yardage on line plunges, he scored the Indians' only two touchdowns in the game. Those were made using the wing shift which completely befuddled the Columbians. Football season was over, but he didn't while away his time waiting for next year.

Wilson Charles had a pleasing baritone voice and used it to sing solos and in groups as well as to orate. In May, he entertained the faculty by singing in a mixed quartet with Edith Bartlett, Delfina Jacques and Walter Comah. He, Philip Tousey, Phineas Wheelock and Wallace Denny closed the program with a humorous dialogue. A week later, he performed well in the annual inter-class track meet, placing third in the 100-yard dash, second in the broad jump, and second in the 120-yard hurdles; he tied for first in the high jump, and placed first in the 220-yard dash. He did almost as well in a dual meet with

Dickinson College a week later, winning both the broad jump and high jump events, placing second in the 120-yard hurdles, and coming in third in the shotput. He didn't do nearly as well in the dual meet with Penn State, placing second in both high jump and broad jump.

Coach Warner remarked about Wilson's improvement in pre-season football practices. He played quarterback in the first half of the Lebanon Valley College game to start the 1902 season. His brother, Elias played fullback for the Printers. Wilson was shifted to right halfback for the Gettysburg College game. Newspaper reporters dubbed him the "hero" of that game for his fine running and punting. As the season progressed, he played some at fullback, some at quarterback, but mostly at right halfback. He wasn't a star yet, but he was a regular.

Wilson sang in "the school quartet" with Monroe Coulon, Alfred Venne and Henry Tatiyopi. Their performance during Christmas week received notice in the school newspaper. In January, as a member of the Invincible Debating Society, he sang in a quintet that was received so well that the audience demanded an encore. He also sang a solo that showed off the depths of his vocal range. In March, he serenaded them with "My Old Kentucky Home." No sooner had the New Year started than he was playing on the Sophomores' basketball team—Carlisle didn't have a varsity squad yet—along with Joel Cornelius, Wallace Denny, Randolph Hill and Thomas Gardner. Charles was the team's captain. He was also captain of the school's track team that year. In a pre-season indoor meet to give new team members an opportunity to compete with the old ones, he won the 35-yard dash and shotput events, tied for first in the high jump, and finished second in the 35-yard high hurdles.

After commencement, Wilson was promoted to the Junior Class and was elected Class Treasurer. He decorated the blackboard in the Junior room with a drawing that was "artistic and highly appreciated by his classmates." The Invincibles then elected him Assistant Critic. He helped win a banner for the school and a gold watch for himself at the Penn Relay Carnival as a member of the winning relay team, along with Wallace Denny, James Johnson and Frank Mt. Pleasant. Their time would have been better if Johnson and Mt. Pleasant hadn't coasted to an easy win. As it was, the Indians won the race by 20 yards. He won more hardware at the annual class meet in late April. He was awarded a handsome watch fob for earning more points for his class than any other competitor. His classmates also gave him a gold medal engraved with "Class contest, 1903." In addition to winning or placing in several events, he set school records in the high jump and the broad jump. Wilson also did well in the track meets against other schools that spring, often leading his team in points scored. Against Bucknell, he broke his own school broad jump record. Soon, it was time for summer outing.

It's not known where Wilson Charles spent the summer of 1903, but New Jersey would be a good guess. *The Red Man and Helper* reported that Wilson, Truman Doxtator and Joseph Baker visited the Zoological Gardens, Independence Hall, Academy of Fine Arts and Academy of Natural Science in Philadelphia on their way back to Carlisle at summer's end. Truman Doxtator worked at Beacon-by-the-sea in Point Pleasant, New Jersey as did Wilson's brother, Elias, which would make hooking up with them logical. Wilson was elected Corresponding Secretary of the Junior Class for the fall term.

Charles earned his first football letter playing at right halfback and fullback that year. He did better at halfback because he was small for the fullback position. The football trips gave him something to share with his classmates. After the Georgetown game, William White, Joseph Baker and he told their fellow Juniors some interesting facts about Washington. On the trip west to Utah and California, Wilson wrote his teacher, Miss Wood, a letter to share with his classmates. Later on the trip, he wrote:

It did not seem to me that Christmas was anywhere near while we were in San Francisco. Everything there is so beautiful. The flowers that we saw in Pennsylvania in August are to be seen in California now, while in Pennsylvania there is good skating. I understand that the weather doesn't change much from winter to summer. To-day [sic] it is like summer and so warm we would rather stay in the shade than out in the sun. I have learned much about this country.

In the winter of 1904, Wilson Charles probably played on the Junior Class basketball team, but no team roster has been found. Wilson continued his singing with a solo for the football banquet, at which he got his first letter for football. He also sang in a quartet for a school assembly at which an encore was requested, but they inexplicably did not respond, possibly because they had not prepared another song. Wilson also served as President of the Invincibles. In the spring, he pitched for the school baseball team, racking up several wins. At the 5th annual class contest, he scored the most points of any contestant by winning the 100-yard dash, 120-yard hurdles and the broad jump, and coming in second in the shot put and high jump. Then a member of the Senior class, he scored all of their points. Wilson even found time to compete for the track team. In the meet with Penn State, he placed second in the 120-yd hurdles and broad jump. He again came in second in that event against Bucknell. Not bad, considering that he hadn't spent much time training for track because of his baseball commitment.

Wilson's brother, Elias, worked as a printer in town for *The Evening Sentinel* that winter. In the class contest held in the spring, he finished fourth in the 120-yd hurdles. After taking a short vacation to "visit his old country home near Trenton," he returned to work half-days at *The Evening Sentinel* and attend school the other half.

Due to the lack of a student file and mention in the school paper, all that is known about Wilson's summer is that he returned in time for football season. Playing baseball for a community or minor league team would be a distinct possibility. Football would have been a little frustrating for him in 1904. All the previous year's starters returned for 1904 except the quarterback and fullback. Joe Baker and Archie Libby were great candidates for the quarterback position. That left team captain Arthur Sheldon with one choice—fullback. Coach Rogers explained his dilemma:

> The position of full-back, however, will be a problem, as all the available men with a sufficient amount of weight have been compelled to play in the line and this leaves a wealth of light material to select from. Captain Sheldon, who played regularly at half-back last year, is being tried out at this position. He is the heaviest of the backfield candidates, but does not seem to take to the position quite as readily as he does to half-back. Charles is also trying for the position. He is very light, but is developing into a speedy man and can boot the leather in great style. Nephew and La Roque are also developing promise, especially La Roque who is a new Indian just from the wilds of Minnesota. La Roque has fair weight and can develop speed, but has yet a lot to learn about the full-back position.

Early into the season, Coach Rogers again commented on Charles's play:

> Considerable attention has been paid to the kicking department of the game and to the catching of punts. Captain Sheldon, Charles, and Tomahawk have done the punting. Charles has shown up the best, sending off

long spirals at distances from forty to sixty yards. Sheldon is practicing faithfully in trying to overcome some bad faults. Tomahawk's punts are erratic.

Rogers also discussed the continuing backfield situation. Note that he had settled on a quarterback and did not rotate that position:

> Three sets of backs are being used and developed. One set, composed of Captain Sheldon, Hendricks and La Roque have been given the preference because of their weight and experience, but in fact have not shown that they can play any better than a set made up of Charles, Saul, and Whitecrow, nor of the other set composed of Fischer, Nephew, and Doxtator. There is not much choice between these sets and all are being given a good tryout. There will be plenty of good backs.

Wilson Charles got enough playing time to score a few touchdowns and letter again but wasn't a big star that year. That the 1904 team was a good one with a lot of talent was brought into focus when the game against Haskell Institute the Saturday after Thanksgiving was added to the schedule. The Thanksgiving Day game against Ohio State immediately became less important and was delegated to the second team. Wilson played right halfback part of the game and fullback the rest of it. He also kicked four goals after touchdown—extra points in modern parlance—in the 23–0 outclassing of the Buckeyes. That he didn't get into the Haskell game wasn't as negative as it might at first seem. Ed Rogers, Bemus Pierce and Hawley Pierce suited up for the game and played much of it. Bemus started at right halfback and Hawley at fullback. Their availability moved Wilson down the depth charts for both positions.

While Wilson spent his holiday on the road, his brother Elias spent his Thanksgiving Day on the football field playing fullback for the Printers, occasionally slamming through the Carpenters' line for long gains.

As part of the entertainment for the Annual Football Banquet, Wilson sang in a quartet with Alfred M. Venne, Ignatius Ironroad and Walter A. Komal. After completing their planned performance, they sang two encores and finished with "College Chum." He also sang solos for the Junior Varsity Reception and as part of a quartet with Ignatius Ironroad, Adam Fischer and Fritz Hendricks. He didn't spend the entire semester just in athletics.

In October, he and Elizabeth Knudsen, mixed-blood Klamath from Northern California, Class of 1903 and considered by some to be the prettiest girl on campus, won the cake for best marching at a reception held by the Susan Longstreth Literary Society. Their names continued to be linked together. Since she had already graduated, it wasn't clear exactly what she was pursuing at that time except, perhaps, Wilson. She may have been enrolled in the normal school or commercial program or could have been employed by the school. In February, she led the large girls' meeting, which might mean that she was still a student. Also, she remained active with the Susans.

Wilson graduated in March of 1905. At some point after that, he became an employee of the school, most likely as an assistant in the carriage-making shop. That spring he didn't play baseball or run track for the school, but in the summer he pitched well for the Green Bay in the Wisconsin League. At summer's end, Wilson returned to Carlisle to vie for a position on the 1905 football team.

That spring, Elias carried the Charles mantle while running the hurdles for Carlisle. He also filled in as the acting foreman in the printing office during Mr. Baird's absence. Josephine spent the summer at her outing home. Elizabeth Knudsen sang a solo for the Susans in the spring and, in late July, visited her country parents in Beverly, New Jersey.

Elizabeth Knudsen; *U. S. Army Military History Institute*

Charles played fullback for part of the first game of the 1905 season, a warm-up against P. R. R. YMCA of Columbia, Pennsylvania. Soon Wilson was platooning at right halfback. Later in the season, he played some at left halfback. He didn't get into the Army or Massillon games but, later on the long road trip, starred against Cincinnati by scoring a touchdown on a 90-yard run, kicking a field goal and three extra points. He didn't play in the Washington and Jefferson game but had a field day against Georgetown. Playing just in the second half, he scored a touchdown, kicked a field goal and five extra points in the 76–0 romp. This year, he got enough playing time to letter.

Shortly after commencement, Wilson Charles married Elizabeth Knudsen in an elaborate ceremony officiated by Rev. Alexander McMillan of the Episcopal Church in Carlisle. Over 1,000 people attended the ceremony that was held in the school auditorium. Major Mercer gave the bride away as was the custom at the school. He and the other males participating in the ceremony wore their dress uniforms. Wilson wore the rank of captain and Quartermaster of the Superintendent's staff. Elias Charles, who had just graduated, served as best man before leaving Carlisle to take a course in electro-typing. Frank Mt. Pleasant, Genus Baird, Chauncey Archiquette, Wallace Denny, Charles Roy and William Gardner were the groomsmen. Ida Nori was Elizabeth's matron-of-honor. Josephine Charles, Minnie Rice, Rose McFarland, Stacey Beck, Bertha Dennis, and Mary Runnels were her bridesmaids. The Carlisle Indian School orchestra played the wedding march from Tannhauser as the processional and Mendelssohn's *Wedding March* for the recessional. News services distributed coverage of the wedding across the country. After a wedding trip to West Point and other points of interest in the East, the Charleses set up housekeeping on the school campus.

Wilson Charles went out for baseball in the spring but not track. He twirled some games with success before heading home to Wisconsin for vacation. According to a later account in *The Arrow,* the southpaw pitched again for the Green Bay team.

Wilson played football again but mostly as a back-up. He did start the Cincinnati game and played well again. This time he was credited with a number of long punts and sharp tackling. He didn't get enough playing time to letter this year. He continued to work as assistant coachmaker until late March, when he reported to Danville, Virginia for spring training with the Trenton team of the Tri-State League. In mid-April of 1907, he was back twirling for the Green Bay club. After baseball season was over, he changed his pattern and did not return to Carlisle. Instead, he coached a high school football team in the Green Bay area.

Josephine Charles spent her summer at her country home in Morton, Pennsylvania. Upon her return to school in September

WILSON CHARLES, ONEIDA PITCHER.

1906 Wire service drawing

1906, she cooked for the athletes' training table. Elias spent the fall in the country recuperating from an unnamed illness.

According to an article in the January 3, 1908 edition of *The Arrow,* Charles had been offered a college coaching job for the upcoming football season. The May 30, 1908 issue of *Sporting Life* listed him as having signed with Butler, Pennsylvania of the Ohio-Pennsylvania League for the current baseball season. That October, he wrote *The Carlisle Arrow* that he was at Haskell Institute where he was employed in the wagon shops in addition to assisting with the coaching of the football team.

Wilson's sister, Josephine, Carlisle '08, wrote that she was also in government service, working as an assistant matron at Wahpeton Indian School in North Dakota. The October 7, 1910 issue of *The Carlisle Arrow* indicated that Josephine was "getting along finely with her work in DePere, Wisconsin." The 1910 Federal Census listed her as living with her cousin, Dennison Wheelock, and working as a servant, thus no longer with the government. Whether she worked for the Wheelocks or someone else was unclear. Regardless of which it was, she was soon back in the Indian Service. *The Carlisle Arrow* of June 7, 1912 reported that she was again employed in the Indian Service working at Hoopa, California. It was there that she apparently met her husband. Around 1914, Josephine married Eric Swanson, a woodsman who was not listed on the Oneida roll, perhaps because his father was from Sweden and his mother wasn't Oneida. They lived in Humboldt County, California where they soon had two sons and two daughters.

According to the 1910 census, Elias Charles was living with his brother. His note from DePere, Wisconsin that was published in the May 5, 1912 edition of *The Carlisle Arrow* tells us more about what he was doing:

> As I am one in Carlisle's great family, I want to express my gratitude for what Mother Carlisle has done for me. I have had many experiences since I left the school. For two years I worked at my trade of printing until sickness overtook me. I left the city life and went to work on a farm nine miles from Carlisle, where I worked two more years. I then accepted a position as industrial teacher at the Red Lake Indian School, Minnesota, but to my disappointment the climate did not agree with me. I then went to the lumber camps. Now I am farming here.

Elias Charles had married Lena Schenandoah (Skenandore?) around 1910 and had a son, Paul, in 1911. By 1917, Paul was dead and his parents appear to have split up. Elias lived alone in Wisconsin until he was 50. He then moved to California to live with his sister and her family.

The 1910 census listed Wilson Charles as living in Oneida (town) in Outagamie County, Wisconsin and working as a carpenter. Elizabeth worked as a dressmaker. Elias was listed as a member of the household. Wilson and Elizabeth had two children. Edna was born in 1907 in Pennsylvania and Wilson Junior was born in 1909 in Wisconsin. According to tribal rolls and Wilson Senior's WWI draft registration, the two didn't share a middle name. Wilson Jr.'s middle initial was D whereas Wilson Sr.'s middle name was Beleves. Wilson Jr. was better known as Buster.

A 1914 press release from Carlisle that was picked up across the nation stated that Wilson Sr. was "instrumental in developing athletics in the government school at Toma, Minn." He was likely working at Tomah Industrial School in Tomah, Wisconsin because that is where he worked as an industrial teacher when he registered for the WWI draft on September 12, 1918. The Charleses moved to Flandreau Indian School in Moody County, South Dakota, probably in the early 1920s, where Wilson worked as an advisor and Elizabeth was a matron. Some newspaper articles also credited him with being athletic director.

Buster followed in his father's athletic footsteps and, due in significant part to being larger physically, had even greater success. He reputedly won All-State honors in football in 1926 and 1927 and the state championships in both high jump and broad jump in 1927. After high school, Buster enrolled at Haskell Institute in Lawrence, Kansas. Lone Star Dietz, his coach at Haskell, thought he might become another Jim Thorpe. In addition to having an outstanding career at Haskell, Buster echoed Thorpe by competing in the decathlon in the 1932 Los Angeles Olympics. Unlike Thorpe, he did not win the event as he finished fourth.

After graduating from Haskell Institute in 1932, Buster Charles attended the University of New Mexico. Wilson Sr. joined him there. In 1938, Buster took a job at an engineering firm in Phoenix, Arizona and later retired to Camp Verde, Arizona.

7
Wallace Denny

Wallace Denny lived at Carlisle Indian School longer than any other student—except his wife, that is. Wallace, 17, and his sister, Elizabeth, 14, arrived at Carlisle on August 12, 1896 in the care of Miss Lamason. They were the children of Josh and Melinda Denny, who were both fullblood Oneida. Melinda appears to have died shortly before their enrollment. Of their older siblings, Wilson was already on his own, Charles may have died, and Louisa may have married. Younger siblings Amos, Mary and Ida were still at home. Wallace had 50 months of prior schooling and entered at the third grade level. Little else is known about their lives

Name: Wallace Denny Nickname: Doctor, Chief
DOB: 11/10/1879 Height:
Weight: Age:
Tribe: Oneida Home: DePere, WI
Parents: Josh Denny
    Melinda Denny, deceased
Early Schooling: 50 months possibly at mission school

prior to attending Carlisle because all that remains of their student files are two of Wallace's historical record cards. They may have attended a mission school but there is no documentation of that. None of their siblings appear to have attended Carlisle. Elizabeth may have known some English prior to coming because she was chosen to represent her room, Number 1, in the December Exhibition. Little is known about Wallace's early education, including the part received at Carlisle. Like other students, he went on outings to work on farms. His first assignments were to Bucks County, Pennsylvania where he worked for various members of the Kirk family on their farms located near Newtown and in Buckingham Township. But he was always back for the start of football season. While at Carlisle, he worked in the Clothing Room.

Wallace Denny was an excellent athlete, very fleet afoot. Unfortunately for him, he arrived at a time when the school was loaded with good athletes, particularly football players. He was on the team but didn't play in games. That changed in 1899 when Pop Warner took the reins as head coach. He enlisted Wallace to be his utility man whose duties consisted of those of an equipment manager, trainer (often called "rubber" at that time) and sometime substitute for an injured player. He quickly became Warner's right hand man but preferred to remain in the background. He didn't shift from competition to a support role in all sports, just football, as he continued to run track in the spring. School papers make no mention of Denny working in a shop. Perhaps learning to be a trainer was his trade. When his enrollment was up in 1901, he returned home. He reenrolled for another five-year term at the beginning of football season and soon started getting dome press. From the November 22, 1901 edition of *The Red Man and Helper*:

> While Mr. Denny, "the rubber man" of the football team, was with the boys at Annapolis last week, he had an experience which caused considerable laughter

from the rest of the boys. Mr. Denny becoming very thirsty began to look around in the station for something to satisfy his thirst. On going up to the supposed water-cooler which stood in the corner of the room, he proceeded to fumble around for the spigot, but found to his chagrin that it was not a water tank but a fire extinguisher instead.

As part of the joint Freshman and Sophomore class entertainment in May 1902, Wallace participated in "a laughable dialog" (a skit, one supposes) with Philip Tousey, Phineas

Wallace Denny
Cumberland County Historical Society, Carlisle, PA

Wheelock and Henry Mitchell. He was rising Sophomore at that time. In the summer, he and Goliath Bigjim attended the Y. M. C. A. Student Convention at Northfield, a predecessor of Moody Bible Institute located in northwestern Massachusetts. After the rest of the students returned in the fall, he gave a talk on his experiences there to the large boys. In the winter, he played on his class's basketball team alongside Wilson Charles, Joel Cornelius, Randolph Hill and Thomas Gardner. He also joined the Invincible Debating Society and took an active part in their programs.

In March 1903, over 50 candidates for the track team competed with each other in the school's first indoor meet. Wallace finished second in the 35-yd dash behind Wilson Charles. He didn't only run track, as Coach Warner's assistant; it was his job to help get the track in shape for the season. But that didn't slow him down. In the annual class meet, Denny placed third in the 100-yd dash behind Frank Mt. Pleasant and Wilson Charles. In the 220, he finished a very close second to Mt. Pleasant, so close, in fact, that *The Red Man and Helper* remarked, "Frank Mt. Pleasant and Wallace Denny made the 220 yards dash intensively interesting, so close did they keep together." He joined forces with some of the fastest boys ever to attend Carlisle Indian School to win at the Penn Relays:

> Wallace Denny was the first runner and he came in ahead by about five yards. Wilson Charles increased the lead materially, and James Johnson and Frank Mt. Pleasant then "took it easy" and finished about twenty yards ahead of their opponents. Besides winning a banner for the school the boys each won a gold watch with the names of the contesting colleges engraved on the back.
>
> The team could have made much better time if it had been necessary to exert themselves in order to win.

Wallace Denny spent the summer at Carlisle and received praise for filling in for a school employee, Disciplinarian Thompson, who was also in charge of the large boys. In the fall, it was reported, "Wallace Denny is again at his old work as 'Doctor' of the football squad." Doctor Denny continued his work throughout the season and accompanied the team on its postseason trip to play football games in Salt Lake City, San Francisco and Los Angeles.

In the spring of 1904, Denny again donned his track togs. In the annual class meet, he finished third in the 100-yd dash and 220-yd dash. Against other schools, he placed second in the meet with Bucknell and received kudos for his teamwork against Penn State:

> Although he did not score any points, much of the success of the team is due to Wallace Denny. Besides taking good care of the boys he went in the quarter-mile run and set such a hot pace that, in trying to prevent him from getting the lead the State College man so exhausted himself that Mt. Pleasant easily passed him in the home stretch, and won in a jog. Denny could have probably scored points in the 220-yds. dash but through an oversight or error of judgment was not put in that event.

That spring, Wallace gained a stepmother. His widowed father married Isabel Cornelius, Oneida, a Carlisle graduate and teacher of both white and Indian children, on Easter Sunday. In the years following the union, his father and 26-year younger bride gave him two half-siblings, Josh Jr. and Grace. Wallace was surely unable to attend the wedding due to distance and school obligations.

Wallace's 2-months' outing that year was spent with a Mrs. Jennie Cook, a widow who ran a boarding house in Chautauqua, New York. It's fair to assume that he assisted her to operate during the resort season and that he attended some lectures in his spare time.

Pop Warner left Carlisle before the start of the 1904 football season, but Wallace Denny retained his position as utility man. Among his tasks for home games, of which there were few, was the lining off of the field. After the Harvard game, the *Boston Herald* reported, "[Umpire] Bill Edwards was kept busy watching the Indian medicine man. There was a strong suspicion that the Indian was carrying messages from the side lines." Carl Flanders, the former star center at Yale who later assisted at Carlisle, shed some light on the possibility that Denney was in fact carrying in plays along with water:

> Wallace Denny and Bemus Pierce got up a code of signals, using an Indian word which designated a single play. Among the Indian words which designated these signals were Water-bucket, Watehnee, Coocoohee. I never could find out what it all meant, and following the Indian team by this code of signals was a task which was too much for me.

That November, the school had its first ever political meeting, an event that mimicked a political party convention. The band played as students marched in and took their seats. The room was decorated with banners supporting the different candidates. Several people spoke, supporting this or that candidate or party, including Wallace Denny:

> Another Republican from Wisconsin, who was introduced as a great traveler, through which privilege he had enjoyed rare opportunities of feeling the political pulse of the country, then came to the front mid cheers and yells. It was our popular Wallace Denny, class '06, and he surprised the audience by his clear-cut logic and quiet eloquence. His speech was pronounced by all as the best of the evening, in the surprises it held for the

audience. Wallace has had to combat an impediment in his speech, and has labored under the greatest difficulties to pronounce correctly. His address last Monday evening showed how well he has mastered all, and on inquiry, his friends learned he has been drilling incessantly in school exercises, having come out conqueror.

Cool-headed and strong were his arguments in favor of the present administration of public affairs. He showed how Roosevelt had come in closer touch with the people than had any other president. The attacks that had been made upon Roosevelt, every president had suffered.

It was not an uncommon thing for the people to criticize the executive officer of our Government.

Denny took his seat amid storms of applause and the tension of the audience was relaxed by singing *America.*

In December, while participating in the student government, Representative Denny of the Junior Class proposed a bill requiring compulsory education for students from 11 to 14 years of age. His bill failed to pass.

As the calendar turned to 1905, Wallace continued his participation with the Invincibles, with a select reading, possibly as part of his speech therapy. At the Inter-Society Debate in March, he, Albert Exendine and Antonio Rodriquez represent the Invincibles as they defeated the Standards' position as argued by Chauncey Charles, Nicholas Pena and James Parsons. The question the Indians debated was: "That legislation to further restrict and better control immigration into the United States should be enacted." Which side he took was not reported. About a decade later, a student, Lewis Braun, testified that the boys disrespected Denny and, probably confusing a speech impediment with poor knowledge of the language, described his speech as broken English. The transcript of Denny's testimony at the 1914 Joint Congressional Inquiry reflects something other than broken English.

In the spring, Wallace Denny went out for track again, both on the varsity squad and for his class's, the Seniors, team for which he was elected captain. *The Arrow* reported that he would be competing in the 100-yd dash, 220-yd dash and 440-yd dash. He placed third in the 100-yd dash and first in the 440 in the annual Inter-Class Contest, with his points helping the Senior class to win the meet. Later, he placed second in the 220 in the dual meet with Penn State. At the end of the spring term, he left for Chautauqua where he again spent the summer. That summer, he also took a course on massage, a subject with which he was already experienced. At the beginning of football season, *The Arrow* reported, "'Dr.' Denny will

"Dr." Denny with "patient" in sweatbox; *U. S. Army Military History Institute*

again have charge of the 'rubbers.' Better results than ever are expected from him because of his special studies this summer." Although listed on the roster as a player, he didn't play much if at all; his role was ministering to the injured.

Wallace continued his participation with the Invincibles who elected him vice-president. He began to be more involved in social events that year. In February 1906, he stood up for Charles Dillon as a groomsman in his wedding to Rosa La Forge. The next month he was among a group of Episcopalian students invited to attend a party hosted by Mrs. Ege at Metzger Institute, a woman's college located in Carlisle. They played Clap In and Clap Out, Feather and "...some games that taxed the mental powers..." After having refreshments, they danced the Virginia Reel to the tune pounded out by Mrs. Ege on the piano. Also attending were Marian Powlas, Elizabeth Baird, Dora LaBelle, Blanche Lay, Electa Metoxen, Adaline Kingsley, Thomas Eagleman, Thomas Saul, Abram Hill, Ignatius Ironroad, William Jones, Miss Gedney and Miss Nellie Robertson.

Wallace Denny graduated as a member of the class of 1906 in late March. The Commencement edition of *The Arrow* included an article titled "Farming" written by Wallace Denny. In that piece, he advised Indian youth of the day to learn about farming because they were landowners and, while they might never farm the land themselves, could lease the land to others to do the actual farming. He went on to discuss various aspects of farming that they would need to know something about.

After graduation, at about 28 years of age, he became Mr. Denny, a member of the staff of Carlisle Indian School. His duties were not much different than they had been as a senior student. He was assistant disciplinarian in charge of the small boys and was the utility man for the Athletic Association. One of his first tasks was to put the track in shape for the season that was just starting. After serving as a groomsman for Wilson

Charles in his wedding to Elizabeth Knudsen, he headed west to Wisconsin for vacation.

Little was heard of him after his vacation until January 1907 at the annual Athletic Banquet; there he was reunited with his old mentor, Pop Warner, who had just returned as Carlisle Athletic Director. This time he had a speaking part. That was probably due to his becoming an employee of the school and of the Athletic Association. His "...humorous little dissertation gave us the 'Bright Side of Indian Football.'" As an acknowledgement of his position on the staff of the school, he served as starter and timer for the annual cross country race held during Commencement Week during the first week of April that year.

Wallace Denny visiting his family in Wisconsin   *U. S. Army Military History Institute*

On June 12, 1907, a Wednesday, Wallace Denny married Nellie V. Robertson in the Teachers' Parlor in a simple but beautiful setting. The ceremony was conducted under a canopy of daisies, the flower most prominent in the decorations. Anna Goueutuey, Pueblo, a teacher at the school, was maid of honor. Hastings M. Robertson, cousin of the bride and graduate of Dickinson School of Law class of '07, was best man. Miss Ella G. Hill played the piano. The bride wore a white gown and carried a bouquet of roses. Wallace was dressed in conventional black. Rev. McMillan of the Episcopal Church in Carlisle performed the ceremony. Nellie's boss, Miss Anne Ely, head of the outing system and namesake of present-day Ely Hall on Carlisle Barracks, gave the bride away. After the reception, Mr. and Mrs. Denny honeymooned in New York City and at New Jersey resorts.

Nellie V. Robertson

On November 6, 1880, barely a year after Carlisle Indian School first opened, Nellie V. Robertson, 9, arrived from the Sisseton Agency dressed as any other American schoolgirl of the day would have been dressed. Nellie, the daughter of a white man, Angus Robertson, and an unknown deceased Sioux woman, enrolled for a three-year term. She had had less than a year of prior schooling and didn't know much English. The 1887 census, the earliest one found listing her, reflects that she had an older sister, Etta, and a younger brother, Wilder. Her school records that remain do not include anything about her father except his name, that he lived in Brown's Valley, and that her mother was dead. She may have had older siblings who were living on their own at that time but that is not known. Nellie must have had learned something in the little bit of schooling she had before arriving at Carlisle because, just eight months later, she wrote a piece that was published in *The School News*, "Nellie Robertson's thoughts on Moses in the Bulrushes." While clearly written by a child, the writing reflects a better command of English than eight months' exposure would suggest. In January 1882, she wrote a short letter to Capt. Pratt to apologize for speaking an Indian word. Alice Wynn spoke to her in Sioux and she reflexively started to respond in her mother tongue. Just one word got out before she stopped herself but she felt so badly about the incident that she couldn't finish her supper and cried. She wrote, "I tried very hard to speak only English." That month she also wrote her father to tell him all about her Christmas and the gifts she received. She wished Annie, Wilder and Etta well. Perhaps Annie was an older sister who was married or living on her own. She also told him how hard she was trying to excel in school.

Nellie spent three weeks that summer and the last half of 1883 on outings, first in Philadelphia then in Willow Grove. She returned home in June of 1884, a year after her three-year term was up. It isn't known what she did for the next

Nellie V. Robertson
Cumberland County Historical Society, Carlisle, PA

three years, but on August 12, 1887 she returned for a five-year enrollment.

Due to being older and an excellent student, Nellie Robertson's name more frequently adorned the pages of the school newspaper, which was then called *The Indian Helper*. She became active in the girls' literary society, often serving as an officer and was placed in charge of C Company. When she was a senior, Nellie started studying with the Normal Department. She also sang alto in the school choir. In January 1890, as part of a school exhibition, Nellie played a piano duet with Miss Moore, a faculty member, to open the exercises. Nellie also served as President of Whatsoever Circle, which was previously known as The King's Daughters' Society.

On April 14, 1890, Nellie V. Robertson graduated from Carlisle Indian School. She began her valedictory address as follows:

> Dear Friends, allow me to take you for a moment out on an Indian reservation as it is to-day. It is a place from which almost all signs of civilization and education are excluded, where broad acres of land lie uncultivated; a prison as it were, where our people, the prisoners waste their lives away in idleness, while their white brothers feed and clothe them. The only homes they know are miserable and comfortless log huts or tepees. Their amusements are of the wildest sorts.
>
> They delight in sun-dances and other barbarous doings where they can torture themselves. Their travelling is done by walking or on horse back. They are an ignorant and uneducated people. True many of the young Indians are being educated at schools, but what will they ever do? Will they ever be the means of bringing the Indians to live and so as the white men?

She then described what her classmates had accomplished thirty years after graduation. All were depicted as functioning well in the white man's world. Some were even prospering abroad. She was accurate about one of them: Dennison Wheelock did become a successful band leader and, later, a lawyer. More research is needed to determine how accurately she predicted the future overall. Nellie had fully absorbed the lesson Superintendent Pratt intended her to internalize. In a later issue, her fantasy piece, "A Trip to the Moon," described a world created in her imagination that would not be unfamiliar to fans of 1950s science fiction movies. After graduation, she and Eva Johnson were rewarded with a pleasant country home for the summer of 1890. They stayed with E. Austin in Oak Lane, Pennsylvania until mid-September, at which time she returned home to her family.

A month later, *The Indian Helper* announced that she and her sister, Etta, were returning to Carlisle. Apparently, Etta had previously attended the school, but her records no longer exist. They arrived in late October and Nellie matriculated at Metzger Institute, a College for Young Ladies, in Carlisle. Its close proximity made it possible for her to continue her participation in extra-curricular activities at the Indian School. She continued to do well in her studies and led the white girls in three of her classes. Etta followed in her sister's footsteps and led her classmates in room number 12 but returned home in July 1891 for reasons that remain unclear. Less than two years after that, she married Solomon Renville, the son of a native preacher.

Nellie filled in as assistant matron over the summer to cover vacations. In September, Nellie and Rosa Bourassa returned to their studies at Metzer Institute. Still participating in Indian School activities, she played another piano duet with Miss Moore at a school exhibition in October. She also played for the Christmas Eve festivities in the girls' quarters. In the spring, Nellie and some other girls gathered arbutus at Hunter's Run.

One assumes that she graduated from Metzger that spring because, after spending her summer in Oak Lawn with E. Austin again, she enrolled at West Chester Normal School in West Chester, Pennsylvania.

Except for breaks in the school year, Nellie stayed in West Chester. She spent her 1893 spring break and summer vacation at Carlisle. In the summer, she filled in as an assistant in the school's hospital. She continued her studies at the normal school until the end of January 1894, at which time she returned home for unspecified reasons and stayed there. Perhaps she was needed to help out at home due to sickness or was ill herself. No quitter, Nellie returned to West Chester in November 1894 and completed her studies. While she was at West Chester, Principal Dr. George Phillips said that she had won the love and respect of them all. She graduated in June 1896. Her article, "Sensitiveness to Sound in English Poets," was published in the school's literary journal, *The Amulet*. It was reprinted in the May-June issue of *The Red Man*.

After graduation, Nellie helped with clerical work in the Carlisle School office for a bit before heading out to the Sisseton Agency to recruit students. She returned with seven pupils. In September, Miss Robertson began her teaching career in room number 7. In November, she gave a talk in front of the whole school on "Helen Keller as a Harvard student." Keller did not attend Harvard, of course, because women were not admitted in her day. She did attend and graduated from Radcliff College cum laude years after Nellie gave this talk. One wonders what the point of her talk was. Could it have had to do with women being allowed in to Harvard or could it have been about the ability of a severely handicapped person to be able to do work at the level required to meet Harvard's standards? Her next talk was on "The World's Advance during Queen Victoria's Reign." She spent the summer of 1897 at Chautauqua as she would many succeeding summers. But not all. In 1899, she visited her family and friends in South Dakota and returned with six girls and one boy. Upon returning, she spent some time at the Jersey Shore.

After four years of teaching, Nellie shifted to doing clerical work under Anne Ely in the Outing Office at a salary of $660 per year. In addition, she held down the fort during Miss Ely's absences. At the celebration of the school's twenty-second anniversary in October 1901, Colonel Pratt said, "I think we ought to hear from a student from among the first who came to us." After several people called out her name, Pratt said, "Miss Robertson, will you please say a word?" She responded:

> I feel that I can add but little to the commendable things that have been heard here to-night, so shall not try, but simply stand so you can see an example of one brought from barbarian into civilization by Carlisle.

Always a sociable person, Nellie acquired a ping pong set in March 1902 and attracted many guests. That summer, she broke with her traditions and summered at Beaver Falls, Minnesota. However, she visited friends and relatives in South Dakota before arriving at Beaver Falls. Much work greeted her on her return as early September was her busy season because she, Anne Ely and Emma Skye had to make the ticket arrangements for 202 boys and 144 girls to return to from summer outings. On November 6, she was the guest of honor at a surprise party to celebrate the twenty-second anniversary of her arrival at the school. She was presented with a dozen fruit knives to commemorate the event.

Nellie continued to work in the Outing Office and to take her vacations at Chautauqua or visiting South Dakota. Suddenly, the rhythm of her life changed.

Wallace and Nellie Denny

After the Dennys returned from their honeymoon, they took up residence at Carlisle Barracks. He continued his work as

Assistant Disciplinarian and she as the Head Clerk in the Outing Office. He didn't give up sports just because he was married. Shortly after their return, he played catcher for the Big Chiefs in a game against the Young Chiefs. Jim Thorpe pitched for the Big Chiefs and Wallace handled his throws with perfection. William Garlow pitched for the Young Chiefs. The seven-inning game ended in a 5–5 tie.

In the fall, Wallace continued his role as trainer for the football team. He even received a little coverage from the school newspaper:

> During the Penn'sy game Mr. Denny, the great Indian trainer, was again in his form of younger days by always following the ball. His brilliant 45-yd. run on the side line was a spectacle.

After their marriage, coverage of their activities became less frequent, but was sufficient to gain an idea of what the Dennys were doing. For example, rather than vacationing separately, they traveled together to see her friends and family in South Dakota, likely stopping off in Wisconsin to spend some time with his. Their working lives changed little at first, other than living together in the small boys' quarters. Wallace kept active supporting the athletic programs and honing his tennis skills.

As far as income was concerned, the Dennys were in an enviable position. In December 1909, Nellie's salary was increased to $900 a year. When she became Outing Manager in 1911, her salary increased to $1,000. Add to that Wallace's salary as Assistant Disciplinarian and the amount paid to him by the Athletic Association for his work as trainer, and you have a tidy sum. Wallace and Nellie were used as success stories in Carlisle publications. In 1910, Wallace and Nellie traveled about the U. S. to the various Indian Agencies and interviewed former Carlisle students to report on their then present conditions. By that time, Wallace's job title had changed to Assistant Commander of Cadets. It brought with it an increase from $720 to

$750 per year and in 1911 to $800. The school's administration was surely happy with their report:

> Their report is very pleasing as they find that while they often pick up the shawl and blanket, they are good housekeepers, good cooks and have many of the lessons taught them in the school, and are making good use of. Mrs. Pedrick aided them in locating the old students and showing them the difference in the Indians who have never attended school and the ones who have graduated.

Wallace and Nellie Denny became institutions at the school after Superintendent Pratt left. Soon, they had more institutional knowledge of the history of the school than other faculty members. Occasionally, articles were written about one or the other of them in school publications. In April 1912, Iva Miller described room number 14, the Seniors' home room as being haunted. She described it as being "...full of sweet memories of classes that have gone forth ready to begin their life battle. Strong and noble characters have left the impress of their personality upon this spot, so that he who understands and realizes the significance of this room, feels that it is a blessed thing to have the privilege of assembling here. It is impossible to recall the names of those who have created the 'atmosphere' of this room, but we all think at once of two names which stand out from the rest: Mrs. N. R. Denny and Charles Dagenette, whose strong personalities seem always with us. They are loved by all with whom they come in contact and are looked up to by all Indians who know them."

That spring, the Dennys set up housekeeping in a cottage next to the athletic quarters and Wallace spent his summer there. No mention was made of how Nellie spent her time, but an item that appeared in the September 20, 1912 edition of *The Carlisle Arrow* may suggest something:

Congratulations to Mr. and Mrs. Denny

A dear little son arrived at the home of Mr. and Mrs. Wallace Denny on the evening of the 12th. His name is Wallace Robertson Denny. Everyone on the Campus extends a loving greeting to Wallace, Junior, and congratulations to his parents in the happy event of his coming.

Nellie was over well 40 at the time and probably had little hope of ever having a child, especially after five years of marriage. So, Little Robertson, as he was called by many, was truly an unexpected bundle of joy for his parents. The school newspaper reported the details of his life. One can only imagine how the students doted on this toddler. He was baptized in March 1913 at St. John's Episcopal Church with Rev. Alexander McMillan officiating. Nellie's cousins, Elsie Robertson and Robert Weatherstone, sponsored him. In October, the Dennys moved back into their old apartment on the first floor at the end of the Small Boys Quarters. The apartment had been improved in their absence and had been given a new coat of paint. It had likely proved a necessity for Wallace to be living closer to his young charges. At age 15 months, Little Robertson joined the Invincible Debating Society by placing his thumb print beside his written name. Two months later, he was walking. With his newfound mobility he was able to patrol the campus when he wanted. At 26 months, it was reported that he visited the stables daily. Two weeks later, it was reported that he had added the laundry to his daily rounds. In February 1915, when he was two and a half, Robert Broker and Ben Swallow made a pony cart for Wallace. In May, he had a picture taken of his pony. Wallace's pony, Steiner Girl, won a blue ribbon at the Carlisle Fair in October. It is likely that both the pony and the cart were intended for Little Robertson. The doting father even had a cavalry uniform tailored for the boy. Winsome,

Little Robertson's second pony, arrived in March 1918. The Shetland ponies became fixtures around campus and in town as well when they pulled a wagon decorated with flags and bunting in the Liberty Loan parade.

The Dennys continued their work at the school. Wallace's responsibilities increased over time while Nellie took a couple of years off during Little Robertson's infancy. She then returned to her former position as head of the Outing Program. When the 1914 Joint Congressional Inquiry rocked the campus, both Dennys were interviewed, even though Nellie wasn't an employee at the time. She testified that the school didn't provide students on outing with adequate shoes and that students complained about a shortage of bread and food was not always properly cooked in the school's dining hall. She also testified that there was discord between Superintendent Friedman and several teachers and that either the superintendent or the disgruntled teachers must leave to eliminate the problem.

Wallace Denny, Robertson Denny & Nellie Robertson Denny
U. S. Army Military History Institute

Wallace Denny testified that discipline problems began when Major Mercer, as superintendent, allowed two or three sociables a week at which students were allowed to dance. When Moses Friedman reduced the number to one reception and one sociable a month, students turned against him. He also testified that school work became more difficult under Friedman. He also told the committee how he had prompted an investigation into the lack of bread for students. As it turned out, the bakery turned out plenty of good quality bread but the Quartermaster would only allow so much to be given to students, citing regulations that limit how much he can give them. Denny was interrogated about a couple of incidents in which he was accused of punching some students. In one case, the student punched him first when he wasn't looking. The other incident involved a tough who came straight to Carlisle from jail. When asked about problems with students drinking, he pointed out that the drinkers arrived at the school with the habit and that they weren't becoming drinkers there. He considered drinking to be a major problem.

The commission recommended that Wallace Denny be reprimanded for punching a student. Wallace continued in his position. After the inquiry, it appears that he did more things to endear himself to students than he had done before. Treats included picnics in parks, watermelons, use of the kitchen, and camping trips. One night after feasting on watermelons, the small boys cheered Denny loudly as they marched into their quarters: "Watermelon, Denny! Watermelon, Denny! Rah, rah, rah!"

Wallace and Nellie became active in the Society of American Indians. Part of their involvement was attending conferences around the country. Nellie became very active in the Alumni Association and returned to work as head of the Outing Department. Whenever Gen. Pratt visited, Nellie and Wallace met and dined with him and stood with him in receiving lines.

In March 1918, Nellie had the great honor of making the presentation of a gift from Pratt to the Susan Longstreth Literary Society at his request. Pratt had 100 letters from Susan Longstreth to him bound in the form of a book. This book was to remain in the hands of the society and members were to be read from it periodically.

Wallace continued to be involved in school athletics, particularly in track, which he coached after Pop Warner left in 1915. Wallace continued to improve his tennis game and in 1916 won the tennis championship of Carlisle and vicinity by beating a number of players from Dickinson College and Conway Hall. He won the trophy by defeating the 1915 champion, Robert E. Woodward. It appears that Wallace didn't serve as trainer for the football team after Warner left because, in later years, he recalled that he had worked with Warner in Pittsburgh. Warner left Carlisle in 1915 to coach Pitt and stayed there through the 1923 season. Denny wasn't needed at Carlisle in 1915 because Head Coach Victor Kelley brought Uncle Charlie Moran up from Texas A&M with him. Carlisle's football program was a shambles the last two years it competed, 1916 and 1917. Denny probably didn't think he was needed at Carlisle when the 1916 season started without a schedule of games in place.

Nellie was mired in a protracted communication with the Bureau of Indian Affairs over her land in 1916, 1917 and 1918. Eventually, she was awarded her share of the Sisseton-Wahpeton Tribal Fund, the patent for her land, as well as a citizenship pin and bag because she became a citizen when she accepted her allotment. At a particularly frustrating point in the process, Superintendent John Francis wrote the superintendent of the Sisseton Indian Agency:

> In response you are advised that Mrs. Denny is an employee at this school, having charge of the Outing work. She has received a patent for all her property and is just

Wallace Denny
U. S. Army Military History Institute

as capable as you or me in taking care of it, in fact Mr. and Mrs. Denny have accumulated quite a bit of property themselves. I dislike even to suggest to her that she should have this money to her credit and supervise.

Apparently, the Dennys were doing quite well financially and owned a significant amount of real estate. Later evidence of this was the 1930 census that valued their home in San Jose, California at $5,000.

Shortly after the U. S. entered WWI, former Superintendent Oscar Lipps wrote Nellie Denny regarding the frenzy of boys enlisting in the armed forces:

> If the war fever strikes Carlisle I am afraid it will greatly interfere with your outing. I should put it up to the boys that they can show their patriotism by taking up the hoe just as fully as by taking up a gun. We are going to need food, and Mr. Sells thinks the Carlisle boys can perform a distinct service for their country by going out on farms and helping to raise food supplies. I think so, too.

Carlisle Indian School supported the war effort in many ways including donating money, making bandages and garments for the Red Cross, and marching in parades to raise support and funds for the war. Although Carlisle Indian School closed suddenly on September 1, 1918—a 9-game football schedule was already in place—Wallace and Nellie Denny stayed on.

Carlisle Barracks was returned to the Army for use as a hospital in which soldiers wounded in France were treated. Wallace served as athletic director for the installation. What Nellie did at this time isn't clear. Because of their longevity with the Indian School and that they remained at the post after its conversion to a military hospital, Wallace and Nellie were in a unique position to dispose of school artifacts. A 1934 letter from the Dennys to Samuel M. Goodyear of Carlisle discussed how various items were disposed of when the school closed.

C. V. Peel of the Indian Bureau authorized them to handle the disposal of the property. They wrote that government property, including records, was sent to Washington; school publications were given to General Pratt, Bosler Memorial Library and the State Library in Harrisburg as were some other materials later, in 1922. Things like pictures and trophies paid for with Athletic Fund monies were retained by the Dennys. Later, when the Hamilton Library (part of Cumberland County Historical Society) established a Carlisle Indian School room, the Dennys

Wallace Denny in Interior Department uniform
U. S. Army Military History Institute

recommended that the State Library transfer its holdings to the newly formed room.

The Dennys stayed in Carlisle until April 1922 when it was announced that Wallace had taken a job as athletic trainer at Stanford University. Pop Warner had accepted the coaching job but would not move to Palo Alto until after the 1923 season because he was compelled to honor the terms of his contract. He sent two assistants ahead to run the Stanford team and teach his system to them. Wallace Denny was part of his coaching team. Andy Kerr, Tiny Thornhill and Wallace Denny coached the Cardinals until Warner was free of his entanglement with Pittsburgh. Wallace's quiet competence quickly caught *Oakland Tribune* reporter Doug Montell's eye:

> The quietest, most efficient and shyest man on Stanford field these days is Wallace Denny, former Carlisle Indian and present Stanford trainer. Denny likes a camera like a cat likes water, claiming that his place is not in the front line before the camera but behind the scenes turning out athletes in the pink of condition. Yet Denny never misses a moment of practice and so thoroughly does he know the ins and outs of football that were Kerr and Thornnill ever called away Denny could conduct practice from where they had left off without a hitch.

Almost nine years later, in April 1931, still at Stanford, Denny drew the attention of Frank Wilton who wrote about him in *The San Mateo Times and Daily News Leader*:

> "I fix you up, buddy!" is the pet expression of Wallace Denny, the Stanford athletic trainer. With the fixing up expression as his introduction, Denny proceeds to do a little rubbing of the sore muscle and a lot of talking about how he used to do it when he was a young man.

Wallace Robertson Denny's doting father wanted him to attend Stanford. Wilton wrote, "My boy is a fine boy. He goes to San Jose State Teachers' College now. I think he will come to Stanford soon and be under 'Pop'." Wallace also told the reporter about his old teammate: "Jim Thorpe was a great Indian. You know, he was a mean player. He was a great athlete—he liked to hit you hard."

After the end of the 1932 season, Pop Warner announced that he was leaving Stanford to take the head coaching job at Temple. Wallace Denny joined him in Philadelphia. Nellie died on May 1, 1935 at 64 years of age. Wallace, being younger than his late wife, continued working after her death. He also remarried. His second wife was Nellie's classmate at Carlisle, Rosa Bourassa, whose husband, Francis LaFlesche, had died a few years before Nellie. The two women probably kept in touch over the years. Otherwise, Wallace would probably have lost track of her.

Al Worden of *The Ogden Standard-Examiner* interviewed Denny in 1936 and got an interesting quote: "Football is just about perfect these days. I've seen hundreds of games since the late 90s and have watched the game improve tremendously. And say, the attendance is certainly ahead of what it was in the long, long ago."

In 1937, at almost 60, Wallace won the campus tennis championship by beating student Meyer Perchonock, Temple's best varsity player, in straight sets. Denny claimed not to have lost a match in 15 years. He continued working at Temple through the 1938 season, after which Pop Warner left. He was replaced by former Temple track and gymnastics star Frank Wiechic, but he wasn't ready to retire yet and neither was Pop.

They found something to do close to their homes in Palo Alto and Santa Clara, respectively. Warner accepted the position as advisory coach at San Jose State Teachers' College and Wallace Denny took his familiar place alongside him for the start of the 1939 season. AP Feature Service Writer Sam Jackson caught up with "Chief" Denny, as the players called him, in San Jose late that year when his team was the highest-scoring outfit in the country. Jackson wrote,

> When you overcome the Chief's natural reticence, he'll take you into the field house and show you the pads and appliances he's concocted to protect various injuries. They're secrets between the trainer and Pop, he says. No other handler knows these exact tricks. Like many trainers, Denny works his psychology hard. He constantly watches the boys on the field, knows how to handle each one to get the most out of him. Problems that a player is backward about laying before the coach are often threshed out with the trainer.

Jackson even got Denny to say a few things on the record:

> Football is harder today than it used to be. The old timers like to think their game was tough, but it wasn't as tough as the open game. Tackling is more deadly. You really need to protect a man more. I don't see any great difference in the physical setup of boys now and forty years ago, but the players today take better care of themselves. I certainly like to win. I used to like to win even if the boys were hurt, but now I protect the boys.

Warner coached and Denny nursed his players one more year. At 1940 season's end, they both retired. Wallace was still in good physical condition and boasted that he had never smoked, drank or chewed. Sam Jackson recalled him saying about Warner, "We've been everywhere else together. When the time comes I guess we'll meet in the Happy Hunting Ground." Pop Warner died in 1954. Denny died the next year at about 77 years of age after a long illness.

8

Lone Star Dietz

O ut of the darkness, a spotlight shone on the opening of a tipi placed in the center of the auditorium. A mystical Indian song emerged from the tipi and soon a young man, Lone Star, in Sioux attire complete with war bonnet, came forth. After demonstrating a war dance, Lone Star gave a talk about Indians with an emphasis on their scalping

```
       Name: William Henry Lone Star Dietz    Nickname: Wicarphi Isnala
        DOB: 8/17/1884                          Height: 5'11"
     Weight: 175                                   Age: 24
      Tribe: Sioux                                Home: Rice Lake, WI
    Parents: William Wallace Dietz, Leanna Ginder Dietz, white
             Julia One Star, Sioux
    Early Schooling: Rice Lake Public Schools, Macalester College
                     Chilocco Indian School, Friends University
    Later Schooling: Philadelphia School of Industrial Art
             Honors: Inland Northwest Sports Hall of Fame, 1963
                     Citizens Savings Athletic Foundation, 1976
                     Washington State University Hall of Fame, 1983
                     Pennsylvania Sports Hall of Fame, 1997
                     Rice Lake Sports Hall of Fame, 2002
                     Albright College Athletic Hall of Fame, 2008
```

proclivities, which he claimed were taught to them by the white man. Such was the introduction pupils at the School of Industrial Art in Philadelphia heard from their new fellow student fresh from the Carlisle Indian School. A *Philadelphia Record* reporter thought Lone Star's talk nearly made one's hair stand on end.

William Lone Star Dietz, old for an entering student at 23, enrolled at Carlisle in September 1907, in time for the fall term and, just as importantly, only six months after Glenn S. "Pop" Warner returned and ready to start football practice. Although he played very little, if at all, he traveled with the varsity squad. His on-field time was most likely with the second team that played a schedule of games with other teams. At the end of football season, he went on outing to the School of Industrial Design where he studied illustration. Most students spent their outings working on farms or at their trade, but a few used this time to get additional schooling. Lone Star was likely accepted at this institution because of the recommendation of his instructor at Carlisle, Angel DeCora, the famous Winnebago artist. While he was still on outing, Angel and Lone Star eloped.

Lone Star is believed to have met Angel DeCora three and a half years earlier when he was doing artwork for the model government Indian school exhibit at the St. Louis World's Fair and she visited the exhibit, if for no other reason than to see the painting purchased from her on display. Angel was thirteen years older than Lone Star and well established in her career while he was still in school. Little is known about their courtship other than they were almost always in different places. However, just three and a half months after he arrived at Carlisle, they were married. But the school kept it quiet until commencement was over in a successful attempt to avoid a scandal. A department head marrying a student 13 years her junior, even though he was 23 years old, would not have been viewed positively, so Dietz was made an assistant art instructor before summer.

Angel and Lone Star soon started a literary magazine that generated much positive publicity for the school. Initially titled *The Indian Craftsman,* its name was changed within a

Lone Star Dietz, 1911
U. S. Army Military History Institute

year to *The Red Man* to avoid confusion with Gustav Stickley's *The Craftsman* magazine. Under Angel's tutelage and with the training he received in Philadelphia, Lone Star became a skillful illustrator and received much praise from critics for his work in Carlisle publications and ephemera.

Angel DeCora broadened Carlisle students' horizons by inviting luminaries from the art world to visit the school and give talks. School visitors reported very positively on what they observed happening in the Native Art Department that Angel headed and in which Lone Star taught. Angel and Lone Star teamed up on some outside projects as well. They illustrated two books together, *Yellow Star* and *The Little Buffalo Robe*, as well as a calendar that was printed in Germany. Articles were published about them and their work in magazines such as *Literary Digest*.

Both gave talks on Indian art with Angel doing more of that than Lone Star because of her greater reputation. In December 1913, they made the claim that Indians had invented Cubism 200 years prior to its being "discovered" by Europeans, citing square eagles that can be found on some Indian art.

Sometimes they mixed their art with other interests. One of Lone Star's illustrations included a dog in a canoe. That dog was a hint as to what else was going on in his life. In 1910, the Dietzes started raising Russian Wolfhounds (today known as Borzoi) in what they called Orloff Kennels behind their apartment on Carlisle Barracks, the old army post that served as the campus for the Indian school. Angel was always an animal lover, keeping a cat for a pet before her marriage, and the regal nature of these dogs probably appealed to Lone Star's theatrical side. He made quite a sight when he exercised these tall, long-legged dogs on local roads, racing along with them on his bicycle with his coattails flapping in the breeze. Before long, they were breeding pedigreed dogs and entering them in shows. The zenith of their success was in 1915 when their top dog, Khotni, won best of breed at Westminster and another of their dogs, Belvina, won a lesser prize. When they broke up their kennel that summer, one of their young dogs sold for $700, more than a year's wages for many people at the time. This dog may have been Nazitka, who later became an American Champion as had Khotni.

Lone Star continued playing football on the second team and riding the varsity bench in 1908. He broke into the starting lineup at right tackle and lettered in 1909. Dietz continued playing in the 1910 and 1911 seasons. Being a lineman, he didn't get the press backs often received, but he got enough to be known nationally. In those days, especially in the Warner system with all its tricks, tackles got to carry the ball occasionally, and he even scored a touchdown in the 1911 victory over Penn. That year's team was arguably Carlisle's best, losing but once while beating two of the Big Four. He then assisted Pop Warner for three seasons with good results, until changes made after the 1914 investigation made it difficult to field a competitive team.

Dietz and Warner became lifelong friends as they both loved football and art. They repainted a backdrop for the school theater together, and Dietz illustrated Warner's 1912 book on coaching football. Dietz did the illustrations for such things as the athletic banquet programs and football posters. One of the figures he developed was used widely both at Carlisle and at other Indian schools after it closed. A color version of this figure was used as the frontispiece for John Steckbeck's 1951 *Fabulous Redmen: the Carlisle Indians and their famous football teams.*

When Warner decided to leave Carlisle in 1915, Dietz had decisions to make. He could stay on as head coach at Carlisle or go to Pitt with Pop as an assistant. Instead, he chose to strike out on his own and lead another team. When Washington State College (WSC) contacted Pop Warner about a candidate who applied for their open head coaching position, he gave a lukewarm reference and informed them that Lone Star Dietz was the man they should consider. After an application process, reviewing references and negotiating a salary, WSC gave Dietz a one-year contract. Initially, he was to coach baseball as well but that didn't materialize, possibly due to cost.

When Dietz arrived in Pullman, Washington, he made quite a splash. No one in this wheat-farming community had seen an Indian dandy before, and there were lots of Nez Perce not far away. His landlady didn't have nearly enough room to store the trunks in which his more than ample wardrobe was transported, so they had to be stored in the gym. The press had a field day showing him shopping in Portland, Oregon, dressed to the nines in top hat, tails, spats and carried an ivory-handled cane. The players weren't too sure, either. Team Captain Asa "Ace" Clark was used to scrimmaging very hard in practice. Dietz focused on conditioning and teaching the players the Warner system: single-wing with a little double-wing thrown in.

Clark and the rest of the players were skeptical. A 3–2 practice game win over the alumni wasn't very convincing, far from it. However, beating the heavy University of Oregon team 28–3 gave Clark reason to reconsider and, after thrashing the Oregon Aggies 29–0, he was convinced.

Dietz, never known for false modesty, claimed he knew the Warner system the best of anyone, and Warner once said Dietz ran the double-wing the best of any coach who tried it. Lone Star had his charges running these formations, mostly the single-wing, to perfection and rolled over their opponents, one after the other. In mid-November, sitting on a 5–0 record with a single, very winnable, game in front of them, Dietz got a surprise—one that would ultimately change history.

On January 1, 1902, the Tournament of Roses unsuccessfully experimented with playing a football game to round out the day after the parade in their mid-winter floral festival. Michigan was brought in as an eastern challenger, and Stanford was selected to defend the honor of the West. Fielding

Yost, Michigan's head coach, had coached Stanford the previous year but was let go because of a rule change that required the coach to be a graduate of the institution he was coaching. He then took the job at Michigan, a school that had no such rule, and led the Wolverines to an undefeated season, scoring 501 points to their opponents' zero. West Coast football was

Lone Star shows off new duds
The Oregonian

*University of Wyoming
Athletic Department*

not up to eastern standards at that time, so Michigan easily rolled over them. To make matters worse, early in the second half, Yost refused Stanford's offer to forfeit the game because they were being thrashed so badly. However, he did allow them to quit when Stanford no longer had eleven men without broken bones. The football experiment failed, so chariot racing became the after-parade entertainment. But good things don't last forever. By 1915, the chariot racing had become very dangerous and the professional drivers who were hired sometimes rigged the races. So, it was time to try something else, and the something was football again.

Coach Dietz received a telegram the day after the Whitman College game, offering his team the opportunity to play in Pasadena on New Year's Day. The opponent would be an eastern power. School officials quickly accepted the offer, but someone was trying to push them aside.

The University of Washington and Washington State did not play that year because a year earlier Washington's coach, "Gloomy" Gil Dobie, took WSC off his team's schedule because he considered them "too much like kindergarten." Also, Dobie rarely played road games and WSC expected UW to play in Pullman, or at least Spokane, occasionally, something Dobie abhorred. When Dobie got wind of the upcoming New Year's game, he tried to elbow his way into it. The only common opponents UW and WSC had that year were Whitman and Gonzaga. UW beat Whitman 27–0 but weather conditions held WSC down to a 17–0 victory. WSC's last game of the year was against Gonzaga, who UW beat 21–7. The WSC team had one last chance to bury Dobie's argument and they took it.

The Washington State players weren't about to let field conditions hold them back against Gonzaga as they wanted nothing to stand in their way of making the trip to Pasadena. Because comparative scores were taken seriously in those days, it was important to WSC, if for no other reason than to silence Dobie, to defeat Gonzaga by a greater margin than had

UW. Also, tacking on another ten points to make up the difference in margins against Whitman wouldn't be a bad idea. Highly-motivated WSC showed Gonzaga no mercy, trouncing them 48–0. Ironically, a Providence, Rhode Island newspaper initially had Brown University playing Washington rather than Washington State. Dietz's sources in the East may have informed him of that.

Something Dietz's sources did tell him was that Carlisle's coach for 1915, Victor M. Kelley, out of spite for Dietz's saying that he wouldn't make good at Carlisle, gave Brown's coach a copy of Carlisle's play book. *The Providence Journal* claimed that Brown knew Carlisle's plays inside and out from having played the Indians so many times. Brown's head coach, Edward Robinson, responded by stating that he would develop new plays for the New Year's Day game. Dietz would spring some surprises of his own but they were largely off-field.

Lone Star packed two trunks of summer attire and led his team to Pasadena. The team stayed in the elegant Maryland Hotel, but the players didn't get much time to lollygag in the lobby: Dietz had negotiated a movie deal for them. The team played the football team in *Tom Brown at Harvard* and got $100 each for their efforts. Lone Star got a bit part for himself. Later, the players figured out that Dietz got the better of them on that deal because, for the $100, he got to hold two-a-day practices. In the movie business, there is a lot of hurry up and wait, so Dietz took advantage of the wait times by having his team run plays during those times. Always the master psychologist when it came to motivating teams, Lone Star found a way to get his team ready for Brown.

Fritz Pollard, the great African-American halfback now in both college and professional football halls of fame, was Brown's big threat. So, Dietz devised a scheme to stop him. He called each of his starters aside (they played both ways then) and told each of them in confidence that he was afraid of Pollard and wanted that player to make it his personal responsibility to stop the scatback. He then swore each confidante to secrecy because he purportedly didn't want the rest of the team to know he was concerned about Pollard. He also had tricks up his sleeve for the media. He told them it was a foregone conclusion that the heavier Brown team would win. He just hoped his team could make it look respectable. Then he went back to perfecting his strategy for victory.

The Tournament of Roses committee hoped to make a great deal of money off the game because the 1902 game, in spite of being a mismatch, was profitable. Promotional materials included blurbs about each team's head coach. The game program also featured two photographs—but both of them were of Dietz, one in formal wear, the other in full Sioux regalia. Dietz also gave the press great interviews. One of the best was the one in which he predicted that California boys would never amount to much as athletes because they relied on automobiles for even the shortest distances.

Two days before the game, it snowed in Pasadena and on the morning of the game it started raining. By game time, the field was muddy, the stands were half empty, and Lone Star had no raingear. Taking no chances that the game would be delayed, Athletic Director and team trainer J. Fred "Doc" Bohler led the WSC team onto the field to warm up. It wasn't unknown in California at that time to postpone games in better weather than that, and Dietz had his team ready to play. But his high-powered offense with its razzle-dazzle plays was ill-suited for sloppy field conditions.

Brown had the best of the first half, threatening to score twice. But, on both occasions, the Dietzmen stiffened, stopping them well short of the goal line. Fritz Pollard later recalled that Lone Star's beautiful white suit was covered with mud early in the game and that, after being tackled, he feared he would be drowned in a mud puddle. At halftime, Dietz made some adjustments.

He threw out all but the simplest plays and focused on linebucking. Although Brown had a heavier line, particularly in the person of tackle Mark Farnum, Dietz felt his warriors could move them out. And they did. By hammering the line, they moved the ball forward and set a rushing yardage mark that held for decades. They also scored two touchdowns and made the kicks after touchdown while holding Brown scoreless. Fritz Pollard was held to less than 50 yards rushing in the 14–0 WSC landmark victory.

That historic game not only demonstrated that West Coast football was the equal of its eastern counterpart but also established what is now known as the Rose Bowl. As Rose Bowl historian Rube Samuelsen noted, this game was indeed the granddaddy of all them all, not just Rose Bowl games but all the New Year's Day games that followed. Recently a credible case has been made for naming the 1915 WSC team national champs. A 1915 Philadelphia newspaper predicted that they wouldn't receive the honor because of the press's eastern bias, even though they would deserve it if they beat Brown convincingly. As expected, the press was silent about it after the game was played. The team returned to Pullman to a hero's welcome; however, their coach wasn't with them.

Dietz had caught the movie bug and stayed behind in Hollywood to negotiate a movie deal. He didn't successfully negotiate a film contract he liked, claiming that the studios wanted him to portray Indians in a negative light. However, after rumors swirled around about Lone Star taking coaching jobs on both coasts and places in between, he negotiated a big raise for himself at WSC.

Expectations of what defined a successful season in Pullman had changed. In the several years prior to Lone Star's arrival, Washington State suffered through a series of losing seasons, but Pullmanites wanted no more of that. In fact, anything short of an undefeated season was considered subpar at this point. The 1916 team was accused of resting on its laurels, and

Dietz was criticized for being distracted by Hollywood because his team had suffered two defeats, both at the hands of the Oregon schools. So in 1917, Lone Star set aside his fancy duds and got out his moleskins.

Some think that 1917 was Dietz's best coaching job because several key players were lost through graduation or enlistment, and he had a lot of green ones to teach the rudiments of Carlisle football. That team went undefeated, giving up just 3 points the entire year. They even beat UW. That was possible because Gloomy Gil had departed and his successor was willing to schedule a game. WSC players and fans were disappointed because they expected to make another post-season trip to Pasadena. However, the U. S. had entered WWI earlier that year and service teams were drawing large crowds. Two service teams were selected for the New Year's Day contest instead.

Like most colleges, WSC wasn't going to be fielding athletic teams in 1918 due to the war and didn't want to pay Dietz a coaching salary if he wasn't coaching the varsity. So, he was let go after three years which included two undefeated seasons, a post-season victory, and only two losses. This was an excellent start to a coaching career, but Dietz wanted to consider other options.

Although Lone Star hadn't caught on in Hollywood, he still had the movie bug and a film career was brought to him. Tyrone Power Sr. blew into Spokane in August 1917, with visions of turning Minnehaha Park into a major motion picture studio. Dietz invested in the Washington Motion Picture Company and signed on to work on both sides of the camera. Funds were raised, a modern studio was built and a script was selected. A month into shooting, Power had a nervous breakdown and left town, never to return. Neither the cast nor the script was the strongest, which made the movie resemble its title, *Fool's Gold*. The film made enough money to cover its expenses but contributed little return for the tremendous investment made for building the studio. Eventually the company went into receivership and was sold for pennies on the dollar.

However, another opportunity came knocking for Lone Star. Ten of his players left WSC and joined the Marines. Stationed at Vallejo, California, they joined the Mare Island Marines football team but lacked a coach. Dick Hanley was dispatched to Spokane to recruit their old mentor. Although a civilian, Dietz trained to become a Marine officer in the morning and practiced the team in the afternoon. Despite being quarantined during an influenza epidemic and a four-game, 3,500 mile bus trip, Dietz's charges went undefeated. Because a Mare Island team composed of different players had competed in and won the 1918 Tournament of Roses game (the Rose Bowl wasn't built until 1923), Dietz's team was required to undergo an arduous post-season playoff schedule. The Marines emerged victorious and were selected to defend the honor of the West on New Year's Day, 1919 against the Great Lakes Navy team.

The Mare Island Marines were beaten up and sick going into the game. Dick Hanley was in bed with pneumonia and unable to play at all. A combination of good play by the Great Lakes team that featured three future NFL hall-of-famers, including "Papa Bear" George Halas, and poor decisions on the part of the Marines' quarterback led to a defeat. That defeat was a harbinger of things to come for Lone Star that year.

For reasons that remain unclear, Angel DeCora had not come west with Lone Star when he first took the job with WSC and had not moved out in the intervening years, so he filed for divorce on the grounds of desertion. The divorce was granted in November 1918, but neither party was allowed to remarry for six months. Angel did not live that long. She was caught up in the influenza pandemic that raged around the world at that time and died in February 1919. Dietz considered himself a widower.

Shortly after the game, the head of the Spokane draft board announced that he was filing charges against Dietz for draft dodging. He and Dietz had previously had words over Dietz's using what he considered an excessive amount of sugar, a rationed item during WWI. A couple of years earlier a reporter, who was familiar with Dietz's background in the Midwest, wrote a column that claimed that Dietz had no Indian heritage. That column served as the basis for the charges. Dietz had claimed to be a non-citizen Indian on the draft forms he filled out in September 1918, with the advice of Marine officers, and the government disputed that claim. The WSC administration reacted by withdrawing its contract offer for Dietz. The trial, held in late June 1919 at the federal courthouse in Spokane, was quite sensational and received national coverage. According to the charges, William Henry Dietz was the natural-born son of William Wallace and Leanna Ginder Dietz, two white people. The Dietzes, since divorced, lived in Rice Lake, Wisconsin at the time of their son's birth and raised him in that community. The prosecutor brought in several witnesses, including neighbors and relatives, from Rice Lake where Dietz grew up. He also brought in Sally Eagle Horse from the Pine Ridge reservation because Dietz had claimed she was his sister.

The prosecution witnesses from Rice Lake testified that they had either seen the young Dietz shortly after his birth in 1884 or they had seen him grow up. They all supported the government's case that Lone Star was really the white child of W. W. and Leanna Ginder Dietz and that he had no Indian blood. Through an interpreter, Sally Eagle Horse testified that her brother, James One Star, had gone to Carlisle Indian School decades before but she hadn't seen him since. Lone Star was too young to have been her brother and didn't have a scar she recalled her brother having as the result of a childhood accident.

Dietz also brought in witnesses from Rice Lake including the woman who raised him, her mother and two of his father's nephews. Two Marines from Mare Island testified about his activities with the Marines. Leanna Ginder Lewis, who had divorced Dietz's father almost two decades before, testified that her son was stillborn in August, 1884 and that W. W. Dietz took the corpse and disappeared. He returned no more than ten days later with a child that he had had with an Indian woman about the same time. Leanna testified that the baby had a clump of coal-black hair and grew up to be the defendant. She brought with her the red shawl the baby was wrapped in when she received it. Leanna's mother (also named Leanna) testified that she was present for the birth and supported her daughter's story. Two nephews of the elder Dietz and their mother, his brother's wife, testified that W. W. had shared with them that his son had Indian blood on his mother's side and to keep it a secret.

Lone Star also took the stand. He told of growing up thinking he was the son of W. W. and Leanna Dietz until, at about age 15, he overheard them fighting and learned part of the secret of his birth. He testified that his parents and grandparents were fair-haired and blue-eyed and that, unlike them, he was dark-haired and dark-eyed.

To say the trial was sensational would be an understatement. It was the O. J. trial of its day. News reports were wired to all parts of the country and created headlines daily for the duration of the trial. High school girls came to the courthouse hoping to meet the famous, handsome football coach. After several days of testimony, the jury was tasked to make a decision.

After considerable deliberation, the jury was unable to come to a unanimous decision. The jury deadlocked 8 to 4 in favor of dismissal. The judge declared the jury hung. The prosecutor immediately refiled charges, this time for filling out draft forms improperly. In January 1920, out of money and unable to defend himself further, Dietz plead *nolo contendre* to the revised charges and was sentenced to 30 days in the Spokane County jail. This sentence was very lenient for the time. People found guilty of lesser offenses were often given much longer sentences.

The judge may have not been very enthusiastic about putting Dietz in jail.

Dietz's reputation and career were ruined. He never obtained a top-tier coaching position again. As Ray Schmidt, editor of the journal for the College Football Historical Society, sees it, Dietz then took on a series of "reconstruction projects." In spite of this, Lone Star persevered and compiled a hall-of-fame-worthy coaching career with stops at Purdue, Louisiana Tech, Wyoming, Haskell Institute and Albright College. When he was between jobs, Pop Warner hired him to coach his freshman teams at Stanford and, later, at Temple. Wherever Dietz went, he immediately increased interest in the football program dramatically. Through it all he continued drawing and painting. He even illustrated Pop Warner's 1927 book on coaching football.

In 1922, he married Doris Ohm Pottlitzer of Lafayette, Indiana, whom he met while coaching at Purdue University. Their union lasted until his death. People who knew the Dietzes described her as a delightful person, very refined and a gourmet cook. She was the society page editor of the local paper when she met Lone Star. The author is dismayed over not finding a single photograph of Doris—Dietzee as the cookie-munching neighborhood children called her. Doris and Lone Star were not blessed with children of their own.

Lone Star's reputation as a strategist persisted, largely because he put out winning teams where others had failed. In 1929 he was called "Miracle Man" for turning around the Haskell Institute Fightin' Indians. Because of his brilliance, he was selected to submit a favorite play to "My Winning Play," a series run by the Associated Press in the early 1930s. Always a showman, Dietz selected the "Dead Indian Play" as one of his favorites. Pop Warner originated the play at Carlisle in 1910, and in 1911 quarterback Gus Welch used it to call his own number against Penn with a 65-yard touchdown run the result. Jim Thorpe was too injured to play in that game and

Warner used the "Dead Indian Play" to offset this handicap. According to Dietz:

> The play is most effectively used in a team's own territory, about the 40-yard line, where a kick formation is a constant threat, with the defensive backs playing rather deep and the defensive line somewhat scattered. The back behind center gets the ball on a "lob" pass, drives into the line between left guard and tackle and is generally tackled by the defensive right halfback, who plays in front of the hole. Naturally, the other defensive backs are drawn up to this point in backing up the play. The offensive line then moves up to the point where the ball carrier is lying on the ground in a rather prone position. Another back, addressing the prone one, says, "Are you hurt?" The ball carrier gets up slowly and responds, "Oh, I'm all right," and throws the ball to a third back who, with the aid of the flanking linemen and backs, circles around the opponent's end, usually for long gains which have resulted in many touchdowns.

Dietz claimed to have abandoned the play but said there was nothing in the rules to prevent him from reviving it.

In 1933, Lone Star Dietz accepted the head coaching position for the Boston Braves NFL team. George Preston Marshall, owner of the team, moved the team to Fenway Park, necessitating a name change for the team. Marshall's granddaughter wrote an op-ed piece to the *The Washington Post* some years ago, stating that her grandfather had renamed the team Redskins in Dietz's honor. Dietz has been embroiled in the Indian mascot controversy for many years due to his central role in the naming of the team.

Dietz's antics in the NFL are the stuff of legends. A favorite is the one that Howard Roberts recalled in his 1953 history of professional football. George Halas brought his Bears to Boston to play the Redskins and secretly sequestered his team in the

Brunswick Hotel. While there, Halas held a team meeting in a room and posted guards at the entrances to keep out all but team members. Papa Bear started the meeting with some game films. After they were over, he turned on the lights to see Lone Star Dietz applauding from his seat in the front row, "Wonderful! Wonderful! Thank you. A great idea, George. I learned a lot." Lone Star had infiltrated the enemy camp. After two years in the NFL, he returned to the college game.

After two season of asisting Pop Warner at Temple, Dietz took the head coaching job at Albright College in Reading, Pennsylvania. In 1937, his first year as head Lion, he led the team to its first unbeaten season. He soon became a fixture in the community. His paid coaching career ended after the 1942 season when Albright College terminated its athletic programs for the duration of WWII. Lone Star put his skills as an artist to work to support himself during the war. After the war he operated Liberty Academy, an art school in Pittsburgh. When the Korean War siphoned off his students to the military or defense jobs, he used his life savings to pay off the school's debt.

In 1956, Lone Star stole the show at the Rose Bowl celebration honoring the 40th anniversary of his team's landmark victory. While on the West Coast, he visited Pullman at a time Washington State was looking for a new football coach. Although he did not formally apply for the job, it was clear he wanted it. However, those weren't the days of septuagenarian coaches. The school did give him a school blanket, a decades-overdue honor.

Dietz spent the last eight years of his life living in poverty in Reading, Pennsylvania where he assisted with youth football and remained involved in the Albright College community. He continued painting and several of his works can be found hanging at Albright. A former player whom Dietz visited frequently at his army surplus store remarked that, every time he saw him, Lone Star had some new idea. He was never defeated and didn't wallow in the past. Lone Star Dietz died of cancer in 1964 holding Pop Warner's inspirational poem, "Keep A-goin'," in his hand.

Since his death, he has had a number of honors bestowed on him but has not been inducted into the College Football Hall of Fame. In 2005, he may have come the closest. However, the selection committee chose to ignore the names of coaches on the ballots and selected two coaches for induction who were not eligible for induction at that time because they were still actively coaching. After Bobby Bowden and Joe Paterno were selected, the rules were changed to make others, should there ever be other coaches in their situation, eligible for placement on the ballot. Interestingly, both coaches accepted the honor and neither publicly questioned why they could be inducted when their names hadn't been on the ballot.

Lone Star Dietz was a fascinating man whose life deserved a book-length biography. Fortunately one has been written. Those interested in knowing more about Lone Star are directed to *Keep A-goin': the life of Lone Star Dietz* by the author who also wrote the book you are now reading. After writing that book while researching his own family background, the author learned of a man from whom he might be descended and who maintained two families, one white and one Cherokee, along the frontier in 1760. Apparently situations such as the one Leanna Lewis described may not be as far-fetched as they might appear at first blush. Also, while looking at census data for Gus Welch, the author stumbled across a Lone Star family in Washburn County, Wisconsin, the county immediately north of Barron County, the county in which W. W. Dietz lived and Lone Star Dietz spent his youth. Research of Frank Lone Star yielded little about the Lone Star family that lived in the Washburn County. Could these Chippewas be Dietz's relatives? The facts of Lone Star Dietz's birth became murkier with this discovery.

After completing Dietz's biography, the author also learned of Joel Platt's enormous collection of priceless sports artifacts.

Included in this collection are objects that were surely in Dietz's possession at the time of his death. A 1974 *Sports Illustrated* article discussed his baby curls. Platt's Sports Immortals web site prominently displays the beautiful pair of gloves Jim Thorpe made at Carlisle and gave to Lone Star. Who knows what else is in that collection?

Dietz's war shirt and leggings

9

Louis Island

Louis Abraham Island was first enrolled in 1898. However, the records of that enrollment have been lost as has documentation of his birth, believed by family members to have been in Canada, if such paperwork ever existed. Island was somewhere between five and eight years old when he first came to Carlisle. His older sister, Carrie, also attended Carlisle and was listed on the 1900 Federal census as being full-blood Oneida. Their father, also named Louis, was alive in 1905 to re-enroll his son for a second term, but their mother was deceased by that time. Like most small boys at Carlisle, he received

```
Name: Louis A. Island                Nickname:
DOB: 7/12/1890 or 7/12/1893          Height: 5' 5"
Weight: 137                          Age: 21
Tribe: Oneida                        Home: Green Bay, WI
Parents: Louis Island, Oneida
         Kate Wheelock Island, Oneida
Early Schooling: Oneida Boarding School likely
Later Schooling: Haskell Institute
                 Chiropractic school
```

Louis Island; *Louis Geoffrey Johnston*

little mention in the school newspaper during his early years at the school. Louis Island's first mention in *The Red Man and Helper* listed him as one of the students returning from summer outing for the new school term in September 1900. His next mention was over two years later when he scored a touchdown for the Blacksmiths in the shop championship game against the Printers.

Island became a freshman in the fall of 1903, at which time he was elected president of the Class of 1907. Louis was very active in school affairs. He joined the Invincible Debating Society where he frequently spoke, participated in debates and became an officer. After the 1905 football season was over, he was named to the school's "All-American Foot Ball team" at quarterback. Later in December, Louis participated in a gymnastics demonstration as part of the entertainment for a sociable. In December 1906, the Invincibles elected him president. Sometime in his Carlisle career, Island shifted from blacksmithing to printing.

Though only 5' 5-1/4" tall and weighing 148 pounds, Louis went out for football and made the varsity in 1906, playing quarterback behind Archie Libby. He got into the early games and onto the scoreboard by kicking a 30-yard field goal against Albright College. After that, his major playing time came with the second team. He drop-kicked a field goal against Dickinson Seminary in Williamsport, Pennsylvania but missed the kick after Theodore Owl's touchdown.

In the winter, Louis Island played left forward on the basketball team that represented Carlisle well against Franklin and Marshall College. In the spring, he played baseball on the school team. Somehow, he also found time to run track. He showed another side of his athletic prowess and chivalry at the Senior outing when he quickly donned a bathing suit to retrieve a purse a damsel dropped into the lake. A week later, he spoke at the local Methodist church he regularly attended. Staying at Carlisle over the summer, he pitched for the Printer's Devils against the Velvet Treaders, a team made of faculty and staff members, trouncing the elders 21–7.

Frank Mt. Pleasant was shifted back to quarterback in 1907, keeping Mike Balenti and Louis Island from moving up on the depth charts. Island and Balenti got into the early-season games and received good reviews. After the Villanova game, *The Arrow* reported, "His [Mt. Pleasant's] successor, Island, worked very creditably." *The Sentinel* echoed those sentiments: "Mt. Pleasant is better than ever in running with the ball and he handles the team well, although Island does as well in the latter respect as he." A couple of weeks later against Bucknell, the reports weren't as positive: "Mt. Pleasant was not in the game and Island filled his position most of the time, until replaced by Balenti. The former ran the team fairly well, but was poor on running back punts and was responsible for some heavy losses. Balenti was also weak in handling the ball. Both seemed to be anxious to get in the lime-light by kicking drop-kicks, and Island did succeed in scoring in this manner." He also kicked a goal after touchdown. Filling in for a player who many thought should have received first team All-America honors is never easy, especially for players who would have been starters for most other teams. Because Mt. Pleasant was injured so badly in the Minnesota game, he had to sit out the big game with Chicago. Student reporter William Yankee Joe observed, "Every student thought that it was up to Island who has been backing up Mt. Pleasant during the season. But when we heard the line-up and with Balenti at quarter back some of the students were a little shaky." *The Arrow* reported that those fears were unfounded: "Balenti and Island ran the play without a hitch, and the accurate kicking of Hauser, coupled with his slashing runs and line plunging, made up for the ground-gaining and scoring abilities of the regular quarter-back."

After football season, Louis focused his attention on his numerous other activities until graduation in April 1908. In addition to his diploma, he received an industrial certificate in Printing, Two-Thirds. Apparently, there was another third to the printing program. However, graduation from Carlisle didn't end his education.

In the fall of 1908, Louis Island enrolled at Haskell Institute. He also joined the football team. The purple and gold Fightin'

Louis Island in Fort Wayne Friars uniform; *Louis Geoffrey Johnston*

Indians played such teams as Missouri, Texas, Nebraska, Texas A & M, LSU and Alabama. After two years in Kansas, 18-year-old Island returned to the reservation but thought of the Cumberland Valley.

From West DePere, Wisconsin, Andrew Doxtator wrote Carlisle, "Louis Island is returned student and he wishes to go back to Carlisle again. This is all puples [sic] I could get." Island re-enrolled at Carlisle, this time in the commercial course, on September 10, 1910, and played football again. Again a solid player but not a star, Louis completed his career at the Indian school but remained nearby.

Island took a job at the Hershey Chocolate Company, which made visits to campus practical. On March 17, 1911, *The Arrow* reported that Louis and William Newashe, also employed at Hershey, played on the Hershey YMCA basketball team against their old school. Their old classmates loudly applauded their pluck. In May the *Harrisburg Telegraph* announced that Louis had registered as a student at Lebanon Valley College in Annville, Pennsylvania.

In the fall of 1913, Louis Island started his professional football career. He played end for the Jackson, Michigan All-Stars or Independents, as they were sometimes called. Made up largely of University of Michigan players no longer eligible because of grades or other infractions, the Independents were a competitive team. In fact, they claimed the southern Michigan championship until defeated by the Fort Wayne Friars in a game played in a snowstorm on the Friars' home field, League Park, in Fort Wayne, Indiana. The Friars were so impressed by Island that they hired him for the 1914 season. He played well enough in 1914 to be brought back in 1915. The Friars went 7–1–1 with him playing right end and quarterback. He would have likely been back for another season, but an off-field accident ended his playing days.

At some point, Louis located in Fort Wayne and took a job as a punch-press operator at the local General Electric plant. In his spare time, he officiated whatever game was in season for area teams. In early May 1916, his playing career ended as the result of a punch-press accident in which his left thumb was crushed. Island lost the best part of a month's work due to the injury but returned to the same job in late May.

That fall, Louis began his coaching career by taking charge of the West End junior team. Because the West End of Fort Wayne, now a historic district, was populated by many of the movers and shakers of the town, Island very likely coached the scions of important families and made contacts that would serve him well in the future. At the beginning of the season, pundits considered it the strongest team West End had ever fielded. Louis's team played well most of the season but lost their last regular-season game to the rival Badgers, throwing the city junior championship into turmoil with three teams making claims to it. Once football season ended, he began officiating basketball games. Island continued officiating through the winter. He had arranged a nice life for a bachelor: he had a job that covered his living expenses and in his free time he participated in his first love—sports. This idyllic life was rudely interrupted by events thousands of miles away across the Atlantic.

The June 27, 1917 edition of *The Fort Wayne Sentinel* crowed, "When Battery D [sic] leaves here the latter part of this week or the first of next week its roll will include the name of one of the best athletes of the city, Louis Island. Louis went to headquarters last night and signed up, ready to do his bit as a true American wherever the unit may be ordered...When he leaves the city it will be with the best wishes of a host of friends and admirers." That day's *Fort Wayne Journal-Gazette* gave him a send off: "Believing that he, a true American, should 'do his bit,' Louis Island, the well-known football player, appeared at battery B recruiting headquarters last night and signed up for service with the artillery...Island should make good with the battery as he had four years' infantry training at Carlisle. It is a sure thing that if he plays the artillery game as hard as he did the gridiron game there are bound to be some German

Sgt. Louis Island; *Iris Davis*

lines smashed and a few plays broken up. Here's to you, Louis, and success."

Three days later, *The Fort Wayne Daily News* reported that Pvt. Island was given the honor of carrying the unit's flag. The flag was purchased with funds raised by contributions collected by Mrs. F. H. Banks. "Lieutenant L. F. Woods received the flag and then handed it to Private Louis Island, saying that he knew of no one in the battery more worthy to carry the colors.'" About six weeks later, *The Journal-Gazette* covered a parade: "When Battery B paraded yesterday as United States regulars, Fred Fosmire, of German and Irish parentage, and Louis Island, a full-blooded Indian, carried the Stars and Stripes and artillery guidon. Thus does Americanism unite all under the flag in common service to the nation." On August 16, Louis A. Island was promoted to the rank of sergeant. It isn't known if the fact that 18 men failed to pass the physical examination affected his promotion.

Battery B shipped over to France, arriving in November 1917, as a component of the 150th United States Field Artillery of the Rainbow Division. He was engaged in fighting at Chateau Thierry, Verdun, second battle of the Marne, St. Mihiel and the Argonne, where he was on the firing line when the armistice was signed. He accompanied the army of occupation into Germany and was stationed at Coblenz until sent home. In April 1919, Sgt. Island and seven others, one of whom was dead, were cited for "especial bravery" for serving the guns while under fire during the American drive at Chateau Thierry. The May 11 *Journal-Gazette* praised him with the headline, "Friar Grid Star Is Welcomed Home With Batteries B and D." A photo of him accompanied the article. "Loie, we greet you. May you live long and prosper."

And that was exactly what he intended to do. Soon Louis Island's name was showing up again on the sports page for coaching football. He continued his life of working at mundane jobs while coaching and officiating on the side until the late 1920s. His employment history during this time included working as a gardener and as a meter man. But in 1928, he had no occupation. This likely means that he was attending a professional school to better his position in life because the next year he was listed on the Fort Wayne city directory as being a chiropractor. The 1930 census listed his occupation as drugless physician, which was likely another term for chiropractor at that time. Indiana didn't license chiropractors until 1955, so he may have been practicing under some other title. In some states, chiropractors practiced as drugless physicians to avoid going to jail for practicing medicine without a license, which happened to some of those who called themselves chiropractors.

Dr. Louis Island; *Louis Geoffrey Johnston*

Dr. Island, as he was now called, had made a major life change in the early 1920s. He married a white woman named Phoebe Harsh from Mentone, Indiana. Phoebe was a farm girl who had four sisters but no brothers. So, Louis was the only young male at family gatherings for a while. Niece Iris Davis and nephew Dick Boganwright knew him only as small children but recall that he was "a nice, friendly guy" who liked children. Outgoing without being loud, Louis was soon well thought of by Phoebe's family. He and Phoebe had a son, Harsh Louis Island. Just as Louis had settled into a career and family life, the unexpected struck. In September 1933, Dr. Island died of tuberculosis. Phoebe lived 22 years more. Their son, who was also known as Louis, died young as had his father. His death was thought to be caused by an infection of a wound acquired in the Korean War.

Louis & Phoebe Island; *Louis Geoffrey Johnston*

10

James Johnson

Carlisle Indian School documents list James E. Johnson as a member of the class of 1901, which implies that he arrived in 1896 or before. Determining specifics about his enrollment is difficult because his file is void of these records. The 1900 census taken at Carlisle placed Jimmie's year of birth at 1878 and indicated he was full-blood Stockbridge with full-blood Stockbridge parents, all born in Wisconsin. From reading tribal rolls and federal censuses, it is reasonable to conclude

```
Name: James Johnson            Nickname: Whirlwind
 DOB: 6/6/1879                   Height: 5'7"
Weight: 138                       Age: 24
 Tribe: Stockbridge              Home: Gresham, WI
Parents: James A. Johnson
         Adis Tousey-Johnson
Early Schooling: Reservation, possibly
Later Schooling: Dickinson College Preparatory School
                 Dickinson College, Northwestern University
       Honors: College Football Hall of Fame, 1969
```

that James Johnson's parents were James A. Johnson, mixed-blood originally from Tennessee, and Adis Tousey-Johnson, full-blood Stockbridge-Munsee. His father was a barber and his mother kept house and took care of the children. Difficulties in finding James A. Johnson on tribal rolls initially gave the impression that he may have died by the time James E. came to Carlisle. However, he shows up on the 1900 Federal Census. A September 5, 1902 article in *The Red Man and Helper* mentions James's brother, Adam, as helping his father at that time. This further supports that the Johnson children had a living father at that time. Later, James was listed as being from Gresham, Wisconsin, the town closest to the Stockbridge-Munsee Reservation. However, later records indicate that he was born in Edgerton, Wisconsin on June 6, 1879.

Records of Johnson's physical size at the time of his arrival are lost, but later photographs and newspaper articles depicted him as being average height or shorter and thin. Mere words could not do justice to Johnson's hair as can be seen in his photo on the College Football Hall of Fame website.

Home for James was in central Wisconsin. The Stockbridge-Munsee Reservation, the relocation home for Jimmie's tribe, is located northwest of the Oneida Reservation immediately adjacent to the Menominee Reservation. The Dawes Act of 1887 and the Burke Act of 1906 caused much of the reservation to be sold off to white people during James Johnson's youth, and by 1910 the Stockbridge were no longer recognized as a tribe by the government. It is highly likely that James did not live on the reservation even if his father farmed his allotment. Thus, James had no on-reservation childhood, and attending Carlisle probably required less adjustment on his part than it would have required from many of his classmates.

James Johnson joined the Invincible Debating Society and, in December 1898, was elected reporter. In March 1899, James and Caleb Sickles teamed up to argue the negative in a debate about whether building the Panama Canal would be beneficial to the United States. They lost but put up a good fight as retold by *The Indian Helper:* "There were more members of the society present than usual, and a spirited debate occurred relative to points of order in which President Martin Wheelock maintained the dignity befitting his office, and rendered wise decisions." The next month Johnson was elected assistant critic. He would remain active in the Invincibles throughout his time at Carlisle.

October of 1899 found Pop as head coach of the Carlisle Indian School football team. Jimmie Johnson was mentioned in *The Dickinsonian* as one of the new men "...who have the look of comers." Johnson had started his varsity career at Carlisle. At the end of the school year, Johnson enrolled in the Dickinson College Preparatory School but still played football for Carlisle. The yearbook described him as, "A renowned warrior of the Indian school. Flourishes black eyes, bandaged wrists and torn ears during the foot-ball season. Wants to be an angel."

The October 5, 1900 edition of *The Red Man and Indian Helper* opined on the upcoming football season, "Johnson, who was substitute for Miller, played in several of the games last season, and who is doing good work this year. He will probably fill the right half-back position..." James shone for Carlisle while attending Prep. He improved in 1901 and got more attention for his play, now at quarterback. Leading up to the Penn game, Pop Warner said, "...Johnson's playing at quarterback has been a feature of the team's play all the season." After the game the *Philadelphia Record* raved, "The star performer for the Carlisle team was Johnson. The speedy little quarterback ran his team with admirable judgment, played a strong game in the backfield on defense and on the trick quarterback run made more ground than any member of the team, with the possible exception of Wheelock." After the season, Walter Camp placed Martin Wheelock on his All-America Second Team and named James as his third team quarterback.

James Johnson graduation photo
The Red Man December 1911

In the spring, Johnson played baseball, also for Carlisle, generally at second base. With his speed, he was a constant base-stealing threat. Surprisingly, he batted third or fourth in the order, places usually reserved for power hitters. So, Jimmie was not just a singles hitter; he must have had the ability to drive in runs.

Over the winter of 1902, he was made captain of the small boys' companies at Carlisle. It appears that he earned money for his education by working at the Indian school. His pay may have included room and board.

That spring in track season he gained renown as Carlisle's star hurdler. However, he and James Phillips were not allowed to participate in the meet against Dickinson College because Johnson was finishing his senior year at Dickinson's prep school and Phillips was a student at the law school. Eligibility rules were evidently evolving. Johnson's school record in the high hurdles was broken by Johnson Bradley in that meet as James watched while officiating.

Jimmie returned home for the summer and wrote back when he found work in Evanston, Illinois, a locale in which he would spend much time in the future. He returned to Carlisle in September as a freshman at Dickinson College proper, ready to star in football—at Carlisle. The Invincibles made him an advisory member of their society, likely because he was no longer studying at the Indian school and, thus, couldn't be a regular member.

James had no problem deciding for whom he would play in the annual Dickinson-Carlisle game because none was played. The teams were unable to agree on the lengths of halves to be played, a negotiable item in those days, and the game was canceled. *The Dickinsonian* placed the blame on Warner, who may not have wanted to play the game for reasons known only to himself. Carlisle had a pretty good team that year, going 8–3. Johnson starred but was overlooked by Walter Camp for All-America recognition. That oversight was rectified a little bit when President Roosevelt invited the team to visit him in the White House after the Georgetown game. A *New York Sun* article, possibly written by the Carlisle publicity office, gave the following account of James meeting the President:

> "De-lighted," exclaimed the President, grasping the hand of Johnson, "you play quarter back. The mass play of your team was splendid. I am delighted."
>
> So was Johnson but he did not show it until he got outside.
>
> "Mr. Johnson," asked the President, "how was it that Yale defeated my college, Harvard, while she played such a good game against you?"
>
> The little quarterback replied, "We did not play a very good game."
>
> "I do not know why Harvard took such a slump," asked the President.

Walter Camp may have snubbed Johnson that year, but Nathan F. Stauffer, columnist for the Philadelphia *Inquirer,* didn't. Stauffer named Johnson quarterback of both his All-American and All-University teams, the distinction between the two being unclear to the modern reader. When naming Johnson, he wrote, "Johnson gave the Indians more life and ginger than any quarter they have ever had. He is a fine general in choosing successful tricks and clever executing such plays. However, he lacks ability in the kicking line." His teammates honored him by voting him captain of the 1903 team.

Although enrolled at Dickinson College, James did not abandon the non-sports aspects of Indian School life. In February, he gave an original oration titled "The Indian as an Individual" to a meeting of the Invincible Debating Society. The Man-on-the-band-stand was impressed by his "deep earnestness."

In March, an indoor track meet was held for boys wanting to be on the team that spring. Jimmie won both high and low hurdle events. That spring he won a gold watch at the Pennsylvania Relay Carnival held at Franklin Field. He ran the third leg on what had to be Carlisle's fastest team ever. Wallace Denny led off, followed by Wilson Charles, then Johnson and anchored by Frank Mt. Pleasant. In June, he was off for the Midwest, likely to Evanston to earn some money, over the summer.

1903 was an historic year for Carlisle football in many ways. James Johnson played a role in a play that continues to be talked about today. For the Harvard game, Pop Warner dusted off a trick play he had used at Cornell in 1897 against Penn State.

Prior to the game, Warner had local haberdasher and Carlisle school tailor, Mose Blumenthal, install elastic cord in the hem of a player's jersey. The elastic cord would cause a football placed under the jersey, either front or back, to remain in place without being held there by the player. Warner saved the hidden ball or hunchback trick for the second half kickoff in the big game with Harvard. After kicking his first attempt out of bounds, the Harvard kicker arced the ball high and deep down the middle of the field to the waiting Jimmie Johnson. As he fielded the kick at the goal line, his teammates huddled around him facing outward. He slipped the ball under the back of Charles Dillon's jersey and shouted, "Go!" The team scattered and headed toward both sidelines, some for one and the rest for the other, each faking that he had the ball. The actual ball carrier, Big Dillon, ran straight for the Harvard goal line, arms swinging as if he were going to throw a block. Harvard's safety, Carl Marshall, not wanting to get blocked out of the play, sidestepped Dillon. While Dillon, a guard, was steadily making his way to the goal, several of his teammates raced to the end zone because someone had to remove the ball from Dillon's shirt in order for it to be touched down. Accounts vary as to who removed the ball. It may have been Al Exendine or it may have been Johnson or it may have been someone else. Regardless, the Boston crowd, always supportive of the Indians, loved the play, but the Harvard team was incensed at having been made

Wisconsin natives on the 1903 team: Charles Williams
(2nd from right in back row), Wilson Charles (3rd from
right in second row) & Capt. James Johnson (holding football)
Fred Wardecker

to look like fools. The Crimson played with desperation and came back to win 12–11.

Walter Camp named the 5'7", 138-pound quarterback to his 1903 All-America First Team. The football team, Carlisle's best to that point, closed its regular season against Northwestern University in Chicago. Jimmie Johnson starred in that Thanksgiving Day game played in a snowstorm that was blinding at times in South Side Park, then home of the Chicago White Sox baseball team. The Indians defeated Northwestern, that year's Co-Champions of the West, 28–0 with Johnson responsible for 23 of those points. The *Inter-Ocean* praised his play: "Little Johnson was easily the most brilliant player on the field. He ran his team in a masterful way, carried the ball for good gains, and finally climaxed his performance by shooting the ball between the posts for a place kick." Northwestern was weakened a bit when guard James Phillips refused to play against his former teammates from Carlisle. *The Red Man and Helper* reported, "Watching the contest from the stands, Phillips said that had the field been free from snow Carlisle's speedy back would have doubled the score."

The Indians then made the longest trip to play a football game since the Indians' 1899 trip to San Francisco four years earlier. First stop on the trip was in Salt Lake City for a game against the University of Utah. Warner benched Johnson for an infraction of an unspecified team rule. The Indians still won handily, 22–0. An hour before the Reliance Athletic Association game on Christmas Day in San Francisco, Johnson was still fuming over having been benched for the Utah game. While Warner was giving Johnson and his backup, Joe Baker, instructions, Johnson shouted, "Listen Pop. I don't care if I never play in one of your ball games!" Warner immediately informed Baker that he would be taking Johnson's place that day. Other players overheard the outburst and asked Pop to give Johnson a second chance. Warner cranked up the heat by saying, "Baker really did a fine job for us against Utah. And besides, I couldn't play a player whose heart would not be in the game." Johnson then spoke up, "Well, Coach. If the other boys want me to play, I will."

The Indians then handled the highly touted Reliance A. A. 23–0. San Francisco *Examiner* expert, C. M. Fickert, opined, "The team worked as one man, or rather Captain Johnson worked them as one man. He is the greatest quarterback that has ever played here. He exhibited great generalship in handling his team and in sizing up his opponents' play. He is very active, very aggressive, always on the ball, and he is continually urging on his men. With him off the team the score would have been different. And the crowd guessed right when they yelled that there was 'too much Johnson.'" On New Year's Day 1904, they defeated Bemus Pierce's Sherman Institute team 12–0 in Riverside, California near Los Angeles.

James Johnson demonstrating his unique puntcatching technique
Chicago History Museum

The June 3 issue of *The Red Man and Helper* announced that, after a visit with his family in Chicago and Wisconsin, Jimmie was to matriculate at Harvard University in the fall. Instead, he enrolled in Northwestern University's dental school and played on the university's football team. The Northwestern University football team experienced two of its better seasons when James was on the team, going 16–4–1. Two of the losses were games he missed due to injury. Even though 26 years old and banged up with injuries, Jimmie continued to score at will, leading Northwestern to wins over Marquette, Ohio Northern and Michigan Agricultural College (today's Michigan State). Because Northwestern had little depth, injuries were more costly and, very likely, more prevalent than for many of their opponents. Players had to play hurt more often and rest less often than they would with other teams who had deeper benches. Ten minutes into the game against the powerhouse Minnesota, James suffered a career-ending injury.

Johnson owns a bit of NU folklore in that he is the only person to have played against Northwestern in one game (NU's last game of 1903 against Carlisle) and to play for Northwestern in its next game (the 1904 opener against Fort Sheridan). He wrote a footnote to history in the last game of the season, scoring the last touchdown to be made on Sheppard Field, the game-winning touchdown over Illinois. He was elected cocaptain with Harry Allen for 1905 but, over time, his name has been dropped from the captains' list. Perhaps his being late returning to school for pre-season football practice due to being on his honeymoon had something to do with it.

James married Florence C. Welch, an Oneida, also of Wisconsin, after she graduated from Carlisle as a member of the class of 1905. Florence may have put her Carlisle training to use by working in the Northwestern Dental School secretary's office, as she wrote to Major Mercer on the stationery from that office.

In response to all the deaths and serious injuries experienced in college football around the country, Northwestern terminated football as a varsity sport the following spring, making the 1905 season Johnson's last as a player. He continued his dental course, graduating in 1907. But he was not quite finished with football.

James assisted Pop Warner in coaching the Carlisle football teams in 1907 and 1908. Warner may have selected him over others who had been involved during his three-year absence to put his mark on the team. Because Johnson and Warner were away from Carlisle at the same time, Pop may have been more comfortable working with him than with those who led the team in his absence. James also established a private practice at 5301 State Street in Chicago, but it may not have developed

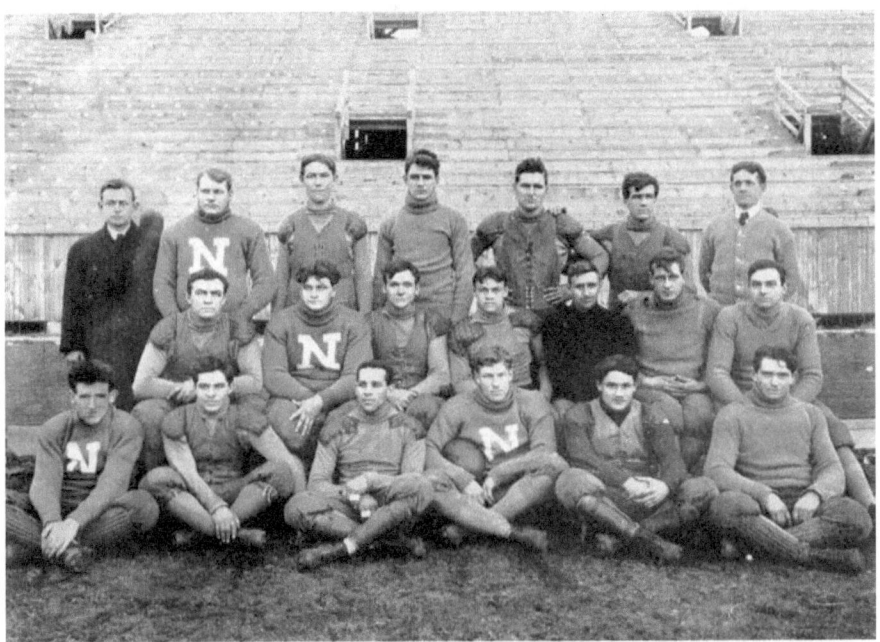

1905 Northwestern University team, James Johnson (front row 3rd from left)
Northwestern University Library

as quickly as he would have liked because he explored other opportunities.

In October, *The Carlisle Arrow* reported, "Antonio Rodriguez, Class '05, received a letter from James Johnson in which he said he will make a visit to Porto Rico [sic] in the first part of next December. I, like the other boys here at San Juan, P. R., who are Manuel Ruiz, Julio Hoheb, Antonio Rodriguez and the undersigned, were glad to hear that Carlisle's star quarter-back of the 1903 football team and all-American quarter-back for the same year, will soon land on our shores. We will do all we can to make his stay here as pleasant a time as he ever had."

The December 11 *Arrow* provided more detail: "Assistant Coach Johnson, together with Mrs. Johnson, left here last week for a two months' visit in Porto Rico. After their return from there they will go back to Chicago, where Dr. Johnson will continue his practice of dentistry." In May 1909, Enrique Urrutia, one of Carlisle's Puerto Rican students, wrote that Johnson had opened a dental office on the island. That fall, the Johnsons wrote that he was "following his profession with profit to himself and relief to the natives." Florence had taken a job as a clerk with the Department of Education.

James Johnson responded to the requests for information from former athletes by Major Mercer in 1907 and Moses Friedman in 1909. Johnson provided the information that was requested but elaborated little. In September 1910, an issue of *The Carlisle Arrow* carried two articles about the James Johnsons. They had spent ten weeks vacationing in the United States. Dr. Johnson's business amounted to $4000 the past year and Mrs. Johnson earned $1200 a year as a stenographer and typist for the Bureau of Education. Mr. and Mrs. Siceni Nori hosted a surprise party for the Johnsons the evening before they left for their return trip to Puerto Rico, where they expected to remain for three years more. The income figures were included because they were so large. Florence Johnson was earning more than the average working man at that time. When the two incomes were added together, they were likely among the elite of their community, as were many of his patients.

In 1912, James Johnson wrote about his automobile tour of the U. S. The bulk of his writing dealt with the former Carlisle students he visited along the way and how well they were doing and how they had assimilated into white society. The May-June 1915 edition of *The Red Man* contained a photograph of the Johnsons' richly-appointed parlor and dining room in their home in Puerto Rico. The *Fond du Lac Commonwealth* reported on Johnson's purchase of the 70-acre Buskirk farm on Lake de Neveu Road just a half mile outside the city limits, referring to him as "a prominent dentist of San Juan, Porto Rico." He had vacationed in Wisconsin the previous summer and, while visiting with relatives in Wittenberg drove to Fond du Lac. Johnson planned on remaining in Puerto Rico for two more years, after which he planned on making the farm his home.

In 1916, James wrote the superintendent asking for a statement of credit for the biology and physics courses he had taken in 1900 and 1901. He was applying for admission for a medical course to prepare him to specialize, possibly in oral surgery. The principal, Mr. Blair, was directed to prepare the requested statement. Those plans may have been interrupted by America's entrance into the Great War in 1917.

A later census lists James Johnson as a veteran of the World War. Given his age, about 39 at America's entrance into the war, it seems likely that he did not see combat but was assigned to a hospital or clinic, possibly stateside. If he didn't enlist, he was likely drafted because of the Army's need for dentists during the war. When the war was over, he returned to civilian dentistry.

The 1930 census listed James Johnson, 51, as living at 559 East 63rd Street in Chicago with wife Teresa, 30, and daughter

Jacqueline, 4 years 6 months. He was practicing general dentistry. Whether Florence died or they divorced is unclear, but census records make divorce appear more likely. This stint in Chicago must have been short-lived because, according to his obituary, he lived in Puerto Rico for 30 years, returning to the states when he became ill in the fall of 1941. James Johnson died on January 18, 1942 at about 63, at Kahler Hospital, part of the Mayo Clinic, in Rochester, Minnesota of stomach cancer. His sister, Ida, wrote their brother and sister in Wisconsin from Chicago that he had died and that his wife wanted him buried alongside his sister (presumably) Mary.

James Johnson's obituary in the *The Chicago Defender,* a weekly newspaper that served the African-American community, sheds some light on his background. Johnson's funeral was conducted in Metropolitan Funeral Home, a black-owned business, and he was buried in Lincoln Cemetery, a traditionally black burial ground. A further indication that *The Defender* considered Johnson to have been African-American was the sentence, "At Northwestern, he was referred to in the daily papers as an 'Indian.'" "Daily papers" may have been code for white-owned newspapers. In contrast, *The Chicago Daily Tribune* referred to him as a Stockbridge Indian and made no mention of his burial arrangements in its initial obituary on January 19, 1942. On January 25 it mentioned the address, but not the name, of the funeral parlor but did say that he was buried in Lincoln Cemetery.

If many white Chicagoans considered James Johnson to be black may explain why his dental practice there did not flourish as he hoped and would explain why he practiced for many years in Puerto Rico.

11
Frank Lone Star

Frank Lone Star was an orphan when he arrived at Carlisle on August 21, 1903 at about 12 years of age. Frank was apparently living with his older brother and guardian, John, Ke-wa-ge-zi-qne-ba, who enrolled Frank because their parents had both died of consumption as had their sister and "There is no proper school for Indians here." Frank's heritage is murky at best. He is not listed under various spellings of his name on tribal rolls due to being form "the lost tribe of Chippewas," which his brother later helped get government recognition as the St. Croix Tribe Chippewa Indians of Wisconsin. The only censuses that list him are the ones taken at Carlisle Indian School while he was a student there. A note

Name: Frank Lone Star	Nickname:
DOB: 2/2/1891	Height: 5'7"
Weight: 128	Age: 20
Tribe: St. Croix Chippewa	Home: Shell Lake, WI
Parents: James Lone Star, deceased	
unknown deceased	

in his student file indicates that, in addition to being his guardian, John was his brother. John didn't show up on censuses until 1905, some years after he married and started a family. John attended Carlisle from February 1891 to April 1895 when he left to escort his sister home. One assumes that she was ill with tuberculosis at the time. John re-enrolled in September 1895 but was sent home at the end of the month because he was "not strong enough." The January 15, 1897 issue of *The Indian Helper* mentioned receiving a note from John in which he requested to return. No record exists of his wish being granted but six years later his younger brother was granted admission.

Like most of the small boys (Carlisle's term for the younger male students), Frank received little mention in school publications. That doesn't mean he wasn't active in school life. However, he spent the majority of his first three years at Carlisle in the country on outings at farms in eastern and central Pennsylvania. While in the country, students normally attended the local public schools, often alongside the children from the farms on which they were living. He apparently had enough of that in August 1907 because he ran from the Irwin W. Miller farm in Philipsburg, New Jersey. In less than two weeks, he returned or was returned to Carlisle, where he stayed for the remainder of his first enrollment.

Upon his return, he was assigned to work in the office as an orderly. Frank must have liked being at the school more than being in the country because he soon joined the Invincible Debating Society. After working for awhile in quarters, he was assigned to work in the office. *The Arrow* reported that he liked his work in the new surroundings. However, his surroundings were about to change.

Major William A. Mercer, second superintendent of Carlisle Indian School, requested to be relieved of his duty at the school and returned to regular duty with the army. At the end of the year, the Commissioner of Indian Affairs requested that the Secretary of the Interior ask the War Department to revoke the detailing of Mercer to Carlisle Indian School. Charles H. Dickson, Mercer's replacement on a temporary basis, arrived on January 22, 1908 and immediately began the transition. Dickson had formerly been Superintendent of Riverside Indian School in Anadarko, Oklahoma, so he was able to hit the ground running. *The Arrow* reported his visits to the meetings of the various debating and literary societies shortly after arriving. Soon, a new one was being mentioned without its formation being noted. The Dickson Literary Society was for small boys where the Standards and Invincibles were primarily for large boys. Frank's name soon appeared in coverage of the Dicksons' meeting. He was apparently on the cusp between large and small boys. However, he continued to be active in the Dicksons after commencement and, in the fall, was named President. He was apparently being groomed for the position as evidenced by his visiting a meeting of the Mercers as early as February. The Dicksons continued as an organization after the permanent replacement, Moses Friedman, arrived.

The changes in scenery, the school's administration, or his attitude or all three resulted in Frank's name appearing in the school newspaper on a regular basis since his return from the country in late 1907. On February 28, 1908, he received his first mention for athletics:

> Frank Lone Star is hard at work training for the "Class Contest" next spring. He has joined the track team for that purpose. We hope that he will make a success of whatever he undertakes to do.

Frank received no mention for his competing on the track team, but the March 13 *Arrow* provided a reason for his further participation:

> It has been decided to hold the annual cross-country race as one of the Commencement events the same as

last year, and the date will be March 31st. This leaves only about two weeks' time for training and those contemplating going in the race should lose no time in getting into condition. No one will be allowed in the race who has not trained for it.

The first prize will be a gold watch, second prize a silver watch, and other prizes will include sweaters, roller skates, jerseys, base balls, bats, gloves, and other prizes of which there will be at least twelve.

There will also be a handicap small boys' race immediately following the big race but over a shorter course. Boys under 12 will be given a start ahead of boys under 13; then will come boys under 14 followed by boys under 15, while boys under 16 will start last. This plan will give the younger boys a fair chance. There will be ten prizes for this race, the first prize being a pair of five dollar roller skates.

The course for the small boys' race will be from the laundry to Wetzel's corner then turn to the left and take every left hand turn to Guard House lane and finish at the cross walk between girls' quarters and small boys' quarters.

Frank didn't win the roller skates but, by finishing fifth, won a prize of value to a boy.

His five-year enrollment was up at the end of the school year and Frank returned home on June 24, 1908. But he didn't stay there long. On August 18, Frank's brother and guardian, John, completed an application for a three-year enrollment. The only previous education listed on the form was Frank's recently completed five-year term at Carlisle. Both vouchers of disinterested persons stated that there were no proper schools for Indians at Shell Lake. Frank, then 17, was re-enrolled on August 30 in the 7th grade.

That fall, he spent his mornings doing academic work in the classroom and the afternoons working in the print shop. The December 18, 1908 issue of *The Carlisle Arrow* listed Lone Star as one of the apprentices who printed the school newspaper. He must have had ink in his blood or at least liked it better than anything he had tried previously.

Angel DeCora and Lone Star Dietz started a literary journal about that time. Apparently the print shop didn't have enough printers for the increased workload as reported in the February 12, 1909 edition of *The Carlisle Arrow:*

First Issue of The Indian Craftsman

The first number of the *Craftsman,* our monthly publication, is out. The work on it is a credit to all the boys. All the composition was practically executed by this year's apprentices and the press-work was done by four boys who never before attempted to handle a cylinder press. These boys are taking hold in the right way and each number will probably show an improvement in the press-work, as they become more familiar with their work and with the machinery. These boys are: Frank Lonestar, Chippewa; Harrison Smith, Oneida; Roy Large, Shoshone; and Louis Roy, Sioux.

In April, Frank and three other boys from the print shop went out to the country on outing. The paper commented, "We miss them in the shop, but hope they will be benefited by the change." Whether the administration felt they needed a change is unclear. He was with the George W. Hibbs family, RFD Bristol, Pennsylvania until the 10th of August. When he returned to school, he was elected secretary of the Sophomore Class, which met in Room 12, (Carlisle Indian School classes did not correspond to public school classes). His scholarship improved from good to excellent over the next two years while his printing ability dropped from excellent to good. His conduct was generally very good.

Frank continued to receive kudos for his work in September: "Frank Lone Star, Chippewa, is getting to be a very good hand at bookbinding. He made up some books for Mr. Kensler's department that were first-class in every way." He also received praise for printing the cover of the program for the Athletic Celebration on a platen press. Frank was also active with the Invincibles that school year as he often participated in debates on topics such as the American Navy is a bluff. Although he argued valiantly for the negative, his team lost this debate.

His summer outing for 1910 was spent with the Thomas B. Delker family in Hammonton, New Jersey. Back at school in the fall, Lone Star took up the snare drum with hopes of making the school band. No record was found of that happening, but he was elected sergeant-at-arms of the Junior Class. He was also elected recording secretary of the Invincibles. By January 1911, he had charge of the school's cylinder press and was credited with doing good work. A month later, he started working half-days downtown at John S. Rudy and Son, printers. In May, after commencement, William Bishop and Frank Lone Star went to work for a Charles L. Story in Wilmington, Delaware. Bishop set type as a job compositor and operated a platen press. Lone Star was a cylinder pressman. They got these jobs because "...Edward Eaglebear's work had been so good that his employers requested two more Indian boys."

Here, Frank's Carlisle record is murky. In one place, his student record said he ran from his country home in June 1911 and was listed as a deserter in July. A returned student record dated March 21, 1911 implies that his second enrollment had been completed. Regardless, two other cards indicate that he re-enrolled two more times: in September 1911 and again in March 1912. Both cards state that he ran shortly after re-enrolling both times and is listed as a deserter on both cards.

However, he kept in contact with both students and administrators at the school.

In June, Frank wrote a post card to Sue M. Brooks from Buffalo, New York. Unfortunately, only the address side of the card was copied for the file. She apparently took offense to what he wrote and contacted the school. Superintendent Friedman then wrote Lone Star:

> It comes to me that you have been sending objectionable post cards to a respectable young lady in Waynesburg, Pa., and I would advise you for your own welfare to discontinue this at once. The relatives of this young lady are in a position to take up the matter with the postal authorities and make trouble for you, unless you do as I advise you.

Lack of further correspondence about the matter implies that he heeded Friedman's advice. The November 29, 1912 issue of *The Carlisle Arrow* reported that Peter Jordan, a former student then living in Chicago, "...often sees Frank Lonestar, who is a former member of the same class."

Chicago Typothetae, a printers union, requested a reference in December. Superintendent Friedman acknowledged that Lone Star had been a student and had deserted. He also acknowledged that Frank had experience as a printer but disavowed any knowledge of the quality of his work even though his returned student report addressed the matter: "This boy should be given a position in a printing office with good men. He works well and is well advanced at his trade. He is capable of earning good wages." It's not clear if Frank gained employment in Chicago because, a year later, a check for $15.82 to close out Frank's account at the school was mailed to an address in Chicago, but Frank never received it. By then he had moved to Cleveland. Frank was still trying to get the check replaced in April 1914. It's not clear if he succeeded.

The last anyone heard of him was in a piece in the November 12, 1915 issue of *The Carlisle Arrow* which reported:

> Through a letter from Mrs. Adeline Greenbrier Shawandosa, '10, of Cleveland, Ohio, we learn of the death of Frank Lonestar, who was one of Carlisle's faithful students. He died at Shell Lake, Wis., at the home of his brother, October 30, 1915. Carlisle extends her heartfelt sympathy to his relatives and friends.

Readers may be confused as to why football was not mentioned even once in this chapter. It is because no mention has been found of Frank Lone Star ever playing football at Carlisle, although he may have played on the printers' team. There is nothing to lead one to believe that he played on the varsity. The reason he is included is that, in 1920, a Frank Lone Star played three games at tackle and guard for the Columbus Panhandles, a charter member of the NFL.

There is no reason to doubt the report that Frank Lone Star died in 1915, which makes his playing in the NFL impossible. Playing professional football under assumed names was commonplace in those days. Lone Star Dietz, who went by William Lone Star at Carlisle, was sentenced to a month in the Spokane County jail by a federal judge in early 1920 and was looking for a coaching job. Also, in his playing days, he played tackle. The fact that he only played three games would attest to Dietz being too old to play professional football competitively. Dietz would likely have been aware of Frank's death due to the notice being printed in *The Carlisle Arrow* and that his hometown in Wisconsin was in the county immediately south of Frank's home. Also, a cryptic note on a census implies that Gus Welch, Dietz's teammate at Carlisle, was related to John Lone Star's wife. It is remotely possible that Dietz was related to John and Frank Lone Star. Perhaps more clues will surface in the future.

12

Jonas Metoxen

Numerous members of the Metoxen (believed to have been Met-the-oxen originally) family attended Carlisle Indian School. Jonas Metoxen first arrived at Carlisle on June 28, 1891. The 1885 census, the earliest found that recorded him or his father, listed Jonas as having an older brother, Adam, and sister, Susan. However, he may have had other siblings who, as adults, were no longer listed with their parents. Other Metoxens at Carlisle may well have been his cousins. He surely found a number of other familiar faces given the number of Oneida children at the school.

Name: Jonas A. Metoxen
DOB: 1873
Weight: 187
Tribe: Oneida
Parents: Abram Metoxen
    Jerusha Metoxen
Early Schooling: unknown

Nickname: Man-afraid-of-his-wife
Height: 5' 9 1/2"
Age: 24
Home: Oneida, WI

Jonas Metoxen; *Cumberland County Historical Association, Carlisle, PA*

After nine months at the school, Jonas began going on outings in the spring that lasted until mid-September. Each year he returned just in time for the start of football season. In 1893, the school played an abbreviated schedule and it isn't known if he was on that squad, but in 1894 Carlisle began to play football at the college level in earnest. Jonas Metoxen played fullback on this team and would not relinquish this position for some time. The Carlisle Indians recorded but a single victory in 1894 while their fullback labored in obscurity. That didn't last for long. In 1895, Carlisle played Yale for the first time and Jonas got positive press for his efforts. *The New York World* observed, "The Indians repeatedly worked in wedge on centre, and every time it netted five yards. Occasionally Metoxen got fifteen and twenty." In the last game of the season, he injured his knee while running back a kickoff against the New York City Y. M. C. A. team, a team that was bolstered by several members of the Crescent Athletic Club. *The World* reporter opined that the Indians would have scored three more touchdowns had it not been for Referee Underwood: "'Those Indians will go away with a poor idea of Christianity if that robbery keeps up,' growled Harry Stevens. 'Talk about your hold ups!' He went on to say, 'When Metoxen was carried off the field with a wrenched knee, he surprised everybody by blubbering with pain. So much for the inherent stoicism of the race.'"

Just before the 1896 season, columnist Owen Langdon commented on the team's prospects and appearance: "The Indians are remarkably good players, everything considered. One of their best men last year, Pierce, a fine guard and worthy of a great Varsity team, has very pronounced Indian features. Metoxen, the fullback, Wheelock, the left guard, and others of the team were less pronouncedly Indian in appearance. The team as a whole was decidedly good and will probably be no worse this year." In the infamous Yale game in which the Indians were robbed of a touchdown and a victory, former Yale star Harry Beecher discussed the game for *The World*. He described the

Indian ball carriers' work on what should have been the decisive drive: "Seneca, Metoxen and Pierce made decisive gains, and seemingly had no trouble in fooling with the Blue's rush line. They ran, crawled and rolled ahead, always with the ball." The November 6 *New York Times* commented on an editorial titled, "What is important is that the Carlisle football team of 1896 has given no irrefragable proof of the ennobling power of education on the Indian," from what the *Times* called "an interesting neighbor of ours." The *Times* went on to say that the article was intended, "...to be complimentary to Metoxen, Lone Wolf, and the other red gladiators of the gridiron." From this one can conclude that the eastern newspapers considered Jonas Metoxen to be one on Carlisle's star players.

So important was the game after the Yale game, the one with Harvard, was that the *Michigan Daily*, the University of Michigan student newspaper, sent a reporter to cover it. Its reporter observed, "...Metoxen, with the longest, blackest kind of football hair, throwing a Harvard half-back right over his head. It was a perfectly clean game, no slugging, but four Harvard men had to quit because they ran their heads too hard against the Indian line, which might just as well have been made of brick."

After the game the following week with Penn, *The Atlanta Constitution* ran an article titled, "A Scalp for Pennsy," and subtitled, "Mighty Metoxen Powerless: Great Indian Full-Back Plunged Uselessly Into the Line." A section of the article contradicted that a bit:

Metoxen's Great Playing

Two plunges and Metoxen and H. Pierce carried the ball to Pennsylvania's ten-yard line. Cayou went around the left end for five yards. Then he went around the right end and was thrown by Overfield two yards from the coveted chalk line. It was the first down, and it looked as if nothing could save a touchdown. From thousands of

Pennsylvanians' throats came the appealing cry, "Hold them, Pen." Straight into the mass of men Metoxen plunged. The line held, but none could tell if beneath that mass of men the Indian back had gone over for a touchdown. A wild shout rent the air when the players were pulled off each other and Metoxen was seen lying with the ball on but not over the goal line.

There were still two downs, and one Inch, to gain. Not a sound arose from 15,000 people as the men lined up. It was a grim grapple, and not one of those twenty-two men but would have broken a limb or even his neck to make or save the touchdown. The Quakers crouched close to the ground like so many wild beasts waiting to spring. With clenched teeth and fierce faces the Indians hurled themselves upon their foes. There was an awful crush and swaying of fighting men, and the great human mass went down in a heap together.

Again came that dead silence as the men sullenly rolled off each other in response to the referee's whistle. Then again that triumphant shout arose, for the white men had met the onslaught and Metoxen had again been stopped right on the line. One more chance remained. As Metoxen dashed into the line the Quaker rushers heaved forward and threw the entire Indian team back, and the touchdown was lost by six inches. Then the referee's whistle blew and the game was over.

When interviewed before the Thanksgiving Day game with Brown, Metoxen commented on the Indians' play against Penn:

It has been our custom when about to take part in a big game to sleep the night previous in the town where the game is to be played. This resulted in giving our team plenty of rest. We didn't follow the plan this time, however, but remained in Carlisle over night. Then, in order to make time, we were called very early in the morning, ate our breakfast at 5 o'clock, and took the train for Philadelphia. Rising so early and traveling several hours in the train tired the boys very much, and they were quite listless when they went on Franklin Field.

Due to an injury in the game with Cincinnati, Jonas did not start the game with Brown. It became necessary for him to play when, early in the second half, McFarland was injured. He was ineffective when playing injured. Although Carlisle lost to each of The Big Four in successive weeks and to Brown on Thanksgiving Day, the 5–5 season was considered a success because it included thumpings of Penn State, Cincinnati and Duquesne and a decisive win over Wisconsin, that year's Champions of the West, under the lights in the Chicago Coliseum. Jonas starred against Wisconsin and there was a humorous sidelight to the game. Two of Bemus Pierce's kickoffs hit the iron arches that supported the Coliseum's roof. By playing the toughest possible opposition, and on the road, Carlisle was developing a reputation as were its stars. A wire service article printed across the country featured a full-length drawing plus a write up:

AN INDIAN FULL BACK

Jonas Metoxen, a Pillar of Strength to the Carlisle Football Team

One of the best men on the famous Carlisle Indian school football team is Jonas Metoxon, the full back. His name in its original form was Met-the-Oxen, but in the process of civilization the included article "the" was assimilated and the decidedly Christian title Jonas was prefixed. But "the play's the thing," and the play of Jonas is of a kind that gives it rank with that of the best on any gridiron. Metoxen is an Oneida Indian. He stands 5 feet 9 1/2 inches high and weighs 187 pounds. The strongest feature of his work is line bucking, and in this he is admittedly excellent, and many of the best scores made by the Indians during the season have been directly traceable to the strong plays of Metoxen.

In March 1897, the following item circulated around the country:

The Carlisle Indian football team will be greatly weakened next year by the loss of many of the best players.

JONAS METOXEN.
Wire service drawing

Metoxen goes to Princeton, Lone Wolf and Cayou to Chicago University and two more of the players to Wisconsin.

Lone Wolf returned to Oklahoma; however Cayou and Metoxen remained at their usual positions for the upcoming season, although Cayou wasn't expected to play because of injuries. He later went to the University of Illinois.

The 1897 version of the Carlisle Indian team continued to show improvement, especially in the kicking game, but still included losses to the Big Four teams played that year. Before the season started, *The New York World* depicted Jonas falling on a loose ball. After the game with Penn, the *Record* observed, "Metoxen—he's harder to stop than a whole team of oxen." Jonas's punting improved to the point that he was considered better than any man Yale could put up against him. The team had a winning season but lost to the three Big Four teams they played plus Brown.

In the spring of 1898, Joseph Metoxen, Jonas's uncle, announced that the Wisconsin Oneidas had formed two companies of soldiers to fight in the war against Spain. Neither company had officers because they preferred to be led by "...army or militia officers, who understand white man's style of fighting." The would-be soldiers practiced drilling on the reservation under the direction of several war veterans well past the age limit for enlistees. They also organized a band that was to accompany the troops. One supposes that a Wheelock was involved with the band. The elder Metoxen reported that his nephew wrote him from Carlisle to inform him that his classmates were ready to organize a company to fight in Cuba. Joseph also said that he attempted to form, as he expressed it, "plenty big Injun army" that would have included soldiers from the Menominee and Stockbridge reservations as well as some from Brothertown on Lake Winnebago. It appears that his attempts failed.

That October, Jonas Metoxen scored a touchdown in an early-season loss to Cornell, but the Indians' play impressed their opponents' coach, Glenn S. "Pop" Warner. The 1898 team posted another winning record, but yet again a victory over one of the Big Four eluded them. After the season ended, Jonas returned home as his enrollment had ended. He didn't just lie about. In the summer, he played for the Oneida team against Green Bay at the annual Oneida Fair.

In April of 1899, *The Evening Sentinel* reported that Connie Mack, manager of the Milwaukee baseball team, planned on fielding a barnstorming football team in the fall made up of former Carlisle players who were then living on the Oneida Reservation near Green Bay. Jonas Metoxen was to coach the team.

For years, pundits had declared that all the Carlisle Indians needed to become a championship team was a good coach. In 1899, Superintendent Pratt finally hired one and Pop Warner took the helm. However, Jonas wasn't there; he was back home playing for the local Wisconsin National Guard team, Company I of Marinette, but not for long. Exactly why Jonas returned to Carlisle on October 18 is unclear but it is known that the Oneida team folded.

It took Jonas awhile to learn Warner's new signals and his new position at right halfback. Shuffling players in response to injuries incurred in the loss to Princeton on November 11, Warner shifted the badly bruised Metoxen back to his old position at fullback for the game with Oberlin. That was a good move because he proved to be a human battering ram against the hapless Oberlin line and left the game at half time due to having run up an insurmountable lead. Jonas closed out the regular season by routinely plunging through the Columbia line for 10 yards at a clip. That victory earned the Indians a trip to San Francisco where the Indians defeated the University of California on Christmas Day. This game made the Indians the first team to play games on both coasts. On the way back,

Jonas and his teammates played the mismatched Phoenix Indian School team to complete the school's best year to that time. Jonas closed out his Carlisle career with a 9–2 season that included Carlisle's first win over a Big Four team, Penn. Metoxen returned home shortly after the season ended.

Before the post-season games were played, sports writers announced that Jonas would be entering Lawrence University in the fall and would be trying out for the football team. He selected Lawrence, located in Appleton, Wisconsin, because of its close proximity to his home. But when fall came, he played for the Marinette team.

The announcement of Jonas's upcoming marriage provided the reason for the switch. He married Phoebe Baird (Ya-go-win in Oneida), a former student of both Carlisle and Hampton Institute, on November 4, 1900, in the Hobart Episcopal Mission Church on the Oneida Reservation. Miss Baird, approximately 22 years of age, was the daughter of Cornelius and Margaret Baird. Wedding guests included the Honorable Isaac Stephenson, a wealthy lumberman and early Progressive politician, as well as the officers and members of Company I of Marinette. Stephenson presented a beautiful set of silverware as a wedding gift from the group.

Jonas's name didn't disappear from the sports pages as he continued to play football on the local Marinette Company I team and someone named a racehorse Metoxen, presumably in his honor. However, not everyone noticed. As early as January 1902, an unattributed newspaper column reported on his absence from the pages of the national press: "James [sic] Metoxen, the Indian who a few years ago was the star player on the Carlisle football team and received many ovations from patrons of the sport and much notice from eastern newspaper scribes is now living in semi-obscurity in the little village of Preble." His obscurity was broken by a November 1902 newspaper article that stated the Marinette team lost a game to South Bend because Metoxen didn't play. According to the reporter, Jonas's wife wouldn't let him. That led to locals dubbing him "Man-Afraid-of-His-Wife."

A February 1904 wire service article titled "Metoxen, Fullback, Now Works on Farm" told of Jonas's life on the farm cutting cordwood in winter and driving a team (of horses or mules) to deliver it to a paper mill in Appleton, Wisconsin. It also mentioned that he found a way to get involved with a local football team each fall. When interviewed, he seemed more pleased with the results of his labor than from any government largess: "We get a few cents from the Government for Christmas, but that's all." He picked up a silk-lined overcoat from the seat next to him and said: "That's what I used to get when I

Wisconsin players in photo are:
James Johnson, Jonas Metoxen, Caleb Sickles & Capt. Martin Wheelock
Cumberland County Historical Association, Carlisle, PA

played football, and now, umph, get darn little." The reporter opined: "With the reputation this man had he could easily be demanding a comfortable salary from some big university as a coach, had not his native instincts been so strong that as soon as he was out of college he went back to his former haunts on the reservation." When contacted about this, Superintendent Pratt pointed out that not one of the football players had drifted back to idleness, although some had not done as well as Jonas, who was saving up to buy more land.

By 1910, Jonas and Phoebe's family had grown to include sons Elmer and Irvin along with daughters Eunice, Josephine and Helen. Soon, daughters Nellie, Birdena and Alice were added to the brood. In 1910, Superintendent Friedman wrote to former football players to inquire as how they were doing and also requested photographs. Jonas sent him one of his farmhouse. The next year, he submitted a Record of Graduates and Returned Students. He indicated that he had taken no further schooling after leaving Carlisle and that he was married to Phoebe Baird. He described their home as a three bedroom, two-story frame house that he built shortly after they were married. The farm consisted of 82 acres of land on which were stables and a granary. He planned to build a barn the following spring. His livestock consisted of three horses, 5 cows and a calf. Jonas had never worked for the Indian Service but had worked off the farm one winter as a blacksmith.

In 1914, Jimmy Callahan, manager of the Chicago White Sox, told of an experience he had two years prior to that:

> With several others I left Camp Jerome, Comiskey's camp, on a long tramp after a world's championship games two years ago. Our course took us through the clearing which skirted Little Bass Lake in Wisconsin. We went through the swamp land across the Flambeau River and then around Turtle Lake. That was some walk and took us through some wild country. Jogging

along—and talking in a loud voice, which is excellent when hunting—we came to the edge of a small birch forest and into a dense thicket. Turning at an abrupt bend, we almost ran into an Indian in tattered trousers, ancient Mackinaw coat and leather leggings. He was taken by complete surprise. The Indian grinned a greeting of "Howdy," and to our astonishment, asked: "Say, can you tell me who won the world's series?" That man was Metoxen, one of the greatest football and baseball players ever turned out of Carlisle.

Jonas spent the 1914 to 1916 football seasons as a member of the Altoona Indians, according to a 1942 article in the *Altoona Mirror*. That Keith McClellan's extensively researched *The Sunday Game* makes no mention of him being with the team, places doubt on the validity of that assertion. Also, Metoxen would have been in his early 40s at that time. He could have been playing under an assumed name but he would have had little reason for doing that—unless his wife objected.

In 1917, as the U. S. entered WWI, Jonas attempted to organize an Oneida troop to be part of an Indian regiment from Wisconsin. It appears that the War Department did not form Indian regiments but integrated the 13,000 Indians who enlisted into existing units.

By 1930, Jonas and Phoebe had moved off the farm and into Menasha, Wisconsin where he worked at a paper mill. A local newspaper article with an accompanying photograph informed residents of his exploits on the gridiron after an old fan recognized him and told the newspaper about Metoxen. Jonas related a humorous story about an incident that occurred in a game played in Wisconsin after he left Carlisle. A Menasha man on the opposing team was carrying the ball when he saw Jonas bearing down on him. Rather than letting Jonas tackle him, he simply tossed him the ball.

Phoebe died in February 1934 at about 55 years of age and was buried at Oneida after the funeral at St. Thomas Episcopal Church in Menasha. The cause of her death is unknown. The 1937 census listed Emily Doxtator as Jonas's second wife. According to an April 1939 newspaper article, Jonas and Mamie King filed for a marriage license. The January 1939 Tomah Agency roll listed Emily Doxtator King Metoxen as married and George King as divorced. Mamie might have been Emily's nickname and they must have put off getting a church wedding for a few years.

Jonas was injured seriously in an automobile accident in September 1939. He had 6 broken ribs and a broken left leg. His wife, Emily or Mamie, one assumes as her first name wasn't included in the newspaper account, had her right leg broken in addition to some other unspecified injuries. His son, Irving Metoxen, the driver of the car in which Jonas was riding, pled guilty to drunken driving and was fined $100 plus costs or 90 days in the county jail. His driver's license was revoked as he had a history of public drunkenness. Jonas's other son, Elmer, was also in the car and was fined $10 and costs or 15 days in Winnebago County jail. Both took the jail sentences. Mr. and Mrs. Metoxen were both treated at St. Elizabeth's Hospital in Menasha. She was released shortly after treatment, but he was in the hospital for about three weeks. A 1940 insurance settlement with the Hardware Mutual Casualty Company gave Jonas $2,000, Mrs. Metoxen $100, and Elmer $250, one assumes, for their injuries.

On July 18, 1942, Jonas Metoxen drowned in the Fox River Canal in Menasha. He and his wife were walking along the canal wall when he lost his footing and fell in. He was believed to be 68 years old at the time.

13

Thomas St. Germain

The September 17, 1909 issue of *The Carlisle Arrow* contained an unusual report: "Another visitor, who is also more or less of a football enthusiast, is Mr. Thomas St. Germain who paid a visit to friends at Carlisle, while enroute to Washington, this week. Mr. St. Germain played on the teams of Harlem Park at Des Moines and at the University of Wisconsin. He is now engaged in the practice of law at Ashland, Wisconsin." Mention of this visit was peculiar because the visitor was neither a dignitary nor an alumnus. Given the number of students from Wisconsin, it would not be difficult

```
Name: Thomas Leo St. Germain        Nickname: Whitecloud
  DOB: 2/16/1880                     Height: 6' 1"
Weight: 224 1/2                      Age: 26
  Tribe: Chippewa                    Home: Lac du Flambeau
Parents: Joseph St. Germain, Chippewa, deceased
         Mary St. Germain, Chippewa & French Canadian
Early Schooling: Haskell Institute, Harlem Park College
                 University of Wisconsin
Later Schooling: Yale Law School
```

to believe that he had friends at Carlisle. Perhaps more peculiar was that Thomas St. Germain enrolled in the commercial course. Why would someone engaged in a law practice enroll at Carlisle?

A review of his enrollment records from the University of Wisconsin showed that St. Germain had already completed a three-year law course at Highland Park College in Des Moines, Iowa and had been admitted to the Iowa bar. In August 1904, he applied for admission to the University of Wisconsin Law School and was admitted on the weight of his transcript from Highland Park College. St. Germain attended Wisconsin for one year where he played football and was goalie on the water polo team. He apparently returned to practicing law in Iowa after that. Why would school officials encourage him to enroll? Perhaps he knew one of the administrators or was a star athlete. The fact that he was 26 years of age, being 6'1" tall and weighing 224-1/2 pounds may have had something to do with it. Soon his name started appearing regularly in the school publications.

On September 25, 1909, barely two weeks after his initial visit, St. Germain started at center against Villanova. No one ever moved into Carlisle's starting lineup that quickly, and especially to a skill position. The next week, against Bucknell, he played one of the guard positions. Later in October, he sang bass in a 32-member co-educational choir organized by the band director. The YMCA boasted a new member: "Thomas St. Germain read a story on the 'Criminal Neglect of Duty' and followed his reading with words of advice and counsel." On Thanksgiving Day, the Indians pounded St. Louis University in a game played in Cincinnati: "Pete Hauser and his brother, Wauseka, and [St.] Germain were the stonewall combination of the Indian line."

In December, Thomas attended the Susan Longstreth Literary Society's annual reception at which dancers competed for prize cakes and didn't go home empty-handed: "The booby prize was awarded, amid much applause, to Thomas St. Germaine and Miss Gaither, who led the grand march."

In February, St. Germain read a short passage at a service at the Second Presbyterian Church, during which a special offering was collected for Indian missions. In April, he was elected reporter for the Invincibles and gave "a brief but inspiring talk" to the YMCA boys. At term's end, he departed to take a government job in Washington, DC as a clerk at the Land Office. On June 1, he wrote Superintendent Friedman, "I am able to say to you, in confidence, that while 'my official title' is that of Asst. Messenger I am assigned the duties of a stenographer. It is my plan to prepare for the regular examination for clerk & stenographer to be held some time this summer here." Friedman responded, "I take this opportunity because I am a friend of yours, to urge that you pay close attention to your work in

University of Wisconsin 1905 water polo team
Thomas St. Germain (top center), goalkeeper
University of Wisconsin

the office with a view of pleasing your superiors, and winning their confidence. I would also strongly counsel you to so shape your life outside of the office and so choose your companions as to reflect credit upon yourself and win you the approbation of the people with whom you come in contact." Did Friedman know something about him that wasn't widely known? The October 21, 1910 *Arrow* informed readers that St. Germain, then about 31 years old, had enrolled as a member of the Senior Class at the Yale Law School. Oh, he also joined the Yale football team and played on the scrubs!

After spending the summer of 1911 working at the Sac and Fox Agency in Cushing, Oklahoma, St. Germain returned to Yale to continue his study of the law. He reputedly assisted with the coaching of the football team as well. On September 13, 1913, in response to a query from Superintendent Friedman, possibly prompted by a visit from St. Germain, John W. Edgerton wrote, "I beg to say that Thomas St. Germaine [sic] graduated with the degree of Bachelor of Laws in June 1913. He was not a brilliant student but by hard work managed to get through.—He was faithful and diligent." Yale listed Thomas as having been a member of the Yale Senate, Kent Club, University Wrestling Association and University Water Polo Team. He was quite active in extra-curricular activities, particularly for a law student. In September, he visited Carlisle, renewing old ties and spoke briefly to the Catholic meeting on Sunday evening. Then he headed east again.

The fall of 1913 found Thomas St. Germain holding down the position of head football coach at Villanova University. Perhaps Tom's being there had something to do with Carlisle and Villanova not scheduling an early season game that had become a tradition. He went 4–2–1, which was an improvement over the vast majority of his predecessors.

St. Germain attended Carlisle's 1914 commencement and advised the students: "Faith in yourself, no matter what the world thinks, will win. Be a useful citizen is my motto." *The*

Arrow reported that he also impressed the fact that to be a Carlisle student meant something.

He was looking for a job in the fall of 1914. Perhaps factors other than his coaching prowess were involved. He wrote Oscar Lipps, stating, "Because of Villanova's unwillingness to re-engage me with my terms, the State College at Jonesboro, Arkansas' final decision to get a Newbraska [sic] man instead of hiring me to act as their Athletic Coach the year round, I find myself out of a coaching position for this fall." He then asked Lipps to hire him as an assistant and specified the terms of his proposed employment. He went on to say, "This is not much, but it will enable me to get on my feet nicely when I return to Oklahoma where I am arranging to go into a prominent law firm after the football season is over." He was in New Haven, Connecticut at that time, where he had been tutoring a professor's son for the past month. Lipps replied, "'Economy' is now the watch word throughout all the Departments of the Government, and I am sorry that I am unable to make you any offer whatever."

Thomas needed a job and in the worst way. He had quietly married a white woman and they had a child on the way. Thomas Jr. was born on October 8 and Thomas Sr. needed a way to support his wife and child. He reputedly coached Princeton Township High School football in Illinois and practiced law in Iowa and may also have been in the real estate business in Wisconsin. He and his wife were soon divorced. The exact chronology of events is not clear. After being out of the public's eye for a few years, his name jumped off newspapers nationwide in January 1917.

Miss Jeanette Black, daughter of a wealthy Philadelphia realtor, appeared before Judge Stelk in the Court of Domestic relations in Chicago holding her two-year-old son. She told the judge her story of meeting Thomas St. Germain at Villanova and that he had promised repeatedly to marry her. But, on January 8 of the previous year, 1916, the day set for their marriage, he instead made Miss Janet Wilkins of Crown Point, Indiana his second wife. Miss Black said, "After my baby came, my father was going to prosecute St. Germain under the Mann Act and I prevented it because he had promised to marry me." Thomas told the judge that her parents objected to the marriage because he was an Indian. As the *Chicago Herald* put it: "Thomas St. Germain, Indian athlete and lawyer, winner of many football games and women, was released by Judge Stelk in the Court of Domestic Relations yesterday on his promise to pay $100 within a few days to Miss Jeanette Black of Philadelphia, mother of his two-year-old boy." The judge ordered him to pay Miss Black $100 plus nine annual payments of $50 each. He claimed to have already paid more than the judge required.

Thomas St. Germain
Cumberland County Historical Society, Carlisle, PA

It appears that St. Germain lived and worked as a lawyer in Iowa, at least to 1920 when the Federal Census listed him as being a roomer with the Thomas Trissel family in Mason City, Iowa. Lac du Flambeau rolls list a second son, Joseph, as having been born in 1918. Janet and Joseph were living with her parents in Davenport, Iowa at that time. In the fall of 1922, at an age considered to be too old to be playing football— 37 according to some sources, but 43 according to others— St. Germain came out of retirement and played the interior line positions for the Oorang Indians, at least for the first half of the season. He was the starting center in the Oorang's first game. Assistant Postmistress Hazel Haynes remembered him well: "He was a lug! He filled up that whole, great big, old window. He was nice. 'Well good morning to you, and have a nice day,' he would say to me each day he came to the post office." For whichever reason, injury or the threat of divorce, prevailed, he again retired from the game. This time it appears to have been permanent.

A third son, John, arrived in 1922 and daughter Margaret A. St. Germain was born in 1923. It's not clear where, or even if, wife Janet, was living at this time. The 1930 Federal Census listed the two children's mothers as Chippewa. It also listed an Emma St. Germain as Thomas's white wife from Delaware. Either the census is wrong (a distinct possibility) or Thomas's two youngest children came from a marriage or liaison with an unknown Chippewa woman. For all we know, they may have been from Janet Wilkins.

According to Yale's obituary, St. Germain was the first Indian lawyer to be admitted to the Wisconsin bar. His areas of practice were Federal and Indian law. He served with the U. S. Indian Service, with Lac du Flambeau School and Agency, as a justice of the peace, and on the Objiwa Tribal Council. According to the 1910 census, his Chippewa name was Me-ni-si-no-wi-gi-jig, which may translate to Whitecloud. He died on October 4, 1947 at about 69 years of age of coronary thrombosis and was buried in the Protestant Cemetery in Lac du Flambeau.

St. Germain's oldest son became known as Thomas St. Germain Whitecloud II. He received his medical training at Tulane University and was also known as a writer. Whitecloud II's son, the late Thomas St. Germain Whitecloud III, followed in his father's footsteps and became the head of the Orthopaedic Surgery Department at Tulane. He also turned down Vince Lombardi's offer of a contract to play football for the Green Bay Packers. His son, Jacques, followed in his footsteps and is now Assistant Professor of Orthopaedic Surgery at Tulane.

14

Caleb Sickles

Caleb Mathew Sickles, a 12-year-old Oneida, arrived in Carlisle in August 1891 and enrolled for the standard-at-that-time five-year term. He was 4'6" tall then, but his weight was not recorded. At the end of the summer after graduation in 1898, he re-enrolled for an indeterminate period, listed then as age 21. The enrollment forms that were found included good information, including that his father's name was Martin, that he was half blood, and that he was from the Sagola Agency in Wisconsin; however, much information was missing or unclear. His mother was listed as living, but

---

Name: Caleb Mathew Sickles
DOB: 12/27/1880
Weight: Unknown
Tribe: Oneida
Parents: Martin Sickles, Oneida
        Semantha Titus Sickles, white
Later Schooling: Dickinson College Preparatory School
                    Ohio Medical University

Nickname: Sick
Height: 4'6"
Age: 12
Home: Little Rapids, WI

Caleb Sickles with his mother; *Justine Souto*

her name was left blank. Perusing census records and Carlisle Indian School publications leads one to conclude that Caleb, sometimes misprinted as Carl, was the son of Martin Sickles, a full-blood Oneida, and Smantha or Thimantha but likely Semantha Titus Sickles (her name was spelled differently on each census), a white woman. Caleb was born in Munsey, Ontario as his father was from the English-speaking part of Canada. Semantha was born in Michigan, and their other children were born in Wisconsin. The 1910 census listed Semantha as the mother of 13 children, 12 living, one of whom was Raymond O., who was living with Caleb at that time.

Several other students named Sickles attended Carlisle but don't appear to have been Caleb's siblings. One newspaper article specifically mentioned that Martha, Florence and Arthur were siblings but omitted any mention of Caleb, something that would have been unlikely, given his notoriety, had he been their sibling. However, the August 26, 1898 issue of *The Indian Helper* casually mentioned Arthur as being Caleb's brother. Superintendent Friedman asked Caleb about Arthur's whereabouts in 1910. From his response, it is difficult to determine if they were brothers, cousins or no relation at all. The vagueness of his response may have been due to familiarity of the issue for both parties.

Home for the Sickleses was in central Wisconsin. The Oneida Reservation extends from Green Bay to Outagamie County, the next county over. While some Oneidas lived within the Green Bay city limits, Martin Sickles was listed on the various censuses as being a farmer in Outagamie County. In 1898, Dickinson College listed Caleb's home as Little Rapids, Wisconsin. Later Caleb wrote, "I have never lived among the Indians to any extent." He may have meant that he had been at boarding schools since an early age as were many of his peers or that his family, although listed as Oneida, lived 5 miles from the reservation at Little Rapids. Thus, Caleb did not have an on-reservation childhood, and attending Carlisle probably required less adjustment on his part than it would have required from many of his classmates.

Caleb received his first newspaper coverage in the November 15, 1895 edition of *The Indian Helper* in an article that stated, "Misses Ely and Burgess, and Masters Johnnie Given, Caleb Stickles, George Conners and Ernest Peters went by wheel to Mechanicsburg late Saturday afternoon, returning in the deep shadow of the evening." Apparently he had taken up cycling, which was all the rage at that time. It's not clear whether the Misses, Carlisle faculty members, chaperoned the boys or whether the boys went along as protectors. On modern roads, assuming a time when there is little traffic, and on modern bicycles, that 10-mile ride would be a breeze. However, in pre-automobile times, Trindle Road, the most direct route between Carlisle and Mechanicsburg, would have been a rural dirt road with many hazards.

Caleb started to work in the print shop after the holidays, according to *The Indian Helper.* He continued there for some years and became a valuable worker. By April of that year, 1896, Caleb had joined the Invincible Debating Society. He was given high marks for what was likely his first major public speaking appearance: "Caleb Sickles made a happy hit in a recitation very naturally rendered..." A week later he, James Wheelock and Albert Nash participated in the entertainment given by the YMCA in town. Unfortunately, the nature of his participation was not mentioned.

By this time he was allowed to leave the school for the summer, but it is not known whether it was to work somewhere or to return home. Most likely it was to work somewhere because in later summers he earned money working at the New Jersey shore. After returning to school and the print shop, Caleb, now a Junior, was elected secretary of the Invincibles.

John S. Steckbeck, in *Fabulous Redmen,* lists Sickles as playing on the varsity football team in 1897 and 1898. Game reports make no mention of him and don't include his name in the lineups. He was most likely a substitute, no mean feat on teams that included the likes of Ed Rogers, Frank Cayou, the Pierce brothers, Frank Hudson, Metoxen (met the oxen) and Martin Wheelock in the starting lineup. This was the start, not the end, of his football career.

Caleb graduated from Carlisle in the spring of 1898 and enrolled in the Dickinson College Preparatory School at age 21. Dickinson College's first game of the season was on September 24 against Susquehanna University. Caleb's name was not in the line-up, but a Mr. Sickles of the Indian School umpired the game. In mid-October he got into a game. He played quarterback for the Dickinson College Prep School team in a game against Harrisburg High School and got press clippings for doing "the best work." The next game, a scoreless tie with nearby Shippensburg Normal School, found him at left end, the position he would play the rest of the year. He carried the ball a lot in Prep's offensive scheme and consistently made good yardage. He was a star at the prep school.

After football season ended, Caleb went out for Prep's basketball team and was a starter at one of the attack (known as forward today) positions. In the spring of 1899 he ran track in a meet with Mercersburg Academy and Franklin and Marshall College, coming in second in the 120 yard special event and third in the special open 120 yard dash. His best event that day was the relay race, the first and arguably most exciting event. *The Dickinsonian* gushed, "...But when the crowd saw young Sickles of Dickinson take his place at the line and wait on tiptoes to touch the hand of his panting colleague, and then dash off on the last lap with an astonishingly increasing speed, the chances for our Preps, because suddenly bright, but the distance was too great to be made up, and Mercersburg came in first, although their lead was quite perceptively decreased by Sickles who was heartily cheered."

In May, he played left field and pitched for the Indian School baseball team in a game against Dickinson College and lost 3–2. His relief pitching may have made the difference that day as he walked three batters and committed a balk. However, the reporter thought he had the potential to become a good left-handed pitcher.

In July, *The Indian Helper* shared that Caleb had written them a "friendly letter." The article reported, "At the Beacon by the Sea [in Point Pleasant], New Jersey, a number of our boys are spending their summer waiting on table, and doing other work demanded of them. The other day they played a game of ball with the Trenton Military Academy and won by the score of 21 to 3. Siceni Nori, '94 who is living near Trenton, pitched for the Academy team."

October of 1899 found Pop Warner coaching the Carlisle Indian School football team for the first time. Caleb was still at the Dickinson College Preparatory School but played right end for Carlisle as a substitute for Joseph Scholder. His moment in the limelight came when he played the entire game at right end in Carlisle's win over Penn, their first against one of the Big Four.

Sickles completed his education at Prep in the spring and left for summer employment, first in Philadelphia, then on the Jersey Shore. In July 1900, *The Indian Helper* reprinted an article from a Point Pleasant, New Jersey newspaper, *The Beacon,* about the Independence Day races held as part of their festivities: "The running of Sickles, the Carlisle student, was the chief feature of the foot races. At the tape, he won by a few inches. Sickles is such a clean, good fellow that he deserves all he won, and the crowd was with him, and the red man's praise became the 'white man's burden' at the end of each race."

A month later, *The Red Man and Helper* reported, "Caleb Sickles, '99, spent Sunday with us on his way to Columbus, Ohio, where he intends to work his way through Medical College. Caleb has been spending a part of the summer working at the sea-shore. He looks in splendid condition, and has kept himself under athletic training. He intends that his athletics shall play no small part in getting him his M. D. diploma. The name of Dr. Sickles already runs through the ears of the Man-on-the-band-stand, and we desire him to realize his highest hopes." Pratt was not the only one pleased to see one of his students strive for professional education. Whether Caleb changed his mind or the newspaper got it wrong is unclear, an M. D. diploma was not in his future. Other opportunities awaited him instead.

At the end of the 1901 season, the *Ohio State Journal* had a large write-up titled, "Good for the Indian Captain," that celebrated Caleb's election as captain of the Ohio Medical University football team for 1902. He was described as being 21 years of age, likely wrong, and a junior in the Dental Department. Either he changed majors or Miss Burgess had had it wrong earlier. When writing about Sickles' play, the *Journal* reporter wrote, "In his time he has gained the reputation of being one of the best, if not the very best end in Ohio. He is a hard and sure tackler, as well as very fast in the interference and a sure man when called upon to advance the ball." Dr. W. J. Means of the Athletic Board was quoted as saying, "The choice of Sickles for Captain is very satisfactory to me. We always like men who are well up in their classes as our athletic leaders, and Sickles, in addition to his football ability, is one of the best students in the university."

In April 1903, *The Red Man and Helper* reported, "Mr. Caleb Sickles '98, a student of the Ohio Medical College, Columbus, Ohio, is with us for a brief visit. He is taking a course in dentistry and hopes to finish in another year. This spring and summer he will earn some wherewithal on the New York State Baseball League, and is now on his way to Syracuse. Caleb had pneumonia a year ago and does not look as robust as before he was taken ill, but says he is feeling well now. He intends starting out in business for himself as soon as he finishes. Sickles, Sickles, Sickles! Rah! Rah! Rah!" Superintendent Pratt could hardly constrain his enthusiasm. Or was it Marianna Burgess? It's not always clear. In its next issue, *The Red Man and Helper* wrote, "Dr. Caleb Sickles has gone to Syracuse, where, as was stated last week, he will play ball on the N. Y. League, this season. He says dental Seniors in the Columbus University are called Doctors, and we wish to be one of the first to give him the well-earned title." A May 8 article shared some bad news: "...finding that his injured arm did not permit him to play ball as actively as the League requires...He will get employment in

Columbus for the summer and finish his Dental course next year." A week later he was negotiating with the Portsmouth, Ohio team. In June he was playing left field for the Lancaster, Ohio club.

Caleb Sickles ably captained the 1903 Ohio Medical University football team and, in October, was called on to help his former O. M. U. coach, John Eckstorm, prepare Kenyon College team for their big game with Ohio State. At the end of the school year, Sickles graduated from dental school. In late May or very early June 1904, Caleb wrote Miss Burgess, his supervisor when he worked in the Carlisle print shop:

> It has been some time since you have heard from me. I am through school now and am in the employ of the State. I have a position here at the State hospital. I have been here over three weeks. The day I graduated I was about "broke" but since, I have been getting a few dollars together, and am on my feet again, as it were. I am drawing pay here as an attendant on a good Ward, and doing the dental work-for the employees and some of the patients; combining the two I make quite a little sum. I have also had the good fortune to be selected to coach for Heidelberg University at Tiffin, Ohio. They have quite a school there. While the position does not pay so very much compared with salaries that some coaches get, yet it will be a great help to me this fall. I will get $275 and all expenses for my services for nine weeks. I can never make $275 any easier. They want me to be Athletic Director the year round at a salary of $700. The town is a good one and I have a chance to locate there permanently. I think it would be a good thing for me to accept, but I want to locate in the West and grow up with the town.
>
> One thing I am glad of, that is I have lost interest in playing baseball and football. I play here every Saturday

for the Hospital, that's how I came to get my position. I have a good many privileges with it. Business has been rather brisk with me for the past few days. The other day I made $7.50, and yesterday I made four. Friday I'll make four more, besides my pay as an attendant goes on every day and I am getting all my expenses too. By the time fall comes around I'll have a little money.

His change of heart regarding playing the games must have been very recent as just a month earlier *The Newark Daily Advocate* published an article about his baseball playing: "Caleb Sickles, the full-blooded Indian who played several time in Newark last season, is now covering center field for Manager James' Unions. The fleet-footed red man gave an exhibition of the speed that has made him famous on two occasions Sunday. In the sixth he dumped a slow one down the third base foul line which Snyder quickly gathered in and made a perfect throw to Francis, but Sickles had already crossed the bag. Again in the eighth, Sickles nearly beat out an infield hit, many believing he got to first ahead of Durch's beautiful throw, but Richards called him out." Apparently, after acquiring gainful employment and a coaching job, he lost interest in getting bumps and bruises as a player. Or, knowing the disdain schools had for their coaches playing professionally, he may have spoken pre-emptorily.

The October 13, 1904 issue of *The Arrow* shared that Joel Cornelius was then in Tiffin, Ohio with Caleb Sickles. He was taking a business course at Heidelberg University and, of course, playing football. Like many others from Carlisle, Caleb gave his former schoolmates opportunities when he had the chance.

That October he got rave reviews for his work on the Heidelberg University sidelines from *The Advocate:* "Caleb Sickles, the Indian who is remembered by every Newark baseball fan, as a star center fielder, is coaching the Heidelberg team and has developed the best team the Tiffin institution has ever had." He later received accolades for keeping the Dennison game close when his players were outweighed by almost 40 pounds per man, and some of his best players were unable to play due to injuries sustained in the Ohio Medical College game.

Although he thought about heading west, Caleb set about rooting himself further in Seneca County, Ohio, for which Tiffin was the seat. A controversy rose in 1905 when he was elected delegate to the county convention, probably as a Republican. The issue was whether a non-citizen Indian who could not vote could hold an elected office. Indians as a group were not granted citizenship and the right to vote until 1924. Individual Indians had become citizens decades before that when they received allotments in many cases.

Caleb's dental practice flourished, due in part, surely, to his fame as an athlete and coach. In the fall of 1905, he coached the Heidelberg team again and in November supported his alma mater when the Indians played the Massillon Tigers. In December, Caleb plunged into matrimony by marrying Mabel Teachnor, a white girl from Manchester he met in Columbus. She was about the same age as Caleb and had been a seamstress. *The Newark Daily Advocate* reported, "'Sick' managed to keep the news of his wedding well concealed and escaped from Columbus before many of his numerous friends became aware of the fact that he had passed from the ranks of bachelordom. Dr. Sickles met his wife when attending O. M. U. She was connected then, it is said, with the Protestant Hospital." Caleb established himself quite well in the dominant society of the community and freely shared his experiences with Carlisle students.

The good people of Tiffin were also glad to have Caleb in their midst. The Heidelberg University school newspaper raved about his performance as their football coach:

Heidel is proud of her teams and managers, but prouder of her loyal coach. Dr. Sickles needs no introduction to the athletic world, nor to the students of Hedelberg University. He is a perfect gentleman and a better football coach is nowhere to be found. He has the ability to work out new plays as well as to use old ones to a great advantage. He always has perfect control of his men, for they have confidence in him. The standard of athletics at Heidelberg has been raised fifty per cent since he has come to coach her teams. Three cheers for Coach Sickles!!

In his history of the college, E. I. F. Williams gave Sickles credit for elevating Heidelberg's athletic program:

> The credit for this move should be given to Dr. C. M. Sickles, who had charge of coaching the athletic teams. No longer was the university janitor to be the football manager and students of penmanship the members of the teams. Heidelberg joined with other colleges in maintaining high standards of scholarship and sportsmanship in conducting the game as a prerequisite for a student['s] participation.

Caleb Sickles responded to the requests for information from former athletes by Major Mercer in 1907 and Moses Friedman in 1909. His responses went into detail and he began a correspondence with the school that lasted until its closing. From this correspondence, we learn much about the man and his experiences. Dr. Sickles wrote a piece that was printed in the April 10, 1908, issue of *The Arrow* and is included in its entirety:

> Carlisle has done many things for me—good things. Entering when quite young my life was shaped there, it gave me an insight for higher things in life. When I left I strove four years to attain or rather fit myself for a useful life in the community in which I choose to live. I will advise every graduate of Carlisle to continue their

studies. When you finish your course at Carlisle it is indeed a commencement—you are just beginning. Take up some special branch of work. A graduate of a technical school or of any special branch can always find employment and command a good salary. For my life work I chose a profession—that of dentistry. I put myself on a footing with the white man, struck out boldly in a small city of Ohio in competition with my white brothers, with nothing but my education and nerve. I am not eulogizing myself and do not want you to take it as such, I only want to set forth the facts that might help some one of my own race. I have so far succeeded in life although I have just begun. What I have done others of you can do. You may not all make a success in the "tooth pulling" business but you can do something else equally as well. Since leaving school I have read considerably on the Indian question, which is no question at all. There may be no hope for the old Indians but the young men and women, there is plenty for them to do if they but would. The question is squarely up to you. The success you attain will depend upon yourself. Get away from the reservation and become a citizen of the United States. Work and your success is assured.

A month later, an article titled, "Real Indian Joins Red Men" ran in *The Marion Daily Star*. Using more than a little irony, the reporter announced that Sickles, "...a former football star of national reputation, was among those initiated into the mysteries of the order [Improved Order of Red Men]." The very idea of an Indian joining a secret society of white men was newsworthy, let alone one that used Indian regalia in its ceremonies. Caleb was also a member of the Elks.

In 1909, he wrote again, this time about a different issue: "I am doing all I can to live up to the standards taught me while at Carlisle. It is very hard for the Indian to succeed among the white people on account of race prejudice. I find it no handicap because very few know I have the strain of Indian blood in my veins, but I heard on all sides about this being a white man's country....God bless you and your co-workers in the good work they are doing."

The following year Caleb, at Friedman's invitation, had photos of his home and office taken to be published in Carlisle's *The Red Man* literary journal. Included in the exterior photo were, from the right, his brother, Raymond, who he was educating, Mabel and himself. Their servant is probably included in the unnamed people in the photo. Sickles went into great detail about the demographics of the town, his practice and his financial situation, which was very good. He was contemplating building a new house in two years. He stated with pride that "...I have no little back room, one 'horse-shack,' that a decrier of Indian education would imagine." Recalling some personal history he stated, "I came here without a cent—besides being in debt several hundred dollars—now I have over 1000.00 in cash in the banks here—This might seem as an object lesson to the other students there—that where there is a will, there is a way...P.S. The photographer's bill is 3.00."

Caleb Sickles was doing very well indeed when one considers that he was one of 15 dentists practicing in a town of 1,700 people. He wrote at length describing his practice:

> At present I have all I can do which means I do a business of from 250. to 300.00 per mo. Gross. I started in, in debt and have gradually paid out—all the time adding to my office—now I have over 1000.00 worth of furniture and instruments in my office—the accompanying photograph does not show all—as my laboratory does not show in the picture—among some of my instruments and machines—which are very expensive—I number—a Columbia electric engine with Dariot hand peice [sic]—(all cond) fountain cuspidor—Elgin casting

Dr. Sickles at work; *The Red Man* October 1910

machine, electric annealor—Columbia favorite chair—Sharp lamp—Electric lathe—gasoline blow pipe—just those articles represent an outlay of over 450.00. Then there are my countless smaller instruments aggregating over 500.00 more. My office is lighted by electricity. ...

Both dentists—Sickles and Johnson—were doing very well and were proud of their accomplishments. Pratt surely considered them shining examples of what top students could achieve and very likely used them to promote Carlisle's value as an educational institution.

Caleb's next letter to Carlisle was one of sadness to Wallace and Nellie Denny. It was to inform them that Mabel had died. After telling the details of her last days, he wrote, "I know she is in heaven for she was a pure woman." He wrote Superintendent Friedman a year later to offer his regrets for not being able to attend commencement and to philosophize. "It would be a grand thing if all the members of the Class of 1912 could attend college, which would give them a wider range of thought and fit them to fight the battles of the world....We all know there is room for the educated Indian—all we need is a chance. The proof is that today many Indians are holding responsible positions throughout our cities. Success to all of you."

Three years later he had better news. Caleb married Miss Nina M. Hankey on August 19, 1915, and visited Carlisle with his new bride on their honeymoon trip to Boston, New York and other points in the East. Sickles was rightly proud of what he had accomplished including owning his own automobile and farm. His July 15, 1916 letter to Acting Superintendent John D. DeHuff discussed a possible visit to the Indian school and also announced the birth of their son, an 8 1/4 pound boy, on the 13th. The visit took place and Caleb likely gave the talk on proper dental care that was discussed in the letter.

America's entrance into WWI changed many people's plans, and so it was with Sickles. An almost-40-year old Caleb Sickles served as a 1st Lieutenant in the U. S. Army 11th Battalion and was discharged on December 24, 1918 at Fort Oglethorpe, Georgia. It is not clear whether Caleb enlisted or was drafted. Regardless, he was inducted after the armistice was signed and served a very short time. After that, he was back to his dentistry practice.

Caleb returned to his dental practice and did some coaching in the 1920s at the Tiffin Junior Home, an orphanage that was merged into the Tiffin State Hospital in 1944. The 1920 census listed Caleb (39) as living on Webster Street with his wife, Nina M. (32), Caleb M. Jr. (3 years 5 months), and Ralph M. (1 year 9 months). They would have two more sons, Dewight and Eldon, as well as a daughter, Audrey.

A newspaper from the seat of nearby Allen County, *The Lima News*, recalled Caleb's exploits in a 1954 article: "The 1921 team defeated Chicago East Lane Tech, then recognized as national champion although averaging only 138-lbs per man. Passing was their game. In fact, Dee Griffis threw one to John

Starret for 80 yards and it still stands as a national record. Griffis is now a Tiffin policeman and Starret, later to become coach, is now head of a large boys' club at Nashville, Tenn. Dr. Caleb Sickles, a local dentist and former player with the Carlisle Indians, coached such a complicated offense that the officials had to be briefed before each game and the Tiffin captain had to notify the referee before each play. As a pre-game feature, Starret and Griffis would stand on the two 20-yard lines and heave passes back and forth, all of which had a rather demoralizing effect on the opposition."

Caleb must have maintained some ties with his family in Wisconsin as he owned land there until 1938. The local newspaper, the *Appleton Post-Crescent,* reported that Caleb Jr. sold a parcel in the town of Oneida that October. Now in his 60s, Caleb Sr. may have wanted to reduce his holdings to simplify his life. He died of a heart attack in Tiffin on January 30, 1950 at about 70 years of age.

15

George Vedernack

G eorge Vedernack came to Carlisle from the Lac du Flambeau Reservation on August 31, 1909. George's father was a farmer, so it is fair to conclude that he grew up on a farm. At the time of his enrollment, he had four living brothers and two living sisters. His mother and one brother had died of unknown causes. His younger brother, Frank, also attended Carlisle about the same time. George started off in Room 8 and worked in the tailor shop. A year later he was promoted to Room 9 and shifted to working in the stables. Six months later he began his training as a painter. At first his ability was deemed only 'fair,' but it soon improved. A

Name: George Vedernack　　　　　Nickname: Cotton
　DOB: 4/16/1890 or 4/16/1892　　　Height: 5' 6"
Weight: 140　　　　　　　　　　　　Age: 21
　Tribe: Chippewa　　　　　　　　　Home: Jenny, WI
Parents: Joe Vedernack, possibly German
　　　　 Mary Vedernack, 3/4 blood Chippewa, deceased
Early Schooling: Lac du Flambeau Reservation Boarding School

couple of months later George Vedernack's name, spelled various ways, started showing up in Carlisle Indian School publications.

In the spring, he was active in two sports as he earned his first Carlisle "C" in lacrosse and also placed 3rd in the pole vault at the Annual Class Track Meet in April 1911. If he weren't already on the track team, Warner would surely have tried to recruit him. Pole vaulters tend to be wiry and George's physical dimensions imply that he was just that. After spending the summer in Martin's Creek, Pennsylvania, working for Henry McEwen, George returned to school in time for football season.

After playing on the scrubs in 1910 and possibly 1909, George forced Warner to put him on the varsity squad. He was very small but the quality and intensity of his play demanded that he be promoted, although he was only a substitute. In what many consider Carlisle's greatest victory, Vedernack stood strong. The *Philadelphia Ledger* raved, "Carlisle's defeat of the Harvard team strengthens the conviction that not only has Glenn Warner developed one of the greatest of Indian elevens, but that this 1911 team is about the best among the Eastern colleges." It went on to report that a major cog was missing: "Carlisle was without the services of Captain Burd, [sic] who is considered as having few equals as an end. He was so seriously injured, in the Penn game that he could not play against Harvard." *The Arrow reported,* "Vedernack, who played in Captain Burd's [sic] place, was in the game every minute and very few gains were made around his end." Not bad at all for a first-year man. His contributions were significant enough that Santa Claus, in the person of Jim Thorpe, selected George as only one of nine athletes to receive special gifts at the Catholic reception on Christmas night.

George didn't spend all of his fall on the football field. He was active in the Invincible Debating Society, made extemporaneous speeches, was elected Sergeant-at-arms and visited a girls' debating society meeting. He was also elected mayor of his classroom's model city, Oglala.

Putting his training as a painter to work in January 1912, George made a sign puzzle that students had difficulty solving. About that time, he teamed with Peter Jordan to argue the negative of, "That the divorce laws of all the states should be made uniform" at an Invincibles meeting. Ovilla Azure and Andrew Dunbar, arguing the affirmative, won. In the spring, George placed third in the high jump at the Annual Handicap Track and Field Meet, then headed home, his enrollment commitment fulfilled.

George Vedernack, now 22 years old, returned to Carlisle on September 6, 1912, and enrolled for another year on October 3. Perhaps he waited to see if he was going to make the starting line-up before he committed. *The Carlisle Arrow* summarized his play: "George Vetternack, [sic] right end, is 5 ft. 6 in. tall, weighs 140 pounds, and 21 years- old. He is a Chippewa from

George "Cotton" Vedernack
Cumberland County Historical Society, Carlisle, PA

Wisconsin. 'Cotton,' as he is called, forced his way up from a scrub to a substitute on the team last year, and won his place as a regular by his hard work and his aggressiveness. He was about the smallest player on any first-class team this year, and his success in winning a place on the team shows what fighting spirit and 'pep' can do."

Gus Welch often told a story about that year's Carlisle-Army game:

> I remember the game well. Jim [Thorpe] took the opening kickoff and ran through the Army team for a touchdown but we drew a penalty and the touchdown was nullified. Thorpe was our captain and went to the referee to ask what the penalty was for. The referee said our little end Vedernack, who weighed only 130 pounds, was holding. Thorpe told Vedernack to go to the sideline on the next kickoff and keep out of the way. The kickoff rolled into the end zone. Jim loafed a little, as if he was going to down the ball for a touchback, then suddenly picked up the ball and ran more than 100 yards for a touchdown.

Joe Guyon told another story about that game in which Vedernack was a key ingredient:

> Cotton Vedernack, a Chippewa weighing 137 pounds, played end. He was the best tackle on our team but lacked the blocking equipment. Consequently, the tackles and ends switched positions on offense. Thorpe and I were detailed to block Army Captain All-American [tackle] Devore.

George spent the summer at home in Wisconsin. Apparently, Superintendent Friedman requested that he recruit students for the school. On August 15, Vedernack wrote Friedman: "Received your letter some time ago and was out trying my best to get students for Carlisle. I have about seven so far that want to go for three [years] and not any longer. Otherwise they won't go." Friedman responded promptly, "A three year term of enrollment will be allowed those students who are eighteen or more years of age, but those who have not reached the age of eighteen should be enrolled for the longer period of five years. If there are any exceptions, however, that should be made, Superintendent Everest will recommend to me what action should be taken." On September 18, P. S. Everest, Superintendent of the LaPointe Agency, wrote Friedman to inform him that Vedernack was bringing Frank Holmes, Jr., Arnold Holliday, Francis Obern and Eliza Denomie to Carlisle with him.

Cotton returned for the 1913 season and, though not much larger, had improved. After the opening game against Albright College, *The Arrow* noticed his improvement: "Pratt, Vedernack, Kelsey, and Wallette showed up well enough on the ends to show that Carlisle will be stronger in those positions than last year." After defeating the tougher Penn team, the reporter observed, "Pratt and Vedernack on the ends did not allow a single gain around them and they spoiled every trick play Penn attempted. They also got down the field better than did the Penn's ends on Guyon's long punts." *The Washington Star* noticed his fine play against Georgetown:

> Vedernack stands out as one of the best ends in the East, and that despite his rather small stature. He is short and stocky, and seems small to be playing the position, but there is no doubt that he delivers the goods. He gets around and through the interference in a way that is astonishing. It seems to be almost impossible to eliminate him from the play. It is seldom that he fails to get his man, and yesterday he went through four or five Georgetown men time after time and dropped the man with the ball. He uses splendid judgment in going in to help out on plays through the line and off-tackle,

and seems to know just when not to get in fast in order to prevent an opposing back from slipping around him. He would compare favorably with much larger and heavier men who are playing end positions in the big universities.

Two weeks later, early in the Dartmouth game, Vedernack suffered a wrenched elbow and was through for the day. Fortunately, his elbow had recovered enough for him to play part of the game against Syracuse the following week. Back at full strength, he played the entire game against Brown a week later to end the season and his football career at Carlisle. George Vedernack had been a significant cog in the legendary Carlisle teams of 1911–1913 that had lost but one game each year and ranked highly among the best teams in the country each year. However, his athletic career at the Indian school wasn't over.

In December 1913, George was promoted from Private to 1st Sergeant of Troop E, a position that brought considerable responsibility. For instance, in March 1914, he supervised the oiling of the floors in the Large Boys' Quarters. Earlier that month, football lettermen, "C" men, drew for game balls from the previous season's victories. He won the ball from the Syracuse game. Cotton kept in shape that winter and early spring playing—practicing mostly—lacrosse until commencement. After receiving his certificate in painting, he was off to Altoona to work in a railroad shop, but not before withdrawing his money from agency and school accounts.

Although no longer at Carlisle, George kept in touch with old friends there and occasionally visited them. He played for the ex-Carlisles football team which was also called the Altoona Indians—that is, when he wasn't playing for someone else. In 1915, he became one of a handful of players ever to play for three professional teams in the same year: Altoona Indians, Pitcairn Quakers and Youngstown Patricians. At Pitcairn he was joined by his younger brother, Frank, another Carlisle alum who worked as an expert painter of passenger railcars. Frank received $4 to $5 a day for his work. Compared to this, $50 a game playing football looked great. In 1916, George just played for Pitcairn and Youngstown and in 1917 just for Youngstown. That was probably because he had moved to Youngstown where he was working as a shipping clerk. Although these were the ragtag days of professional football, the better teams often included All-Americans, against whom Cotton more than held his own.

He was in Wisconsin, probably visiting, when he enlisted in the National Army on June 29, 1918 at Eagle River. He listed 22 New Court Street in Youngstown as his residence. Private Vedernack spent the war at the Machine Gun Training Center at Camp Hancock, Georgia and was honorably discharged on March 26, 1919.

After the war, the Patricians attempted to reform a team and signed George Vedernack. Reeling from a 27–0 thrashing by Massillon on October 5, 1919, the team disbanded. George appears to have missed playing in the NFL by less than one season. After this, things get fuzzy due to lack of information. A 1929 census lists George as married and living in Columbus, Ohio. However, he was likely married some time prior to that and had at least one child, a daughter, Carol. He died on July 14, 1936, of "Lob. Pneumonia and Pyloric obstruction" while living in Youngstown, Ohio. Carol's wedding announcement described her late father as a "professional football star," so it is likely that his football career continued after the demise of the Youngstown Patricians.

George Vedernack catching a pass
Cumberland County Historical Society, Carlisle, PA

16
Gus Welch

Gustavus A. Welch, Chippewa, arrived at Carlisle from Spooner, Wisconsin, on September 22, 1908, accompanied by his younger brother, James. The Welch children were orphans. A logging incident took their Irish-born father before the turn of the 20th century, leaving their mother, Mary Hart Welch, a widow with seven children. They lived in Washburn County, Wisconsin, according to the 1900 Federal Census. That census listed Susan, Lizzie, Robert and

> Name: Gustavus A. Welch Nickname: Gus
> DOB: 12/23/1890 Height: 5'9"
> Weight: 162 Age: 19
> Tribe: Chippewa Home: Spooner, WI
> Parents: James Welch, Irish, deceased
>   Mary Hart Welch, Chippewa, deceased
> Early Schooling: Tomah Indian Industrial School
>   Hayward Indian School, possibly
> Later Schooling: Conway Hall, Dickinson School of Law
> Honors: American Indian Athletic Hall of Fame, 1971
>   College Football Hall of Fame, 1975

Gus as being "at school." James, Robert and Gus were on the roll of the Tomah Indian Industrial School in Monroe County, Wisconsin. In 1905, John and Robert, the two oldest boys, were living together on their own: tuberculosis had apparently consumed their mother as well as several siblings by this time. Brother John, being the oldest, signed the Carlisle enrollment papers for James and Gus. Gus's birthday varies widely across the several official papers that can be found. However, his short, handwritten autobiography puts his date of birth as December 23, 1890, near Spooner.

Gus Welch punting; *U. S. Army Military History Institute*

Before coming to Carlisle, Gus spent a lot of time with his maternal grandmother, Chemamanon, wife of the chief of the La Couriterielle band, Kewanzee. Washburn County is adjacent to Barron County, where Lone Star Dietz grew up. Both counties were heavily timbered and dotted with lakes. The local towns were in early stages of development when the boys were young. Chippewas lived among and around the early white settlers. Living in the northwoods with fellow Chippewas, young Gus learned many of the traditional skills, including paddling a birch-bark canoe, harvesting wild rice, collecting maple syrup and trapping furs. He put the latter one to great use when he decided that he wanted to enroll at Carlisle in order to play on their sports teams in 1907.

Learning that the Carlisle Indians would play the University of Minnesota in mid-November, Gus trapped a wolf and used the proceeds from selling its pelt for trainfare to Minneapolis. After arriving in the Twin Cities, he located the practice field used by the Carlisle Indians' football team and watched the players prepare for the game. He positioned himself behind the goal post that kickers were attempting to split for field goals. Eventually Frank Mt. Pleasant made one. Gus outran all the other boys who were standing around, including two Carlisle substitutes, and retrieved the ball. Before anyone could take away what looked to him like a shiny new ball (mistaking a well-used practice ball for a new one is understandable because he had never seen a real football before; he had only played with homemade balls stuffed with leaves.), Gus kicked it back through the goal post over Mt. Pleasant's head. So impressed with the kick was the Carlisle star that he escorted Gus over to meet Pop Warner. The Old Fox invited Gus to apply for admission to Carlisle and let him watch the game from the bench dressed in a Carlisle uniform.

Shortly after arriving at Carlisle, James and Gus often gained mention in the school newspaper. James was at the head of his class, Room No. 4, in the October Merit Roll. He gave an impromptu talk to a meeting of the Dicksons in November in Room No. 4 1/2. He had apparently been promoted. In December, Gus participated in a debate for the Standard

Debating Society, developing skills he would use in later life. He and David Robinson successfully argued for the negative for the proposition that business training is of more importance to the Indian than agriculture. In February 1909, Gus received positive mention in *The Arrow* for his recitation in the auditorium the previous week, "Men to be Honored." On the Final Merit Roll in April, James was first in his class, Room No. 5. Apparently he had been promoted a second time. The Welch boys definitely stood out academically.

Gus's first recognition for athletic prowess came for his victory in the July 4, 1909 school games. Gus and Joseph Trepania won the 100-yard three-legged race, winning new swimming suits for their efforts. Gus then went on outing to work on a farm where he earned $15 a month. Back at school in the fall, he studied blacksmithing, was elected President of the Sophomore Class, was ranked first in his class on the December Merit Roll, debated as a member of the Standards, was frequently called upon to make orations at school events, and was promoted to first chair in the cornet section of the famed Carlisle Indian School Band. *The Arrow* noted an immediate improvement in the band's sound. He also participated in athletics but not on the varsity level.

Gus continued to be in the first rank of students in all aspects of school life except, to the naked eye, athletics. He made the varsity football team in 1910 but did not start. In track the following spring, he made a small splash, placing in some meets and running one of the legs for the winning team at the Penn Relays. 1911 was Gus's breakout year in football. It was also the year his idol, Jim Thorpe, returned to Carlisle, and Welch was assigned to room with him in the athletic quarters. Gus thought Warner was joking when he told him to move in with Thorpe and had to be told again the next day before he believed it. Although Thorpe and Welch were opposites in many ways, they got along. Pop wasn't called the Old Fox for nothing. Where Thorpe was inclined to do wild, risky things,

Welch was sensible; Thorpe was quiet while Welch was talkative; Welch was studious, but Thorpe would rather be playing or hunting outdoors. Both were orphans with American Indian mothers and Irish fathers. Jim had lost his twin early in life where Gus had lost several siblings. Perhaps this combination helped them to bond.

1911 was a special year for Gus as well as for Carlisle. Gus wore several hats and received numerous honors, including president of the Senior Class, orator, quarterback of the football team, president of the school's model republic, captain of the track team, sometime football scout, and subject of a limerick written by a classmate for publication in *The Arrow.*

Pop Warner considered the 1911 Carlisle eleven their best team ever with star players at every position. So strong was the team that it could defeat major opponents without the services of its left halfback, the incomparable Jim Thorpe. Although everyone else played in Thorpe's shadow, Gus got his share of media coverage and became known around the country as one of the best at his position. The quarterback in Warner's single-wingback formation is generally called the blocking back for good reason. Welch was a good blocker and led the way for Thorpe, the tailback. But the blocking back also called the signals, which in those days included selecting the plays to be called. Sometimes he even called his own because Warner developed plays in which the blocking back got the ball to keep the defense honest. Gus also ran back kicks and punts with the best of them. The game against Andy Smith's Penn Quakers provided a stage for Gus to display his talents. Both teams' stars, Thorpe and Mercer, were too injured to play, which made the contest all the more interesting. The Philadelphia *North American* described the contest in colorful terms: "The redskins scalped, raged, plundered and ravaged. The fleet Arcasa and the rapid-moving Welch skirted the Penn Ends as though the gentlemen set to guard these points were stakes driven into the skirts of tepees [sic] to foil the wind." Later in the game Gus made his big play as the *North American* reported:

> ...it was on the 15-yard line that Welch started for an end run. Coming sharply from midfield, he ran toward the north line. Running toward the south at a long angle, he finally formed the apex of a rapidly moving triangle. Only one man had a chance to catch him, but no player had the fleetness of foot of the Indian, and Welch, maintaining his burst of speed, pulled steadily away, and went over the line for a touchdown after a run of 95 yards.

The 1911 Indians lost but a single game, 12–11 to a weaker opponent, Syracuse, due to overconfidence. But the loss was not due to anything Gus Welch did or didn't do; he tried everything he could to salvage a victory. Because he was laid up with a bad back most of the week leading up to the game, he did not dress for it. When things didn't go well for Carlisle in the first half, Welch went to the locker room at half-time and suited up. His play and generalship nearly overcame the deficit that accumulated in the first half.

Gus also had a good track season in the spring of 1912, particularly in the 440-yard dash and 880-yard run. He made the U. S. Olympic track team but wasn't well enough when the time came to make the trip to Stockholm, Sweden. After graduation, he enrolled in Conway Hall, Dickinson College Preparatory School. At the end of May, he left for Browning, Montana, with Sampson Bird. *The Carlisle Arrow* didn't speculate about the reason for their trip. The always short-of-funds Welch was probably looking for an opportunity to make money. The following September, when reporting that he returned too late from roughing it in Montana to be ready to play in the first game, the *Arrow* commented on how fit he appeared. Elsewhere in the issue, the reporter mentioned that Welch had spent the summer in the harvest fields of North

Dakota. Although playing baseball is always a possibility, he more likely worked on threshing crews those summers.

In the fall, Gus was back to studying at Conway Hall and playing football for Carlisle. The team was loaded with talent as most of the stars from the previous year's team returned. Once again, the Indians went through the schedule with one loss. An ankle injury kept Welch from performing at top form and was likely the cause of his not being named first team All-American. The *New York Evening Sun* chose him for its second team, stating, "Welsh [sic] of Carlisle had to handle probably the most versatile offense any team has shown this year, and he is therefore chosen as the second-best quarterback of the year."

Gus filled in as captain of the track team until Bruce Goesback was elected. After the 1912 Olympics, *The Carlisle Arrow* seldom mentioned Gus with regard to track, but he was still an integral part of the football team. Note of Gus's activity with organized religion began that fall when he gave a short talk to the Boys Catholic meeting on the good that can be accomplished by attending the meetings of the Holy Name Society. He even gave a talk about the Penn-Carlisle game to a Union meeting (presumed to be boys and girls together) of the Holy Name Society. Gus soon spent some more time at St. Patrick's for a major media event.

As soon as the World Series was over, Jim Thorpe returned to Carlisle to marry Iva Miller, a Carlisle student. Gus Welch, Thorpe's old roommate, was best man. This may have been Gus's first film appearance as Thorpe sold the movie rights to his wedding to two motion picture companies.

With Thorpe now gone, Gus had three new backfield mates in 1913; Pete Calac and Joe Guyon were moved from line positions to the backfield while Edward Bracklin was installed at right halfback (wingback). The team didn't miss a beat and had a one loss-one tie season. Gus led his team three years running to one-loss seasons and to three of Carlisle's greatest victories ever over Harvard (1911), Dartmouth (1913), and Army

(1912). Several players, including Welch, were mentioned for All-America honors. So successful was the team that year that Gus and Superintendent Friedman were invited to speak at the Dickinson College football banquet.

Sadly, the Carlisle Indian School was in disarray at that time due to an incompetent administration. Teachers and students alike were at the point of mutiny. Impoverished, Gus wasn't happy that football players and band boys generated thousands of dollars in revenue for the school but were paid little for their efforts. He thought Warner to be profane and unprincipled. He also believed that Warner and Friedman had let Jim Thorpe take the fall for having played minor league baseball when they were likely aware of it well before the Olympics. Welch drafted a petition and got 214 students to sign it. He then delivered it to Rep. A. H. Rupley, who lived in Carlisle. When Gus's brother in Wisconsin fell ill in early January 1914, he wanted James to go help with the family. Perhaps sensing the upcoming investigation brought about in part by Welch's petition, Warner and Friedman insisted that Gus go and paid his expenses out of athletic funds. Although he was away for a month, he returned in time to testify. He felt that Warner exercised no moral authority over the boys and should be removed from his job. That didn't happen, but changes to the school and athletic program decreased Warner's power and the ability to field competitive teams.

In March, Gus, being the school's best orator, gave the welcoming address to Mother Catherine Drexel, the philanthropist nun who spent millions of her own dollars aiding Indians. He began the talk by saying, "We always welcome a friend of the Indian, especially a true and sincere friend such as Mother Catherine Drexel has shown herself." Earlier in the month he was informed by the acting supervisor that Washington would not pay his remaining tuition at Conway Hall. That was a severe and probably unexpected blow to a young man already living on the edge financially.

By summer's end, the superintendent started getting letters requesting that Gus repay some money he had borrowed, usually from former students. Edward Leo wrote from Atlantic City, almost frantic to get his $11 back in order to cover his travel expenses home. His letter was forwarded to Welch at Conway Hall, where he was apparently staying at that time. A few days earlier *The Carlisle Arrow* reported, "Gus Welch and Henry Broker, Carlisle '12 and '13, respectively, returned last week from a very enjoyable and profitable summer in Atlantic City." Apparently it was not profitable enough to cover his law school tuition, room and board. By that time, Gus was preparing for the start of football season.

Having finished his preparatory school courses in the spring, Gus was now a student at Dickinson School of Law and the coach of the Conway Hall football team. Although he had a year of varsity eligibility remaining, he had no intention of playing that year. The Carlisle Indian School was restructured after the investigation was completed, resulting in a student body with fewer boys of the age and size needed for a competitive football team. A few stars remained in 1914, but there weren't enough supporting cast members to generate the results Warner had been producing. After some disappointing games, Peter Calac was made team captain and Elmer Busch, who had been elected captain the previous spring, was relieved of that commission. November injuries had further depleted the team, and the Notre Dame game was coming up soon. Left halfbacks Fred Broker and Jesse Wofford were both on the injured list, making it necessary to bring up Grant White from the reserves. James Crane showed promise at quarterback until he got hurt. The Indians were short a field general and faced a tough opponent. Exactly how it came to be is not known, but Gus Welch suited up as quarterback for the Notre Dame game.

With their old captain leading them, the Indians had a fighting chance against the Irish, going to the locker room down 17–6 at halftime. But the tide turned against them when Gus was seriously injured in a collision with Notre Dame fullback Ray "Iron Eich" Eichenlaub. The injury was so serious that Gus was taken to Chicago's Mercy Hospital. Without him on the field, things went downhill fast. What began as a beating by a superior opponent became a thrashing to the tune of 48–6, Carlisle's worst loss to that time. It was also Gus's worst injury. He was hurt so badly that he remained behind in the hospital when the team returned to Carlisle.

School administrators wrote Gus that his brother, James, would not be visiting him because James was in the hospital in Philadelphia. They were concerned that he had a tubercular knee. Fortunately, their fears were not realized and James made a full recovery, just not in time to visit Gus in Chicago.

On November 20—the Notre Dame game was played on the 14th—Gus wrote to Oscar Lipps, the acting superintendent, telling him that he was feeling fine and expected to return soon. Dr. W. E. Morgan wrote Lipps on the 21st stating, "He not only sustained a fracture of the cheek-bone (which he feels) but he had also a fracture of the base of the skull in front (which he don't [sic] feel) but which requires absolute rest to insure a future without invalidism, such as epilepsy, paralysis, deafness or loss of sight, any one of which might develop in after years from recklessness or negligence at this time." On the 23rd Dr. Morgan wrote, "Mr. Gus Welch still continues with his gradual improvement and seems more contented than before. I believe he has decided to be good and mind the doctor. Has promised me to-day to do just as I say. He's a fine fellow and I can't take any chances with him." The next day the good doctor wrote, "I am sorry to say that our patient Gus Welch deliberately kicked over the traces to-day and in spite of all advice to the contrary, left his bed, and dressed himself, declaring that he would assume all responsibility." Gus's rashness came back to haunt him later.

Gus pulled into Carlisle on November 30th while the team was away on a four-game road trip to New England, Alabama and Georgia. The New England games were played before his return, and newspaper accounts don't list Welch as having played in either the Alabama or the Auburn game. His playing days at Carlisle were finished.

Three weeks after Gus returned to Carlisle, the superintendent received a letter from Wesley Talchief demanding repayment of $10 loaned to Welch when he, Peter Jordan and Henry Broker were stranded in Buffalo, New York the previous August. Talchief sent another letter in January. On January 16, 1915, Welch wrote Superintendent Lipps that he had attended to the matter. Yet another letter from Talchief arrived in March.

Gus's inability to repay his debts apparently didn't influence Lipps's high regard for his indigent ward because, in June 1915, Oscar Lipps hired him as first assistant football coach. The job paid "$150 per month in cash for the months of September, October, and November" plus room and board for the entire school year. The contract contained clauses that required Welch to maintain high standards of conduct and "...see that our football players observe strictly the rules governing amateur athletics; and that they refrain from any conduct that would in any way reflect upon the school or affect their amateur standing as athletes." In other words, no pro football for Gus or his players, at least not this year.

Immediately after Pop Warner's departure in early 1915, several Carlisle alums applied for the vacant head coaching position, apparently viewing the job as a plum. Instead of one of the better known and more involved former players getting the job, it was awarded to Victor M. Kelley. Kelley had attended Carlisle for a year. Well, not exactly. He played for Carlisle in 1908 while attending Dickinson School of Law. Welch attributed Kelley's hiring to Texas politics. Influence from Texas politicians at the national level is probably more accurate.

The 1915 season was even more of a disaster than 1914 had been. The annual Thanksgiving game with Pasadena-bound

Brown brought the 3–6–2 season to a merciful end. The 39–3 trouncing by the Bears was a fitting end to a season filled with dissension. A news piece out of Carlisle said that, as assistant coach, Welch did not want to take the blame for the poor showing. It reported that, "Kelley asked him to assume charge of the squad after he found out that he could not develop it himself, and that three weeks before Thanksgiving Kelley was secretly deposed as coach by the school authorities, although allowed to remain at his own request on the campus until the season's end." *The Providence Journal* mocked Carlisle in a cartoon, depicting the team as a fat caricature of an Indian player long past his prime dreaming of better days. Gus returned to Carlisle with the team and continued his study of the law.

In April 1916, surely with mixed emotions, Gus received his inheritance from his mother. He could no doubt use the $149.35 for his portion of Wa-wi-ens's estate, but he had to sign over another check, this one for $85.00, to pay for the casket in which his brother, John, was buried. Now his oldest brother was gone.

There was much ink spilled speculating about whether Carlisle would field a football team in 1916, but it seems improbable that Gus wanted to be associated with it after what he had gone through the previous year. But he did accept a position as Indian Assistant at $20 per month plus room. The announcement in *The Carlisle Arrow* gave him the title of Assistant Disciplinarian at the Large Boys' Quarters. Also in *The Carlisle Arrow,* Superintendent Lipps provided reasons for Welch's history of financial problems when he wrote:

> Unlike many of the Indian boys who attend higher schools after leaving the Indian school, Gus has not had the wherewithal to see him through college. He has had to work hard to meet expenses but by his push, willingness to do any hard work, by his stick-to-it-iveness and by his

inimitable good nature, he has almost worked his way through college. It is good for the young Indian boys to have among them one of their own who has struggled as Gus has had to struggle for an education and all other things that tend to make a man.

While completing his last year of law school, Gus played football for Dickinson College. He threatened to quit, likely due to poor performance in the first game of the season, but agreed to stay after Dickinson College's student body prevailed on him to continue. Gus led the Red Devils in scoring for the year, which turned out to be a very successful one. After the college season was over, he and his coach, former Dickinson star Frank "Mother" Dunn, shored up the Canton, Ohio professional team. The Bulldogs were somewhat depleted by injuries over the tough season and needed some fresh players. Gus became part of an unofficial national championship team and part of what Bulldogs' manager Jack Cusack considered his best Canton team ever as he shored up their bench. After a quick scan of the team's roster, there can be little doubt as to how he became aware of that opportunity as his old roommate was starring for the Bulldogs. When not on the gridiron, he kept an eye on the future.

When Hervey B. Peairs, Superintendent of Haskell Institute, visited Carlisle for an unrelated purpose, Gus took the opportunity to approach him about the position of athletic director. Following protocol, Peairs made an offer of $1,000 per year for the position of Assistant Disciplinarian and Athletic Director through the new Carlisle superintendent, John Francis. In a letter to Peairs, Francis responded that he had discussed the matter and Welch would be available to start on July 1. However, a war intervened.

On June 7, John Francis informed Superintendent Peairs that Welch had enlisted and was at the Reserve Officers Training

Camp at Fort Niagara where he was hoping to land an officer's commission. A week later he received his last pay check from Carlisle, along with a bill for unpaid board to the tune of $36.00. Second Lieutenant pay of $1,700 per year plus benefits, of which there were many, must have looked very enticing to an impoverished orphan.

Gus Welch, Captain, U. S. Army
Cumberland County Historical society, Carlisle, PA

Later in the month, Gus wrote Francis about his experiences, mostly good, at the army camp so far. But then he had to go to the rifle range. Gus was concerned about not qualifying for a commission because of his prior impatience:

> I am somewhat worried over the result of the shooting. Three years ago I had my face injured, and this is the first effect I have experienced as a result of the injury. The shock received from the rifle fire causes me to have a severe head ache, while shooting the pain almost blinds me.

Because his scores were good, he said nothing to his officers about the pain and volunteered for the aviation corps at his first opportunity. He and Francis corresponded regularly throughout Gus's training. The superintendent suggested that he consider making a career out of the military, given its job security. Just before the end of the letter, Gus wrote, "I have done my best, keeping always in mind that I was a Carlisle man. I also had to remember that I was the only Redskin in camp, and of course my errors would naturally look larger than the other fellows'."

It being the army after all, Gus wasn't assigned to the air corps. Instead he was sent to Harvard—Harvard Reserve Officers' Training Corps, that is. The newly-minted 2nd Lieutenant spent his days attending lectures in Harvard Stadium, the site of some of his fiercest battles, listening to lectures given by six French officers, each of whom had been wounded multiple times. He found staying awake no problem, "About the time their [sic] think that the students are becoming weary, they spring one of these hair-raising experiences, and then you are ready to listen for another hour."

His next assignment was as an instructor at Camp Meade, Maryland. In his off-hours, he played halfback and captained the officers' football team and competed with teams from other military bases, sometimes at Penn's Franklin Field. On November 9, Jim Thorpe wired the Indian School from Canton, Ohio, inquiring about Gus's whereabouts. John Francis sent him the following response:

```
Lieutenant Gus Welch with 14th Training Battalion
Camp Meade, Maryland.
Signed, Francis
Western Union Collect
```

Thorpe was looking for Gus because his Canton Bulldogs had suffered some injuries in the Youngstown game and needed reinforcements, especially with two games against archrival Massillon coming up soon. Gus earned his pay in the home game against Youngstown with an 80 (89 in some accounts) yard touchdown run while Thorpe and Dunn nursed injuries on the bench and rested up for Massillon. Welch, Dunn and Thorpe started the first game against Massillon, and Pete Calac came in as a substitute. The game was played in a snowstorm but Canton prevailed. It's not clear if Gus made it to Detroit for the Thanksgiving game against the Heralds or the away game against Massillon because he, like most of the Canton team, played under an assumed name. Keith McClellan and PFRA Research deciphered game reports and determined that Welch generally played as "Wells" but might have been "Moore." Getting away and back in time for military duty may have been difficult at times. But he must have devoted adequate time to his military duties because, before long, he was attached to the depot brigade and promoted to 1st Lieutenant. A few months later he made captain. Gus argued long and hard to be sent overseas but was considered too valuable where he was. Finally he located a unit that was having difficulty finding officers to lead it and volunteered for the 808th Pioneer Infantry, which shipped out of Hoboken on August 28, 1918, and arrived in France in early September. The 808th was a regiment consisting of 2,721 black enlisted men and 81 white officers. For these purposes, the Army counted Indian officers as white. That summer, Gus made Captain and was reputedly the first Indian to attain that rank in the U. S. Cavalry.

Very shortly after landing in Europe, the 808th saw action in the St. Mihiel sector in the Argonne defensive initiative and, immediately after that, the Meuse-Argonne offensive that lasted until the armistice. The 808th Pioneer Infantry followed closely behind the assault troops and took over captured enemy engineer dumps. Many of these dumps were found well stocked with useable munitions and engineering materials which were quickly put to use against their former owners. Near war's end, Gus received a minor wound from which he quickly recovered. After the armistice, Gus may have been able to enjoy the music performed by the 808th band which included former Carlisle student James Wheelock. With the war won, Gus was ready for gridiron battles.

After the war ended, colleges reinstituted their athletic programs. However, many of them needed coaches and players. Washington State College (WSC) supporters were excited and looked forward to the upcoming football season with great anticipation. Under Head Coach Lone Star Dietz, the team lost two regular season games in four years and split in two Tournament of Roses New Year's Day games in Pasadena. The fourth year the team was nominally called the Mare Island Marines, but Washington State considers it their team because ten players and the coach came from Pullman. The yearbook, *The Chinook,* even included a section on the Mare Island team!

Expectations were high because many of the pre-war players were returning. But Dietz was indicted for draft evasion and no longer coached WSC. *The Evergreen* exposed the school's strategy for hiring a new coach:

> When the athletic council commenced casting around for a man to take the place vacated by "Lonestar" Dietz, they agreed that it should be someone acquainted with the Warner system and able to teach it to his men. In

considering applicants, they discovered that Exendine had made application and had an enviable record behind him. So out of a list of over a dozen candidates, he was chosen, and his salary was to have been between $2000 and $3000. That is the story given out by Graduate Manager Kruegel. Coach Bohler stated, however, that Exendine had signed a contract with Georgetown for next year, so there was nothing to the "rumor." So then it goes to the student body just as I heard it—a confirmed and denied rumor.

WSC set about finding what they thought would be the next best thing. Gus Welch was located on a former battlefield in France after two months of searching and agreed to take the job. He promised to be in Pullman by September 10. After 10 months of overseas duty, the 808th returned to the U. S. Gus Welch separated from the army at Camp Lee, Virginia, in time to embark on a coaching career. Former standouts Carl "Red" Dietz and Clarence "Zim" Zimmerman were selected as varsity assistant and freshman coach, respectively. Now all Pullmanites had to do was to wait until September.

Coach Welch arrived in Pullman with much fanfare as local football fans expected him to repeat, or at least closely approach, the success Lone Star Dietz had had on the Palouse. At Gus's first public appearance, Frank Corbett, Nez Perce, greeted him. Corbett had been behind Welch in the depth charts at Carlisle. After leaving Carlisle, he attended the University of Idaho but was now enrolled at Washington State. He told *The Evergreen* reporter, "Welch was unquestionably one of the best players turned out at Carlisle and was a popular favorite with players and students alike. I had heard a lot about the State College and followed the athletic programs of the college closely while Coach Dietz was here, but when I heard that Gus Welch was coming to coach this year I at once made up my mind that Washington State College was the place for me."

Not long after practice started in earnest, *The Evergreen* reported, "Captain Welch has also developed that disease so common to football coaches known as 'gloomia bearitis,' which particularly affects the vocal organs in such a way that he can only talk about the weak points of his team. The poor tackling of his men and the acute shortage of experienced players on his squad are coming in for their share of comment."

Welch spent his spare time on the rubber-chicken circuit. He told the Chamber of Commerce, "We are going to strive to give you the best team that ever represented the State College, but a winning team is not, by far, the sum total of the aspirations of the coaching staff. It is our desire to make Rogers Field a vast classroom for the development of real men. We want to teach them stamina, patience, aggressiveness and determination."

By October, *The Evergreen* bemoaned, "Football Prospects Not the Brightest." With the belated arrival of Walter "Fat" Herreid, WSC had but seven returning lettermen whereas several of her Pacific Coast Conference rivals boasted much larger numbers of experienced players. Hopes dimmed a bit more when the Marines would not release Walter V. "Boots" Brown in time for football season. Brown was quarterback Arthur "Bull" Durham's understudy in 1915 and 1916. He then played in the 1917 Mare Island Marines backfield that won the Tournament of Roses game on New Year's Day of 1918, the year before his former WSC teammates played in the Marines' uniforms. The Crimson and Gray opened the season encouragingly enough, crushing Multnomah Athletic Club of Portland 49–0, with the three Hanley brothers scoring five of the seven touchdowns. Lone Star Dietz gave the team a pep talk before the game "and encouraged the various members in his famous characteristic manner." Next up were Andy Smith's California Golden Bears, considered by many to be the class of the conference. Perhaps succumbing to a bit of grandiosity after WSC's unexpected 14–0 victory over Cal, *The Evergreen* opined, "No team in America could have held out against the crimson and gray on that memorable afternoon, for such fierce and constant onslaught as Welch's men displayed has never before been witnessed in the annals of coast football."

Wins against Idaho and Oregon brought the Cougars, as WSC's teams began to be called after a sportswriter dubbed their fighting spirit in the victory over Cal, to an unscored upon 4–0. Their once-beaten cross-state rival, Washington, invaded Pullman for WSC's homecoming. That Washington's sole loss was to Oregon, WSC's hopes for a Dietz-like season seemed to be materializing. Mother Nature intervened with the result that WSC was on the short end of a 13–7 score in a mud game. The Cougars may have been suffering a bit of a hangover from the Washington game when they played Oregon Agricultural College at Portland and lost 6–0. Welch's charges rebounded against outmanned Montana State, prevailing 42–14 on the road. 5–2–0 is normally a good start for a new head coach, but that record approximated Dietz's worst year, and the only year in which he lost any regular-season games at WSC. Although the Washington State faithful wanted a better outcome, they supported giving Welch another chance and the athletic council awarded him a second one-year contract. He left to practice law and returned in late summer for the start of football season.

Gus started the 1920 season with 13 lettermen and a new assistant coach, Hack Applequist, another player from the 1915 team who took time off from his job with the Anaconda Mining Company to help his alma mater. Carl Dietz was apparently unable to assist as he was battling tuberculosis, contracted when he was suffering from influenza in France during the war. The varsity started off the season by winning the annual game against the alumni. As one former player put it, "Bald heads and forward projections have no place in football." But they put up a valiant fight before succumbing to the younger men. Cougars' hopes of defending the honor of the West on

New Year's Day in Pasadena ran high after defeating Gonzaga, Idaho and Montana, but they were dashed when California ran wild 49–0. *The Evergreen* put it this way: "A superior football team, with all the breaks in its favor, was the cause of the downfall of the Cougars." A win over Oregon Agricultural College and a come-from-behind victory over Nebraska gave Welch and WSC a 5–1 record for the season that, although the best in the Pacific Northwest, was not very satisfying without the New Year's Day trip. In early December, *The Evergreen* editorialized that, contrary to a common misunderstanding on the part of the student body, Gus Welch was not yet under contract for the 1921 football season. It also opined that other colleges were out to hire him and that WSC should sign him when he returned from Oklahoma for a short visit before Christmas. While away from Pullman, he kept his hand in as a player, so to speak, by playing quarterback for Jim Thorpe's Canton Bulldogs in a big game against the Buffalo All-Americans in New York City.

At the end of spring practice, *The Evergreen* thought, with eleven lettermen and Gus Welch returning, that WSC should contend for the conference title in the fall. In the meantime, Gus was busy managing the national Indian conference that summer. He may have rubbed shoulders with an earlier Carlislian who was involved in the event, Frank Cayou. Returning to Pullman in the fall, Gus was ready for a great season.

During training camp, Welch announced that he, Athletic Director J. Fred "Doc" Bohler, and Applequist would be conducting a couple of sessions for the public in the rules and formations used in football. These scrimmages did not turn out as expected. Gus was not pleased with the varsity's performance in a 31–7 pre-season warm up but hoped it would serve as a wake up call for complacent players. Decisive victories over Gonzaga and Idaho gave reason for optimism, but a loss to Cal once again dashed hopes for a New Year's Day game in Pasadena. Completing the remainder of the schedule with only a tie with Oregon gave the Cougars a chance for an invitation to a December 26 game against Centre College in San Diego. They needed to win a play-off game of sorts against Southern California at Pasadena to get the invitation. USC prevailed 28–7 in a game marred by fumbles. Gus's third season at 4–2–1 wasn't terribly satisfying. The editor of *The Evergreen*, tired of annual speculation as to who would coach the team the upcoming year, recommended that the administration sign Welch to a three to five year contract. Just before football season started, the Pacific Coast Conference announced it would enforce rules that disallow seasonal coaches for athletic teams effective immediately. Contracting coaches for a season at a time had been WSC's habit, so Gus was assigned "instruction in gymnasium work" to occupy him outside football season.

The 1922 Cougars went 2–5–0, winning the first two games and losing all the rest. Those five losses included a 61–0 shellacking by Cal and a 41–3 whipping by USC. It was not a happy time. Not surprisingly, Gus resigned on December 23. The factors affecting his decision were surely the losing season coupled with poor prospects for better results the next year, being forced by the conference to remain in Pullman the entire academic year, and his upcoming marriage. Whatever the reason for his resignation, Gus's coaching career was roughly parallel to that of Lone Star Dietz. WSC was the first college head coaching job for both as well as the last major college head coaching position both held in their long careers. Gus did not have the satisfaction of competing on New Year's Day or in the NFL or have a Hall-of-Fame-worthy coaching career, but he was making a name for himself with the trick plays he liked to run. WSC hadn't seen enough of the Carlisle System so searched for another of Warner's Indian proteges to replace him.

Gus married Julia Josephine Carter, daughter of long-time congressman Charles David Carter. The Carters were Cherokee-Chickasaws from Boggy Depot, Oklahoma, but had been in

Washington, DC so long that it had become their home. That year, 1923, he also took the athletic director position at little Randolph-Macon College in Ashland, Virginia, near Richmond. Although only one of his football teams at that institution won two games during his six-year tenure and half won no games at all, he considered his time at Randolph-Macon as being among the happiest years of his life because of the caliber of the young men on that campus. But football wasn't the only sport Gus coached at R-MC.

In 1969 Welch wrote about introducing lacrosse to Randolph-Macon and the South:

> We started Lacrosse, in the south, at R. M. C., and held our own with the best teams in the north. We had no money for our Lacrosse equipment but when I made it known to Mr. Lalle, who owned the only Lacrosse factory, at that time, that I was trying to start Lacrosse in the South, he very generously sent us sticks, and we made the rest of the equipment. Our student body at that time numbered around 225. Some of my happiest days were the six years spent at R. M. C., and I never had finer men at any College where I coached.

In 1929, Gus's last year at Randolph-Macon and just before the start of the Great Depression, he and Julia used their life savings to buy about 500 acres of land in the Blue Ridge Mountains in Bedford County, Virginia, on Apple Orchard Mountain near Natural Bridge. They set up a boys' camp named in honor of Gus's maternal grandfather, Kewanzee, and operated it for 30 years. They had no children but adopted their niece, Serena, and raised her as their own. Serena, the camp boys, and the boys Gus coached were their children.

Welch's next coaching stop was as an assistant football coach at the University of Virginia where he also coached lacrosse. Gus and Jim Thorpe both applied for the open Dickinson College coaching job in 1931, but neither got it. In 1933 the

Athletic Director position at Haskell Institute opened up when Lone Star Dietz left to lead the Boston NFL team. Unfortunately for Gus, then 40, the problems that had plagued Dietz during his last year at Haskell remained. The country remained in the depression and government funding for the school's athletic program also remained low. His contract would have allowed him to stay longer, but reducing Haskell's status essentially to that of a high school created a situation in which the teams could not compete with their traditional opponents. The once-proud Haskell football program was no longer in existence by decade's end. After his stint in Lawrence, Kansas, Gus took a two-year hiatus from sports.

In 1937, Gus got a job closer to home when he accepted the position of director of physical education and athletics as well as head football coach at "victory-starved" American University in Washington, DC. Welch's signing ceremony attracted much media attention but little attention from football players. His AU teams were always playing shorthanded due to few people turning out to play the game. Injuries were catastrophic because he had almost no bench. By early November, things got so bad that he threatened to use a co-ed to kick extra points, should the Eagles score any touchdowns against the Randolph-Macon Yellow Jackets. The season ended with an 0–7–1 record. Only four veterans returned for the 1938 season; the results were better, but only slightly, as the team finished 1–4–0. So few people turned out for the team that pundits accused Gus of dressing cheerleaders and other non-players in uniforms to trick the opposition into thinking he had a larger team. On December 3, Chancellor Gray wrote Welch to inform him that his contract would not be renewed because "...conditions in the University, financial and otherwise, will make impossible a renewal of your contract..." This wasn't the only bad news he got from Washington.

The National Park Service, in a government move only a little less egregious than the recent Supreme Court Kelo decision, planned to extend the Blue Ridge Parkway through Camp Kewanzee. Gus fought the taking of his land through the use of eminent domain in the courts and, after a long, hard fight, lost. The government offered him just $14 an acre for the land they were taking, far less than he paid for it. He did get one concession out of the government. The planned path for the roadway was through an ancient poplar tree. The government rerouted the road a bit to save the tree after Welch protested, but that was about the only concession it would make. When all legal means had been exhausted, Gus said, "The white man has been taking land from the Indian for so long that it has become a habit with him. There's nothing an Indian can do about changing the white man's habits."

From 1942 to 1945, Welch coached at Georgetown Prep School, the nation's oldest Jesuit school, where he went 10–21. The 4–3 1942 team was his best at Prep. During World War II, Gus also served as athletic director for the Alexandria Naval Torpedo Station and organized teams for the Torps in a variety of sports at the recreational level. He also trained soldiers in the Army's specialized training program conducted at Georgetown University during the war. After the war, he taught physical education at Lyndon Hill Junior High School in Prince Georges County, Maryland, adjacent to Washington, DC. In the early 1950s, Gus and Julia bought an 80-acre farm near the Peaks of the Otter in the Blue Ridge Mountains and made it their home. Gus worked with young athletes and ran Camp Kewanzee until his head smashed into the windshield in a car wreck. His vision in later years was diminished by the detached retina which may have been caused by that accident. They sold the camp, which was used as a Methodist Boys Camp for a number of years. Ruins are still visible to hikers interested in seeing the route of the original Appalachian Trail which passed through the camp.

In 1962 Gus spoke at the groundbreaking ceremony for the Professional Football Hall of Fame in Canton, Ohio, as few old-time pros were still alive. Throughout his adult life, he worked for the restoration of Jim Thorpe's Olympic medals, something that did not happen in his lifetime.

He lived to be a little over 76 years old, dying on January 29, 1970. Gus was inducted posthumously into the American Indian Athletic Hall of Fame and the College Football Hall of Fame. The honor he was best known for during his lifetime was the "Brown Derby" award given to the coach telling the tallest tale by the American Football Coaches Association. He won that "honor" five times. The yarn that won him the Brown Derby at the December 1930 meeting of the AFCA, as told by Associated Press Sports Writer Foster Hailey, follows:

> Carlisle was playing Cornell and it was a tough game. Thorpe scored a touchdown against the big red team and the Indians went to defensive play. There was one big guard, 220 pounds, who was laying down on the job. All Gus's urging could not get him to wake up and stop the Cornell plays. Finally it was Cornell's ball on Carlisle's ten yard-line, goal to go. "I was thinkin' hard." said Gus, waving an unlighted cigar. "And I had an idea. I was playin' safety but I called Jim back and went to the line. Then I went over to the referee and I told him 'if you see me slug somebody, it won't be a Cornell man. It will be one of these Indians.' The play came through this big guard. I ran up and there was a big pile up with this guard at the bottom and his face showing on one side. I reached down with my hand flat—like this—I slapped him. The pile heaved and up he came, a nice rosy mark on his cheek. He rushed over and said to the referee: 'Did you see that Cornell slugged me.' The referee laughed and said, 'That's all right. I'll get them the next time.' On the next play this

big bird went through and nailed them for a three-yard loss. On the next play he got a Cornell back for a two-yard loss. On the next play he nailed him three yards behind the line." He and Thorpe worked on the guard for three years with those tactics, Gus said, and won a lot of games. In a game with Pensylvania, Thorpe even bit the big guard in the side to make him play. "After a game with Brown and we were both quitting," Gus continued. "I was talking to this guy and I told him what we had done. He looked at me for a minute and then he said: 'Why, I've said a lot of mean things to those referees. I must write them all a letter and apologize.'" "Here's the brown derby," said Major Frank Cavanaugh, who was presiding.

The Evening Star 2-4-1937

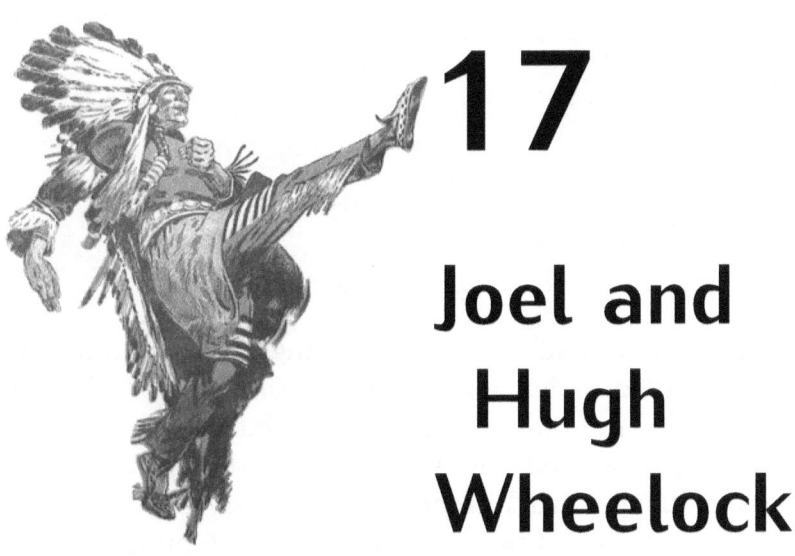

17

Joel and Hugh Wheelock

If the Carlisle Indian School had a first family, it would have been the Wheelocks. Brothers Dennison and James Riley Wheelock were students who, at different times, later held the bandmaster position and made the Carlisle Indian School Band famous. Among other things, Dennison composed two marches named after the Carlisle school. Both Dennison and James attended the Dickinson College Preparatory School after completing their Carlisle studies. After leaving government service, they formed Indian bands of their own and traveled around the country. Dennison set aside his baton and took up

```
Name: Joel Wheelock              Nickname:
  DOB: 10/7/1890                   Height: 5'9"
Weight: 160                          Age: 22
  Tribe: Oneida                    Home: West DePere, WI
Parents: James A. Wheelock, deceased
         Sophia Wheelock, stepmother, deceased
Early Schooling: unknown
Later Schooling: Lebanon Valley College Preparatory School
      Honors: American Indian Sports Hall of Fame, 1971
```

> Name: Hugh J. Wheelock Nickname: Huge
> DOB: 3/2/1891 Height: 5'10"
> Weight: 172 Age: 22
> Tribe: Oneida Home: West DePere, WI
> Parents: James A. Wheelock, deceased
>   Sophia Wheelock, stepmother, deceased
> Early Schooling: unknown

the law, spending much time in Washington, DC. Laurence M. Hauptman relates that many Oneidas today regard Dennison as "an 'apple,' red on the outside and white on the inside."

Sister Ida was quite active in school organizations such as the Susan Longstreth Literary Society. Several other Wheelocks were mentioned prominently in Carlisle publications but were probably cousins. Martin Wheelock comes quickly to mind. But there were also Wheelocks who played football as well as making music with the band—on Carlisle's vaunted varsity. For example, musician James Wheelock led a shop team, but that team didn't play against other schools. However, his younger brothers did.

Joel and Hugh Wheelock were younger brothers of Dennison, James and Ida, children of James A. Wheelock. Why their self-reported birthdates are less than nine months apart is anyone's guess. The May 1, 1896 edition of *The Indian Helper* reported that Sophia Metoxen Wheelock had died recently, leaving James Sr. with several small children to raise. Wheelock Sr. was known to Superintendent Pratt because he had visited Dennison, James and Ida during commencement. Sophia, however, probably wasn't their mother, because she was only eight years older than Dennison. Also, there was a seven-year gap between Ida and Louisa. The older children, Dennison through Ida, must have been from a first wife. He must have remarried and had the younger ones with Sophia. Hugh's enrollment papers list James A. Wheelock as his father and Sophia as his mother. However, Joel's papers list his father as deceased due

Joel Wheelock, 1912
Fred Wardecker

Hugh Wheelock, 1911 *U. S. Army Military History Institute*

to old age and his mother as having died in childbirth. These differences may may been due in part to differences in timing between the boys' enrollments. Their father remarried after the death of Sophia to his third wife, the former Lena Webster, and had children with her. 1905 censuses suggest that he died around that time leaving his older minor children as orphans. His younger minor children remained with their mother, who soon married Martin Wheelock. This lack of a name change for her confuses those who try to decipher the Wheelock family tree. The boys' guardian was their older half-brother, Dennison. At the time they came to Carlisle, each had four living brothers and five living sisters in good health. One brother had died of alcoholism and a sister had died of tuberculosis. Hugh, sometimes called Hughie J. on the census, and Joel enrolled at Carlisle in 1905 and, at times, had an older sibling on campus, sometimes as bandmaster.

Like most children attending Carlisle, their names did not start showing up in school publications immediately upon arrival. Joel's name first appeared in the fall of 1908; Hugh's came later. Most of Joel's early mentions were for athletics, such as leading the "Devils" to victory in a football game played between his shop, the printers, and the blacksmiths. The following January, he played on the school's first inter-scholastic basketball team. In the spring, he earned his letter "C" in track by placing 4th in the 120-yard hurdles at the state intercollegiate track meet held in Harrisburg. He even raked in prizes at the 4th of July track meet held at the school as part of the festivities. Joel won a pair of running shoes for winning the 120-yard high hurdles for boys over 15 years old. He also won two dozen oranges for winning the 220-yard dash and another dozen for his share of the prize for placing 2nd in the 100-yard three-legged race with partner Joseph Loudbear. Lastly, he won a pair of tennis shoes for winning the 220-yard wheelbarrow race with teammates John Goslin and Levi Williams. Joel made quite a haul.

In late September 1909, Hugh Wheelock returned from outing and joined the football squad. Apparently, Joel had been on the squad previously because he ran for a long touchdown a week before in the Hotshots' game against Steelton. That fall Joel got considerable playing time as a halfback, generally at right halfback, and "showed up well" until he twisted his knee in the Bucknell game. He recovered and got into the game with Syracuse, then made the trip to St. Louis to play in that game. A post-season description said that, at 18, he was the youngest man on the team.

Joel wrote a piece entitled "My Trip to Washington" for *The Carlisle Arrow* about traveling to the nation's capitol to play George Washington University. He also was credited as being part of the force that printed *The Arrow* and *The Indian Craftsman* and later for doing part of the composition on the program for that Athletic Banquet program. He played a clarinet solo for his class meeting and was elected captain of the Sophomores' basketball team. He was an all-around man about campus.

To further that image in early January 1910, Joel won first prize in the two-step dance contest with Sara Hoxie as his partner at the Carlisle Indian Band reception. In the spring, he continued to compete in several track events, gaining an occasionally 1st place, and earning his second letter on the cinder path. At commencement, he was awarded his industrial certificate as a compositor, but he remained in school. If anything, he expanded his range of extra-curricular activities to include the Invincible Debating Society without dropping any existing activities. He was made an officer both for his Junior Class (after commencement) and by the Invincibles. He even recited "The American Flag" as a Saturday evening school social.

The following autumn the Wheelock boys were back out on the gridiron; Hugh didn't yet get significant playing time, but Joel did–enough to earn his first letter in football. The *Philadelphia Public Ledger* was quite impressed with his play: "In [Pete] Hauser and [Joel] Wheelock they found backs of the heavy, slashing, plunging type that are as good as any playing in the East today." Although Carlisle failed to win any of its big games in 1910, Joel received frequent kudos for his play. One that stands out was from the *Philadelphia Press:* "Wheelock was another Indian who played a spectacular game. He was able to gain through the line many times, and was strong on defensive play. Wheelock shone particularly at recovering Hauser's long forward passes, standing directly beyond center with his back toward the opponent's goal and by superhuman strength, keeping off Penn men until he had the ball safe in his arms."

In 1911, Joel took time out from his responsibilities as captain of the track team to play in the band, to give clarinet solos to class meetings, to serve as an officer of the Invincibles and of his class, to serve as Lt. Governor of the Model Government afternoon session, and, in the spring, to give his first speech as a Senior, "The Price of Success."

In February, for an assembly of the entire school, Hugh Wheelock performed in, "Brahmin, Jackal and Tiger, a three-act comedy with a good moral, artistic and up to the jungle standard of acting." After spending his summer at home, Hugh returned to school in September, when *The Arrow* reported, "The Seniors are rejoicing over the return of Joel Wheelock, who spent a most profitable vacation in Canada." It failed to mention exactly what he did during that vacation.

Both boys excelled in extra-curricular activities, but neither impressed his vocational instructor. E. K. Miller rated Joel's ability as a compositor as "Fair—Slow" although he considered him a willing worker with excellent behavior. Hugh's instructor was less kind, rating his ability as "not much good as a carpenter."

Hugh and Joel both made the varsity for 1911, arguably Carlisle's strongest team. However, with the return of Jim Thorpe and the maturation of some younger players, neither became a regular starter. Injuries to regulars gave them both opportunities to start, and they made the most of these opportunities. Joel stood out as right halfback, wingback in Warner's scheme, against Georgetown: "Wheelock was especially strong in helping to block opponents upon plays around his end of the line." Both got into the games and played well against the two Big Four teams the Indians defeated that year, Penn and Harvard. *The Carlisle Arrow* bragged, "The Carlisle line out-charged and out-played Harvard in every spot, and it was the Indian forwards who made it possible for the backs to gain. Carlisle was without the service of Captain Burd [sic], our star end, and Newashe was in such condition that he only played a short time, but the Wheelock brothers, Joel and 'Huge,' filled their positions so well that there was no apparent weakness anywhere in the line." Hugh played left tackle in both games, but Joel was needed at right end to stop the Crimson. The *Pittsburg Dispatch* summed up the season in its coverage of the Pitt game: "However, Thorpe wasn't the entire works; there were a few others white men as well as Indians. Newashe and Arcasa were some stars themselves, so were Powell and Wheelock." Both Wheelock brothers got into enough games and played well enough to letter that year.

Hugh must have joined the Standard Debating Society at some time because he and Cora Bresette won a prize, most likely for dancing, at the New Year's Mercer-Standard reception. "Huge" was also active with the YMCA, giving a talk at the April volunteer meeting. Hugh, along with several others, spent the summer of 1912 working at a large brickworks in Mt. Union, Pennsylvania and improving the quality of the town band. Known today for being the home of the biggest Easter grass factory in the U. S., at that time, Mt. Union, located 45 miles southeast of Altoona, claimed to be the world's largest manufactory of silica bricks. Hugh didn't return to his studies that fall. Instead, he got married and continued to work at the brickworks and play in the town band. He may have also played on or coached the town's football team. *The Arrow* did not give any information about his bride. It did report that he visited the school and attended a game at Franklin Field in Philadelphia. Perhaps he married a Carlisle girl.

Joel was even more heavily involved in extra-curricular activities in 1912 than he had been in previous years. He started the new year as the "star" of the Easterners vs. Westerners football game and was elected captain for 1912. A week or so later, he sang "Silent Night" in a quartet accompanied by a lantern light show for a YMCA-YWCA Union meeting. A week after that, he and Joseph Saracino debated successfully the proposition, "That Richard III was a worse monarch than Charles II," at a meeting of the Invincibles. The following week, also with the Invincibles, he delivered the declamation, "The Boss Sees You." And, of course, he competed in track again.

At commencement, Joel Wheelock's name was listed alongside those of other star athletes in the class of 1912, his class, that included future College Football Hall-of-Famers Gus Welch and Jim Thorpe. The Commencement Issue of *The Arrow* include a short poem he wrote:

> **Music is the art of prophets**
>
> When J. W. hath forgot his notes,
> he makes as though a crumb were in
> his throat.

Joel again played football in the fall of 1912 but didn't get as much playing time as before on what was another powerhouse Carlisle team. *The Arrow* summarized his season: "Joel Wheelock is 5 ft. 9 in. tall, weighs 160 pounds, and is 22 years old. He is an Oneida from Wisconsin. Joel won his C by his work in the backfield when he relieved some regulars in important games. All he lacked to make a first-class back was fighting spirit and he showed considerable of this in the latter part of the—season."

Even though he had graduated and was now taking a commercial course, Joel continued his usual dizzying array of extracurricular activities throughout the school year and gained an additional responsibility when he was promoted to captain of a set of troops. *The Arrow* commented a couple of times on his leadership. First: "It seems that everybody takes notice of Captain Wheelock's troop as they march over to the Dining Room." Then later: "If they keep up their good work, Captain Wheelock and his troop will receive some notice at the inaugural parade."

After completing the commercial course at Carlisle, Joel enrolled at the preparatory school for Lebanon Valley College (LVC) in Annville, Pennsylvania where he—big surprise—also played football and ran track for the Dutchmen. Down 10–0 against the Carlisle reserves, he donned a uniform, and according to the *1915 Bizarre*, "His presence fired the entire team with enthusiasm and for the first time during the game they showed what they were capable of doing." He quickly scored two touchdowns to snatch a victory from the Indian second team. Shortly after that the *Manitoba Free Press* (Canadian papers often ran article about Carlisle sports) ran a short critique: "Joe [sic] Wheelock, the famous Carlisle star of other years, is playing end [sic] for Lebanon Valley. Evidently Lebanon Valley plays them to a ripe old age." In a losing effort against Bucknell, he made a gutsy performance. LVC's newspaper, *College News,* reported, "Wheelock, although playing with a twisted ankle, a knee in not any too good shape, and a nose very nearly broken, stuck to his place and played his hardest during the whole time." He not only ran the ball for touchdowns and up the middle for tough yardage, but he was also their kicker. When in Lebanon, Joel probably played in Tyrrell's Military Band when his schedule allowed. He had friends from Carlisle who did, and he surely was acquainted with Mr. Tyrrell.

In the winter and spring, he played basketball and ran track in their respective seasons. Joel visited Carlisle several times during the school year. Could he have left a girlfriend behind? In August, he wrote Superintendent Lipps asking for trainfare from Mt. Union, where he had been working, to Carlisle to assist Pop Warner with the football team. Lipps did not receive the request well: "Athletics are being conducted differently at Carlisle than has been the custom and no inducements whatever can be held out to students who desire to be enrolled or to former students who desire to return to school for the purpose outlined in your letter." He would not be coaching at Carlisle so returned to Annville to play for LVC.

In October 1914, Lebanon Valley College beat Gettysburg for the first time in 20 years due, in great part, to halfback Wheelock's efforts both in smashing through the line and skirting its ends. Joel was named to the All-Pennsylvania backfield at the end of the season. In December, *College News* included Henry L. Wilder's selections for the "All-Time-All-Lebanon Valley team." After just two seasons with the Dutchmen, Joel was named left halfback on the first team of LVC's all-time greats. A couple of months later, he was appointed assistant coach for the Blue and White for the upcoming year.

Joel Wheelock in track uniform
Cumberland County Historical Society, Carlisle, PA

Joel's weekends were filled with football in 1915, assisting with the coaching for Lebanon Valley College on Saturdays and playing for the Altoona Indians on Sundays. He was joined in Altoona by his brother, Hugh. Due to the close proximity between Mt. Union and Altoona, it may have been Hugh that arranged for the two to play alongside several of their old Carlisle teammates. The Wheelock brothers played for Altoona again in 1916.

By June 1917, when they registered for the WWI draft, both Joel and Hugh had found gainful employment, if only for the summer. Joel worked as a tool and die maker at the Bethlehem Steel plant in Lebanon, Pennsylvania and Hugh was a deputy sheriff in Mt. Union but was then single. Either his wife died or his 1912 marriage didn't work out.

Joel served in the army during WWI but, before joining up, served as the head football coach at LVC for the 1917 season. This was quite a feat for a student still in the prep school. According to the *The Quittapahilla 1919:* "The success of the season depended on 'Chief' and he did his best which was excellent. He was unbiased in picking men for their respective positions. He gave them new plays which were very effective, also new tactics on the defence that helped a great deal. 'Chief' had the faculty of bawling you out when you didn't do the right thing, but that only made you fight the harder. On the whole he was a good coach and deserves praise for developing such a fine squad out of so many raw recruits, for we must remember that only a few of our last year's Varsity men came back this year." The school's yearbook recorded 1917 as a 3–4 season but *cfbdatawarehouse.com* includes two more games, a forfeit by Temple and a 73–0 thrashing of Millersburg, giving Wheelock a 5–4 record for his only year as a head coach.

Joel Wheelock making music *Cumberland County Historical Society, Carlisle, PA*

It is not known what Hugh did during that time period, although he did likely serve because he was later a member of the VFW. After the war, Joel organized an All-Indian band which toured widely. Musicians in his large band included former Carlisle students, one of whom was James Garvie. His grandson, Jay Garvie, has a large photograph in which his grandfather is sitting in the front row. Wheelock is dressed in Oneida regalia including a war bonnet. A photo album recently donated to the Cumberland County Historical Society by William Winneshiek's granddaughter includes several individual photographs taken of Wheelock's band members while the band was in Cincinnati in 1929. The musicians are wearing their tribal regalia just as they did when performing.

The 1920 census lists Hugh as divorced, living in Lewistown, Pennsylvania and working as a helper in an ice plant. The 1925 Oneida rolls listed both brothers as being married. In 1930, Hugh, 36, was still living in Lewistown but was then working as a laborer at the steel works. His then wife, Annie Halbert, 49, was a white woman originally from Virginia. He was 19 when first married and she had been 22. If these ages were within a few years of being correct, Annie would not have been Hugh's first wife.

Joel died in Oneida, New York on February 18, 1932. It is not clear if he was visiting family or on a concert tour with a band. He was survived by his wife.

"Chief" Wheelock, Hugh, was well-known in western Pennsylvania for playing bass and tenor drums in various bands including the Tyrone Division (of the Pennsylvania Railroad) band and his brother Joel's all-Indian band, the Veterans Of Foreign Wars Band and the Methodist Church orchestra. He traveled with the J. E. Eshchew Rodeo Indian Band during the 1939–40 season. He worked as a bricklayer's helper at the Standard Steel Works in Burnham for his day job.

Hugh Wheelock died in November 1943, in Lewistown, Pennsylvania, a week after having a gangrenous appendix removed. He was recovering well and was expected to be discharged from the hospital when he was stricken fatally. His cause of death was listed as coronary occlusion.

The Wheelocks were the family who arguably best represented the things that made the Carlisle Indian School famous: its band and its football team. Other band members, such as James Garvie and William Winneshiek, played football on shop or band teams, or in Winneshiek's case, the NFL, but didn't make the varsity starting line-up. The Wheelocks were unique in that regard.

18

Martin Wheelock

Martin Frederick Wheelock was probably a cousin of the Wheelock musicians, who figured so prominently in Carlisle Indian School life. Martin's father was a Civil War veteran having served in the 3rd Wisconsin Volunteers and his mother died when he was about five years old. Martin arrived at Carlisle with a group of Oneidas led by Peter Powlas on September 20, 1890, when he was about 16 years old. Three years later, when Superintendent Pratt relented and allowed the boys to play football against other schools, Martin Wheelock was ready to compete.

```
Name: Martin Frederick Wheelock      Nickname:
 DOB: circa 1874                     Height: 6'2 1/2"
Weight: 200                          Age: 25
 Tribe: Oneida                       Home: Green Bay Agency
Parents: Abram Wheelock
         Mary Ann Wheelock, deceased
Early Schooling: unknown
       Honors: Walter Camp All America 2nd team, 1899 & 1901
```

Martin Wheelock (lower right); *U. S. Army Military History Institute*

By 1896, the team and its players were getting positive press. In *Harper's Weekly,* Caspar Whitney raved, "There is not a stronger nor heavier line in the country than that of the Indians, the centre and guards, Wheelock and B. Pierce, particularly being well-nigh impregnable." By September 1897, the school newspaper considered him one of the team's "big guns" and expressed concern that his ankle sprain was not serious. Apparently it wasn't because in October he received a hero's welcome for playing well in a losing effort against a powerful opponent:

> On Monday morning after breakfast, the football team, who returned the evening before from the Yale game which was played at New York last Saturday, was treated to a free ride across the parade, in the large four horse herdic, drawn by the entire battalion. Capt. Pierce, Frank Cayou, Frank Hudson, and Martin Wheelock occupied the small phaeton drawn by boys, and went in advance of the others. The band played lively marches, as

handkerchiefs waved and mouths shouted. The demonstration was a great surprise to all making a unique scene for such an early morning hour. The school is proud of the record made for clean playing, and were gratified that the boys scored.

In November, Martin was injured in a game played in New York City against Brown University. Apparently the idea of taking a then new technology to diagnose an Indian was newsworthy as a press account of the incident was circulated nationally:

USES "X RAY" ON AN INDIAN.
Right Tackle of Carlisle Football Eleven Examined for Injuries.

Martin Wheelock, right tackle of the Carlisle, football eleven, a big Indian, six feet high, became acquainted with the latest acquisition to the white man's science, the X-ray, in the J. Hood Wright Memorial Hospital at New York City.

During the game with Brown, Wheelock had plunged headlong into a mass play directed against him. He tried to rise, but his right shoulder prevented. It was decided to try the X-ray on Wheelock, to see the exact injury done to his shoulder.

Wheelock was deeply interested in the performance. The bones in his hand were shown him, and he was delighted. Then the ray was turned on his injured shoulder, and it was plainly seen he had suffered a fracture. The physicians declared that the man was the finest specimen of humanity they had ever seen.

The hospital authorities believe that Wheelock will be able to play again during the present season.

With only two weeks left in Carlisle's season, the report was overly optimistic that he would be back in action that year.

But, he was able to continue his studies and complete the school year.

After vacationing at home in Wisconsin that summer, Martin returned, undaunted, to play again in 1898 and again helped to establish Carlisle's reputation. At season's end when Frank Hudson declined re-election as captain, Wheelock accepted the honor. Earlier that month he had been elected President of the Invincible Debating Society, an organization in which he participated actively the rest of his time at Carlisle. He "maintained the dignity befitting his office, and rendered wise decisions."

In May, Martin accepted another challenge as reported by *The Indian Helper:*

> Captain Martin Wheelock of the football team has been detailed as captain for the small boys' company, and assistant to Mrs. Given. While the football management may try his metal, his position as captain of the small boys will try his manhood, and for that reason is a position to be sought for and to hold if possible. The Man-on-the-band-stand wishes him success.

1899 was Pop Warner's first year at Carlisle. Perhaps it was his idea or maybe it was Captain Wheelock's to hold light practices in cool August evenings to prepare football candidates who happened to be on campus for the season. Whether it was Warner's coaching, the Carlisle players' maturing or, more likely, both, the Indians posted their best season to date. Martin's leadership surely contributed to the team's success. The team's two losses were to Harvard and Princeton. Some thought Carlisle would have defeated Harvard, had Martin been able to play. He was injured in the first half and carried off the field on a stretcher. Examined at the hospital, he was not seriously enough injured to be admitted. Walter Camp placed him on his All America second team for his efforts throughout the season.

In March, Martin Wheelock took on another adult task when he was a pallbearer for Miss Bessie Barclay, a teacher who succumbed to "rheumatic and stomach trouble." He reprised that role in an even sadder situation in May at the funeral for Paul, the ten-month-old son of band director Dennison Wheelock and his wife, Louise. Perhaps needing a break from sadness, he took a short vacation at a resort in the mountains near Pen Mar, Maryland, after which he returned to school ready for action.

Ed Rogers captained the 1900 team, and Martin Wheelock was still fighting in the trenches. He also did most of the punting, kicking off, and goal kicking that year. Initially Hawley Pierce was to captain the 1901 team but complaints regarding eligibility were raised. *The Fort Wayne News* complained, "Hawley Pierce, captain of the Carlisle Indian team, has held that office for several years, there being no limit as to the time a man may play on the team of reformed scalpers." It's not clear if such criticisms, offers to play professionally or injury were the source of complaints against Pierce, but Martin Wheelock was selected to captain the Indians again.

That season had to have been difficult for Wheelock because he and Jimmie Johnson were the only regular starters who returned from the previous year. Big things were expected from Nelson Hare and Charles Dillon because they had some experience. This was Carlisle's last losing season until the decline that began after the 1914 congressional inquiry. But Martin Wheelock still played his hardest and was again rewarded by Walter Camp. As in 1899, he was placed on Camp's All America second team.

At his commencement in February for the Class of 1902, Martin was asked to give one of the addresses. The subject of the talk was "The Indian as an Athlete." In his talk, Wheelock said:

The records of colonial times show that he [the Indian] is a born athlete. His very mode of living as a hunter and a warrior, develop his reasoning power, enabling him to plan his campaigns skillfully. The only thing that he lacked for many years has been a knowledge of the real cause of his loss of strength. The Indian youth does not differ much from his white brother in his way of displaying energy and spirit. He had games of his own in which he took as much interest as the pale faces do in their modern sports. Since he has been taken away from his favorite hunting grounds and placed in the remote corners of the country called reservations, he seems to have lost his vigorous manhood. Why is this? Because he has been thrust back into the infant's cradle and bound with limits as a child is bound with clothes when put to sleep. It has caused him to neglect his physical development until he has lost nearly all the energy he displayed before the right of self-guidance was taken from him....

Since being placed in schools he has been obliged to come into close contact with many classes of people. In recent years, the Indian has been competing with his new friends in sports. When he first played the scientific games his greatest hindrance was his inexperience, yet he went into the contest with the determination to win....

Four years did he struggle having had very little instruction, but for the last three years a skillful architect [Warner] has helped him to lay out the same kind of plans as his pale faced brothers have for their athletic foundations. Good fortune befell the Red Man when he secured the services of one who not only presented the usual plans but who improved upon them....

The Indian is repeating the feats of his ancestors on the race track and has made himself famous as a runner. Not only that but he has made athletic science his warpath thereby making the college world dread him as did their forefathers in old colonial days.

Martin did not return to the reservation after graduating: he stayed at Carlisle for another football season. The 1902 season was difficult for him as he was laid up much of the time with pleurisy. However, when the faintest opportunity to play presented itself, he was out on the field. That he played at all in the Cornell game is a story of valor that is told best in an article by Pop Warner, excerpts of which are included at the end of this chapter. Walter Camp didn't award Wheelock even third team All America honors this year. *The Philadelphia Inquirer's* Nathan F. Stauffer explained his reasons for downgrading Wheelock when making his picks:

> There are three strong candidates for centre position, Holt for several years Yale's pivotal man; Wheelock, the Indian chieftain, and McCabe, the Pennsylvanian. Holt, by his steadiness and his great defensive power, has the place, although the Indian pressed him closely for the honor. The Cornell and Harvard teams gave Wheelock a great deal of credit for stopping many of their attacks. His inability to last a whole game, however, places him second.

If Stauffer had had any idea of the condition in which Wheelock was playing, he would have awarded the Indian stalwart something higher than second team accolades.

Martin left Carlisle but didn't abandon football; he joined the 1903 Haskell Institute team in Lawrence, Kansas. Haskell's critics complained about Carlisle players continuing their careers by playing there after exhausting their eligibility at Carlisle. Of course, eligibility rules were just evolving at that time. So, he anchored Haskell's line at left tackle for a year before finishing his college football career.

Now that he was well over a quarter century old, it was time for Martin to put aside the things of childhood and focus on serious pursuits. So, he returned to Wisconsin to farm. On October 18, 1905, he married Lena E. Webster, Oneida, also a former Carlisle student, and they began family life together. Lena was the third wife, and widow, of James A. Wheelock, father of the famous musicians. Tracing her life was difficult due to, among other things, her being listed as Ellen Wheelock on some censuses while she was married to James. They farmed on government land at first and raised Lena's two children, in addition to having four together. Martin also practiced the blacksmith trade he learned at Carlisle and eventually farmed his own land. Family legend has it that he played on the independent teams in Green Bay that preceded the formation of the Packers. Already in his 30s, he probably didn't play semi-pro or independent football for very many years.

In 1916, likely as a reaction to the raids conducted by Pancho Villa across the border into the U. S. and the general suspicion of Mexico at the time, Martin joined other former Carlisle and Haskell students in forming a company of soldiers to defend the country from an invasion through the border with Mexico. Six months later, the Zimmerman telegram was intercepted, and Germany's offer to provide Mexico with arms to be used in taking back their former territory was thwarted. So, the offer was not as outlandish as it sounds almost 100 years later.

Martin Wheelock died in May 1937 at age 65. Some years after he had played his last football game, his former coach paid his former lineman a great compliment. In 1913, Pop Warner selected his all-time best Indian players. He chose Wheelock and Wauseka as two members of the team, saying, "Both tackles were magnificent specimens of manhood, and used their brains to advantage." Warner also talked of Wheelock's bravery two decades later.

Captain Leadership

In 1924 J. P. Glass and George Byrnes interviewed Pop Warner for a syndicated column that was distributed nationally by the North American Newspaper Alliance (NANA). In this interview, Warner told of the heroic efforts in 1902 of several past, present and future Carlisle captains: Martin Wheelock, Antonio Lubo, Charles Williams, James Johnson and Albert Exendine, in a big game with Warner's alma mater. This is the story in Warner's own words:

Two men who were dallying with death and should have been in hospital; a third who would have looked well in an invalid's chair; two pieces of leather, which, joined together, closely resembled a puttee; and, finally, a brace of aluminum plate that resembled nothing so much as the rubbing portion of a washboard—these were the chief factors in making possible a strategy that decided one of the most sensational football battles I ever saw.

It was way back in 1902, during my first term of coaching the famous Carlisle Indian team. In those days our annual game with Cornell was one of the biggest events of the season, notwithstanding that during the course of the hectic schedule which the Indians always played we were apt to engage almost every important team in the country. We set a lot of store on winning from the Ithacans, but this year, as the game approached, it looked as if victory was going to be impossible. In earlier games hard luck gave us a kick that sent us reeling, and Saturday, October 18, the day set for our engagement with Cornell, didn't promise to be an occasion for jubilation....

To begin with, my brother Bill had been a big help. Bill was guard at Cornell and one of the best in the game. This year he was captain of the team and mighty anxious to have it make a good showing. Cornell didn't start its training season until September 15 while the Indians got into action on September 1....

I could picture the rest of my brother's thoughts. He stood over six-feet-one himself and weighed 220 pounds. The Cornell center, Davitt, and the left guard, Hunt, were built in the same proportions. Nobody ever had punctured the Ithacans' lines while those lads were holding forth, but they had done a lot of damage to the other fellows' defense.

So I knew Bill was going back to Cornell to tell his comrades just what he was thinking then: namely, that the Ithacans must keep possession of the ball when they met us a month later and batter our line to pieces. And I had a hunch that the formation he would have in mind for accomplishing this purpose would be their famous guards-back play. In that, you know, one guard got back of the other to carry the ball, with the whole backfield in tandem formation helping them to plow through the enemy's line....

Just then everything went wrong. First, after the initial game of the season, Wheelock, our star left tackle, probably the best man in the position that year and the leading drop and place kicker who did all our booting, was taken sick and sent to the school infirmary. He was thought to have pneumonia, but that was averted and then he had a recurrence of pleurisy from which he had suffered the previous year. His pain was so great that he couldn't bear even to have the bedclothes touch him, and the hospital attendants had to rig up a special apparatus that suspended his sheet above him an inch away that they protected him without coming in contact with his body.

Second, Exendine, our great right end, wrenched his ankle so badly in a succeeding game he could scarcely run.

Third, Schouchuk, who played at center and was as good as there was in the country, was so badly hurt the week before the Cornell game he had to be placed in the hospital.

There I was, with the big battle less than a week away, with a line that my brother Bill had called only "pretty good" completely shot to pieces. What could I do? Exendine partly solved my troubles. He insisted he would play despite his bad ankle. It was out of the question for him to take his end assignment. We bound his crippled limb with tape so tightly that he couldn't move his foot and shifted him to right tackle, sending Whitely, who played the position regularly, to fill the left tackle place vacated by Wheelock's illness.

But I still had no center and no right end. I could throw in a center that might fill Schouchuk's shoes acceptably, but I could not replace Wheelock, whose kicking would be sadly missed. He was my best offensive weapon, having made at least one field goal in every game he played.

It was at this time that I was given two demonstrations of the red man's courage which fully upheld all the legends of their stoical indifference to suffering ever told. In 1901, when he played the Navy at Annapolis, Lubo, our left tackle, a thin, wiry fellow, who made up in bravery and football brains what he lacked in size—he only weighed 160 pounds—had his left wrist smashed and cut open. The injury was slow to heal. We didn't tell him at the time, but the school physician thought he had a tubercular infection. The superintendent of the academy positively refused to let him play any more football. His arm was placed in a sling and he was instructed to indulge in no exercise except walking, and even then he must conserve his strength. Lubo couldn't play, but there was nothing to prevent his watching his team-mates during practice.

Throughout my brother Bill's sojourn, he trudged up and down the field, observing everything that was done, listening to everything that was said. He was a true Indian, talking little but retaining every scrap of information that came his way, although in this case it could be of no value to him.

He was really a pathetic figure. In form, he would have been a tower of strength for us, for despite his size he could hold his own against the huskiest of opponents. But he had been carrying his arm in the sling for a year now and it was shriveled away almost to mere bone.

All the time, though, he was hoping against hope that luck would turn his way. At the start of the season, he applied for permission to play, but the superintendent's only reply was an order to me. 'Don't even give him a uniform,' he said. 'His health means more to the school than winning a couple of football games.' Nevertheless he continued his appeals. And when the injury to Schouchuk capped the climax of our troubles he decided to make one more try.

Four nights preceding the Cornell game a knock brought me to my door. There stood Lubo. 'Coach,' he said without any preliminary, 'I'd give anything if I could play against Cornell. I know how Schouchuk and Wheelock can't play. I'd like to go up there for you and for Carlisle.'

I brought him inside and explained as gently as I could that it wasn't possible. 'Not with that arm,' I said. 'But that wouldn't make any difference,' he protested. 'I've been exercising and have kept in good shape in every other way. Besides, coach, I think I can do as much with my right arm as with two arms. I can protect my left so it won't get hurt.'

I asked where he thought he could play.

'Tackle, in Wheelock's place.'

'No. That's out of the question. A tackle must have both arms.'

'Well, then, center.'

'No, a center must use both hands to pass the ball.'

'Well,' he declared. 'I know I could play somewhere on the team.'

I had to tell him it was impossible, although I appreciated his spirit. But when he left, after two hours of argument, he insisted. 'Somehow, I'm going to play.'

As to when he saw the superintendent I don't know, for it was half past ten o'clock when he left my house. But the next morning the chief telephoned me to come to his office. Lubo had been to see him again, he said, and had asked to be allowed to face Cornell.

'I told him, no,' he added, 'but the boy said he must play—he owed it to Carlisle. He's so fine I'm inclined to be lenient, if you and the doctor think it is possible.'

I didn't because I believed Lubo would be performing merely on his ambition. But when the physician told me that, except for his left arm, the Indian was in fine condition, I began to change my mind. We could at least let him practice a bit. I told him so the next day, which was the Wednesday preceding the date at Ithaca on Saturday.

He was on hand promptly. It didn't take him long to convince me that, handicapped though he was, he was better than any substitute I could use. If only he hadn't had that withered arm. That night he came around to see me again. 'Coach,' he said, 'there must be some way to fix my arm.'

I thought hard. I've always been handy at repairing injured players and finally hit on a scheme. I dug up two strips of leather. These I sewed around his bad wrist, extending from the tips of his finger to his elbow. We stuffed the inside with cotton and bound the whole in tape. It seemed to offer adequate protection.

'Lubo, it looks like you were going to get into that game,' I said.

He just stood there smiling and saying over and over, 'Thank you, Coach, thank you.'

I don't mind telling you I felt pretty weepy.

Of course Lubo couldn't play end or tackle. I decided to switch Beaver, the right guard, who had done some playing at end, to Exendine's old position and use Lubo in his place. News of this decision soon got me into trouble. All the cripples around the place asked for harness that would enable them to play. But the biggest shock I got came when [Martin] Wheelock showed up at my house. He had been in the infirmary three weeks but in the last few days had been allowed out in the air a bit. Still he was in such pain he couldn't bear to have any one lay a hand on him.

Martin Wheelock
*Cumberland County Historical Society
Carlisle, PA*

Antonio Lubo
U. S. Army Military History Institute

'Now look here, Coach,' he said, 'if you can fix Lubo you can fix me. There's nothing wrong with my arms or legs; all I've got is pleurisy.'

I didn't argue with him. Arguments didn't seem to count much with those Indians. We went up to the engineering school and asked for help. Someone dug up two wide sheets of aluminum, resembling, as I said before, the metal portion of a washboard.

'That's the stuff!' said Wheelock. 'First I'll put on a heavy shirt. Then you can fix these on me, one in front and one in back. Bind them with tape, so they won't slip. Put my jersey on over all and I'll be absolutely all right.'

There was left but one vacancy on the team. That was center. Fortunately this would be the one position where Wheelock would suffer a minimum of pain, although he was bound to have plenty of it no matter where he was placed. I assigned him to it.

[Warner then discussed some strategy and the events of the game's first half that put Cornell ahead, 6-5.]

The second half got under way with Cornell rushing us off our feet. And yet, just when it seemed that she was about to score, an Indian would appear from nowhere and throw the man carrying the ball for a loss on third down. Mostly it was Lubo and Wheelock. How Lubo did it with his lame arm I don't know. And time after time Wheelock winced in pain as he came in contact with his opponents. But always they are on the job diving over or under interference and bringing down the man with the ball. Williams backed up both. Johnson was wonderful in running back punts. The lame Exendine, at tackle, more than held his own. Well into the second half we got a break which repaid our cripples for their devotion to the team. Williams, standing on Carlisle's 30-yard line, delivered the best punt of the day. It was a wonderful kick that carried the ball a full 50 yards before it touched on Cornell's 30-yard line.

Brewster, the Cornell quarter [back], apparently figured that the ball would roll clear to the line. He decided to let it pass, so that it could he brought out again on the 20-yard line. But after one high bound, the ball took a backward instead of forward leap, and struck the leg of Tydeman, right end, who had run back to give Brewster interference. This made a free ball of it and Bradley, Carlisle right end, who had charged down the field, grabbed it.

It was Carlisle's ball on Cornell's 13-yard line, and Quarterback Johnson immediately proceeded to the most brilliant strategy of the game. This consisted in using the same formation, with variations, four times in succession....[Warner then described an early incarnation of his single-wingback formation which was designed to protect his crippled players. Johnson's brilliant strategy used fakes, deception and speed to confuse the defense as to where the ball was going and who was carrying it. On the fourth play of the series, Willliams dove over the middle of the line for the go ahead touchdown.]

Lubo was able to continue after this play, but Wheelock's outraged body could endure no more. He fell in an agony of pain and had to be taken from the field. This necessitated the only substitution of the game. We missed the goal after touchdown and the score was Carlisle 10; Cornell, 6.

But the game was won. Williams played center on defense and we held the Ithacans until the whistle blew. Was Lubo happy? Was he! And that reminds me. After the game that night I talked again with Bill, my brother.

'How did Lubo impress you, Bill?' I asked.

'Say, Glenn, was that fellow in uniform when I was down at Carlisle?'

'No, he's the one who followed you around with his arm in a sling watching you at practice.'

'Well, if that fellow can play like that when he's crippled,' replied Bill, 'I'd hate to tackle him when he was in good condition.'

In view of the fact that Bill was placed on the All-American that year by Walter Camp and all the other critics, his performance in the Carlisle game being praised particularly, I consider he paid Lubo a fine tribute. But the boy deserved everything good that could be said about him.

And Wheelock, too. The strategy by which Johnson won the game was fine; but never so wonderful as the splendid feat of these two boys in playing that day. When you get down to facts, it was their devotion to their school and their team that beat Cornell. There's a lesson in it for every lad that aspires to play the game.

Glenn Warner and the story he tells illustrated by a diagram prepared by George Byrnes of the Colgate football department. Key to the Play: A (Johnson, Carlisle quarter) received ball from center and, faking end run, sped to right. B (Williams, Carlisle fullback) who on previous formations had faked line plunge, took ball from Johnson. C (Carlisle right halfback) and D (Carlisle left halfback) ran to right as though to protect A (Quarterback Johnson). With latter drawing attention of Cornell backs, B (Williams) made flying dive over Cornell line, just too quick for a Cornell back to stop him, and scored the winning touchdown.

19

Charles Williams

Charles V. Williams and his sister, Priscilla, enrolled at Carlisle Indian Industrial School sometime in the 1890s, after their mother died, but little is known about their early time there. Charles went out for football in 1900 but received no mention in the school newspaper. He must have been pretty far down the depth chart at that time. The next year, 1901, things changed. The football team was lacking big men for the line that year and Warner was trying everything to put together a winning combination. To illustrate the nearly desperate situation at Carlisle, a single pre-season

Name: Charles V. Williams	Nickname: Bull
DOB: 1880	Height: 5' 11"
Weight: 176	Age: 20
Tribe: Stockbridge	Home: Shawano County, WI
Parents: Andrew Williams	
Emma Williams, deceased	
Early Schooling: unknown	
Later Schooling: Northwestern University	
Sherman Institute	

issue of *The Red Man and Helper* included three mentions of filling holes in the lineup with Charles Williams:

"Williams, Flores and Lubo are so far the best tackles and their work has been very satisfactory.

"Flores is rather light and inexperienced, but if he continues to play as he has, he will secure a place on the team and allow the removal of Williams to full-back where he will greatly strengthen the team.

"Palmer, who was rather counted upon to fill the position of full-back, has fallen off in his work, and it may be that Williams will be taken from tackle and placed at full-back."

Charles V. Williams
Fred Wardecker

Warner wanted to play Williams at his natural position, fullback, but already by mid-October had injured players and couldn't keep him there: "The Indians were slightly weakened in the second half by the retirement of Wheelock, their giant captain, who wrenched his right knee, his place being taken by Williams, Palmer going in as full-back."

Later in the season Warner was able to move Charles back to fullback and was very pleased with his performance:

...the gains being made mostly by Phillips and Williams, who tore up the Navy line for gains of from 8 to 15 yards at a time...

Williams is proving a good full-back, and is in every play, and a hard man to stop.

> Williams has developed into quite a strong punter since Wheelock's injury, and the team should be fairly strong the remainder of the season in a punting game.
>
> ...Williams put up a star game at full-back, especially on the defense.

The coach wasn't the only one happy with Charles Williams' play. After the season ended, his teammates elected him captain for 1902. That season was a vast improvement over 1901, a rare losing season in the Warner years at Carlisle. The players were more experienced and more filled out, making size less of a problem than in the previous year. Coach Warner and Captain Williams were high on the squad's prospects and weren't disappointed. A press report from Carlisle early in the season shows that Warner expected big things of him: "Captain Charles Williams is from Wisconsin, and he is considered one of the best fullbacks in the country. He weighs 176 pounds, is 5 feet 11 inches tall, 20 years old and has played two seasons." It took some heroics on the parts of several players, including some past and future captains, to upset Cornell and beat Penn, but Carlisle put losing seasons behind them, finishing 8–3. Charley distinguised himself with his good play against Cornell. Warner discusses the Indians' heroics in that game at the end of Martin Wheelock's chapter. Charles Williams received accolades for his leadership and play when jubilant students, who met the team at the train after the victory over Penn, picked him up bodily and carried him around in celebration. Although Walter Camp overlooked him at season's end, others did not. *The Philadelphia Inquirer*'s Nathan F. Stauffer placed him on his All America first team:

> For full-back two men run a close race. They are nearly equal in build and offensive tactics. Both are good kickers, fine line plungers and fast runners, but Williams the

Indian is the strongest defensive back in the country to-day, and it is in that department of the game he excels Graydon, the giant player and star of Harvard. I have seen Williams stop a three-man tandem tackle coming between guard and tackle so quickly and so hard that it knocked two of the three for a complete loss, and this has happened so often the opposing team gave up trying to break the line. I overheard Williams remark to his coach: "I liked it to-day because they opened big holes in our line and I could tackle the backs right away."

And he tackles just as though he were carrying the ball and trying desperately to make first down. So hard, in fact, that I have seen half-backs perceptibly stop running rather than have Williams tackle them.

Charles Williams was not just a jock; he was also heavily involved in other aspects of school life. As a member of the Invincible Debating Society, he played the title role in a scene from "Banishment of Catiline." In another meeting of the society, he and Horton Elm argued their affirmative position well against Antonio Lubo and Albert Exendine in "16–1," a debate over the silver standard. In March 1903, the Seniors elected him class critic.

Charley continued to excel at football, but a new player, Wilson Charles, was emerging as yet another great Indian back. Early in the season they split time at fullback but, to get them both on the field at the same time, Warner shifted Wilson to halfback. In his last regular season game (Carlisle made a post-season trip west to play Utah, Reliance Athletic Association of San Francisco and Sherman Institute in Riverside, California) against previously undefeated Northwestern University, Williams shone. According to an AP reporter, "Half-backs Charles and Sheldon, light but fast as the wind, and full-back Williams circled the ends at will," in Carlisle's 28–0 blowout of the Purple.

After commencement for the Class of 1904, *The Red Man and Helper* marked Charles's departure: "Among the graduates who have gone home is Charles Williams of football notoriety. The team will feel the loss of a valuable man, and his friends at the school will also miss him greatly. Charles is a tower of strength wherever he goes." He may have left Carlisle and the world of big-time football, but it didn't forget him. According to the *Chicago Daily Tribune,* Northwestern University football manager F. O. Smith visited the Stockbridge Reservation and convinced Charles Williams to enroll at Evanston and wear the purple on Saturdays that fall. The newspaper also claimed that several eastern universities also attempted to recruit him. *The Red Man and Helper* reported:

> Ex-Captain Williams, of Carlisle football fame, has entered college at Evanston, Ill. He admonishes all the Carlisle students to try to gain and maintain a good standing. He says: A year of determination is worth just as much to a Carlisle student as to himself at Evanston. 'We should be content wherever we are and work to keep loneliness away.' He sends regards to all and especially to 'Class '04' who are still trying to learn more.

On September 28, after only a warm-up game against Fort Sheridan had been played, the *Tribune* announced that Williams "…did not find the atmosphere of the Evanston institution congenial and preferred to finish his schooling at an Indian school. It is understood he took a train yesterday for Riverside, Cal., where he will enter school. He attended recitations on Thursday, Friday, Monday and Tuesday." The October 20 edition of the *Arrow* reported that Williams was "with Wm. Warner at Riverside, California"—as an assistant coach no doubt. It is believed that Charles played some professional football for three years between 1905 and 1910.

The next that was heard from Williams was that he had joined the Marines. The December 1910 *Red Man* shared that he was, at that time, an officer in the Marine Corps. The following September he wrote from Fort DuPont, Delaware: "I wish the school a continued success in everything, especially football. I am following the work of the team with great interest, and enjoy nothing more than to hear of Carlisle winning from Old Penn or Harvard."

Charles Williams made a career of the Unites States Army, retiring after 30 years with the rank of master sergeant. He either changed branches of the service before arriving at Fort DuPont or *The Red Man* was mistaken about his being in the Marines because they were never stationed at Fort DuPont. The 1938 Stockbridge roll listed him as being alive, single, 59 years of age and 7/8 blood. After retiring from military service, he lived at Morgan Siding, an unincorporated village near Gresham, Wisconsin, and joined the Old Stockbridge Orthodox Presbyterian Church. In 1946 Charles married Abbie Doxtator at Shawano. Abbie died on October 5, 1970. Charles lived to be 93 years old, dying on September 10, 1973.

20

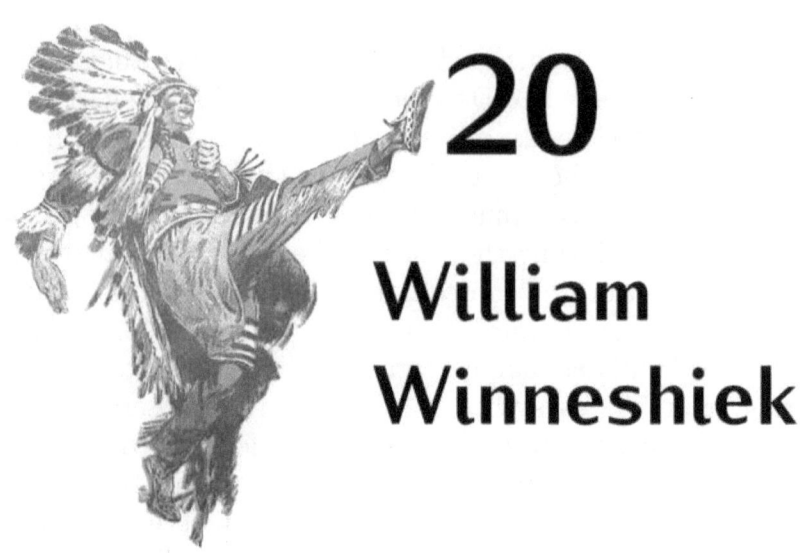

William Winneshiek

Na Hik Sa Wa He Kah

To understand William Winneshiek, we must first know more about his name, his family and his people. Numerous places in Wisconsin, Iowa and Minnesota are named Winneshiek because of his tribe's and his family's numerous moves. As far back as tribal memory reaches, Winneshiek's people lived between present-day Green Bay, Wisconsin and Lake Winnebago. They dominated the western shore of Lake Michigan to the upper peninsula of Michigan in the

---

Name: William Phineas Winneshiek   Nickname: Willie, Bill, Chief
 DOB: 12/24/1895   Height: 5' 8 1/4"
Weight: 150 1/2   Age: 17
 Tribe: Ho-Chunk   Home: Hatfield, WI
Parents: John Winneshiek, Ho Che Kee Way Kah
         Sue Winneshiek, Wah Nauk Ska Wim Kah, deceased
Early Schooling: Tomah Indian Industrial School
                 Sac and Fox Indian School
Later Schooling: Lebanon Valley College

north, to the Mississippi River on the west and as far south as the northwest corner of Illinois. His people spoke a Siouan language, the only people of the Great Lakes to do so. But their culture more closely resembled that of their upper Great Lakes Algonquin neighbors. The people were taller than other American Indians or most Europeans. The French explorer Nicollet described them as brave but lacking in humility, almost to the point of arrogance. They decorated their fringed buckskin clothing with beautiful designs made from porcupine quills, feathers and beads. Both sexes commonly tattooed their bodies.

Winneshiek's people, like some other tribes, are commonly referred to by names given to them by their neighbors. They are often referred to as Winnebago, but that is not what they called themselves. Winnebago comes from a Fox word meaning "people of the stinking water," which was a reference to the algae-rich waters of the Fox River and Lake Winnebago. They call themselves Ho-Chunk, meaning "people of the big voice."

Beginning in the 1640s, the Ho-Chunks started being pressed from the east by their neighbors. First it was from Algonquin refugees and accompanying epidemics that resulted from the Beaver Wars. Later American settlements moving up from Illinois pressed from the south. The Ho-Chunk ceded their land in Wisconsin by 1840 and moved to northeast Iowa. However, many remained behind and refused to move. Over the next half-century they were cast about the Midwest, first to the Crow Wing River in Minnesota, then to Blue Earth County, also in Minnesota. After the Sioux uprising in 1862, in which they played no part, the government removed them to South Dakota with the Nakota (Yankton Sioux). This time they rebelled and scattered to old homes in Iowa, Minnesota and Wisconsin. Some fled down the Missouri River to the Omaha Reservation in Nebraska. In 1865, the government established a 40,000 acres' separate Winnebago Reservation in Nebraska, but many remained in Iowa, Minnesota and Wisconsin. When

Chief Winneshiek
Cumberland County Historical Society, Carlisle, PA

the Lakota raided the Winnebago Reservation in the 1870s and 1880s, many returned to Wisconsin. The government repeatedly sent them back to Nebraska and they repeatedly returned to Wisconsin. Eventually, the government gave up and purchased land for them in Wisconsin. Both parts of the tribes remain today—the Winnebago in Nebraska and the Ho-Chunk in Wisconsin.

The first Winneshiek was an important chief. He became such an important chief that his descendants took his name as their own. Winneshiek is Algonquian (that is, Fox) meaning "a dirty person lying down." His name in the Winnebago or Ho-Chunk language, Wa-kon-ja-googah, means "The Coming Thunder."

Winneshiek was head chief of a Ho-Chunk village at present-day LaCrosse when the Ho-Chunk moved to Iowa. After the move, he was made head chief of the tribe and remained chief of his band. After his death, his brother, Young Winneshiek, and his son, Little Winneshiek, moved back to Wisconsin near present-day Black River Falls. Current-day Winneshieks are descended from these men.

William Winneshiek, a descendant of Little Winneshiek, applied for admission to Carlisle Indian School on June 5, 1911. Most of the information on the application must have come from him because his father, John Winneshiek, was illiterate. Willie's mother, Sue, had died and his father had remarried, but Bill didn't seem to know his stepmother's name. This lack of knowledge was probably due to his being away at school. Bill began his schooling in 1904 at Tomah Indian Industrial School which was located at the Tomah Agency in Wisconsin. After a year there, William transferred to the Sac and Fox Indian School located at Toledo, Iowa. After completing his enrollment at that school in 1907, he spent three months at "Eland Mission," which was probably Bethany Mission operated by the Evangelical Lutheran Church near Eland, Wisconsin. Then he returned to the Sac and Fox school in Iowa, remaining there until it closed in 1911. His absence from his home most of seven years could explain his unfamiliarity with his stepmother.

Shortly after arriving in Carlisle, on June 29, 1911, William received a physical examination and was questioned about his family. He did not know the cause of his mother's death but listed two living brothers and a sister. He had no deceased siblings. His younger siblings attended the mission school at Black River Falls, Wisconsin. His older brother, Frank, had attended Carlisle but his student file can't be found. Due to his own long experience at boarding school and what Frank may have told him about Carlisle, Bill probably adjusted to life there more easily than most.

The Carlisle Arrow first mentioned him in its coverage of the November 17, 1911 meeting of the Standard Literary Society. Although not explicitly stated, one assumes that he had joined the society some time previous to the meeting. He played an instrumental solo, likely on a trombone. The debate topic was "That Aeroplanes will be a benefit in time of war and as a means of transportation."

Winneshiek must have had good writing skills because he was selected as one of the two people from his class to submit papers to a tuberculosis composition contest. Although he didn't win a prize, he demonstrated that he could compete with other students, not only at Carlisle but with those at other Indian schools as well. Along the way, he learned a lot about tuberculosis, which was the primary purpose of the exercise.

He went on his first outing that summer, spending three weeks at the John Rosenberger farm near Wycombe, Pennsylvania. After that he returned to Carlisle for what must have been a quiet year for Bill. His only mention in the school paper that year came in the spring, when he performed a trombone duet with John Arnell for a Standards meeting. According to school records, he spent the summer of 1913 on outing with R. B. Cassidy (probably Ralph Cassady) in Mt. Union, Pennsylvania, working at one of the three brickworks in town. William also played in the Mt. Union Band that summer. His friends, James Garvie and Joel Wheelock, also spent their summers there on outing. Mr. Cassady apparently didn't have room in his house for them, so they lived in the three-story Beers Hotel as did Hugh Wheelock the previous summer. It cannot be by coincidence that all these band boys spent summers in Mt. Union.

The fall of 1913, William Winneshiek must have been active with the Y. M. C. A. because he reported on their activities in the school newspaper. This is something he had not done previously. In January 1914, he represented Room Number 10 in that month's school program and recited McKinley's Dying Prayer. At commencement in April, he received an industrial certificate in baking. Two weeks later, *The Carlisle Arrow* announced, "William Winneshiek left last Saturday for Mount Union, where he will play in the band during the spring and

CIIS Band Trombone Choir, William Winneshiek (right rear) *Cumberland County Historical Society, Carlisle, PA*

summer." His student file reflects that he spent that summer at 19 N. 5th Street in Lebanon, Pennsylvania with George F. Tyrrell. The May 8 *Arrow* reported, "Post cards were received from William Winneshiek, telling of his pleasant surroundings at Lebanon, Pa." Apparently, something had changed. Tyrrell probably gave him the opportunity to play in his band. James Garvie also spent his summer with Tyrrell but, although he had already enrolled at nearby Lebanon Valley College, Joel Wheelock was back in Mt. Union, to make some money, one assumes.

Part of the fallout of the Joint Congressional Inquiry into Carlisle Indian School in early 1914 was the immediate departure of bandmaster Claude Stauffer. The September 11 edition of *The Carlisle Arrow* announced, "Mr. Leo McDonald Will Lead the Band.... Mr. McDonald acted in this capacity last spring, and was so successful in his efforts that he was selected to again conduct the school music." The September 25th edition of the school paper reported that the tailors had made one band leader's uniform and one pair of band uniform pants, presumably for McDonald. It also shared that both the first and second bands were practicing under the direction of Mr. McDonald. Apparently, so many boys were interested in making music that two bands were necessary to accomodate all of them. Because of age differences, the first band could have been for older boys and the second band for younger boys or beginners. The next week readers were informed that band boys were working diligently on classical music for their upcoming concert. On October 8th, the band participated in the Harrisburg Fireman's Parade. The Carlisle Indian School Band was in the second of fourteen divisions. Due to the size of the parade—109 bands and 12,000 firemen—the divisions lined up at different times. The Indians' start time was 12:15 p.m. Mr. McDonald and Grant White, in his full Pawnee regalia, led the band over the 14.5 mile parade route. White executed traditional Pawnee dance steps whenever the band played. The parade ran so long that the last few divisions didn't complete the route. Band members appreciated the crowd's response to their playing and the fine supper they were given after the parade.

As of October 23, Mr. Frank Hollinger was in charge of the band. McDonald's temporary employment had ended, so it seems. A week later, the tailors reported that they had altered the band leader's coat for Mr. Hollinger. On December 2, the band gave its first public performance under the direction of George F. Tyrrell. With no explanation, Tyrrell was in and Hollinger was out.

Tyrrell moved his family to Carlisle Barracks but continued to operate Tyrrell's Military Band in Lebanon, Pennsylvania in his spare time. As alluded to earlier, some Carlisle students, most recently James Garvie and William Winneshiek, also played in that band. George Tyrrell definitely had the credentials to lead the school band. Born in England, he played the cornet for Queen Victoria when he was just six years old. After coming to America, he played with several municipal and military bands, including when on active duty in the Spanish-American War. He even served as bandmaster at Texas A & M College.

When not practicing with the band that year, Bill worked in the barber shop and reported on the shop's activities in *The Carlisle Arrow*. He and Kenneth King, James Garvie and Leon Boutwell spent Christmas at Lebanon, Pennsylvania, with Bandmaster Tyrrell, one assumes.

In February 1915, William contracted erysipelas and was quite sick for several days. Erysipelas, commonly called Saint Anthony's fire, is an acute disease of the skin and subcutaneous tissue caused by a species of hemolytic streptococcus and marked by localized inflammation and fever. For reasons unstated, the school was slow in informing his father of his illness. Superintendent Lipps seemed to be embarrassed by this oversight and wrote of Willie's condition to his father when he was well on the way to recovery.

That spring or summer, Winneshiek enrolled in the Carlisle Commercial College because his file includes correspondence in which he was requesting funds from his accounts at Carlisle and Tomah to be used to cover tuition costs for this school. He dropped out of the commercial school in the fall and withdrew from Carlisle Indian School on October 19, 1915 and relocated to Altoona, Pennsylvania. The next day, he wrote George Tyrrell:

> Struck everything pretty lucky but with one exception and so I am going to do me one favor. Orchestra and band work is easy and steady position is offered me with satisfactory salary. But I am without instrument. I have money in bank at the school and I have telegraphed home to my agent whereby he can make allowance for me so that I can get a slide trombone. Please take your bill and render it to the office and telegraph to Williamsport for the instrument. You can get the money alright if bill is made out against me. So make it out with a price of $80.00. Send telegraph soon as to results.

As the director of two bands, Tyrrell surely had contacts in the music business and would have known which store in Williamsport was involved in the transaction. Acting Superintendent J. D. DeHuff—Oscar Lipps must have been out of town—wrote L. M. Compton, Superintendent of Tomah Indian Industrial School:

> On Monday of last week William Winneshiek requested Superintendent Lipps to give him permission to leave Carlisle. As William had not shown the right attitude for some time, although he seemed to be doing satisfactory work in the Carlisle Commercial College, the desired permission to sever his connection with this school

was given him and he went to Altoona, Pennsylvania. Herewith is being enclosed a check in the amount of $296.89 which transfers to you the entire sum yet to the young man's credit in our School Bank.

His letter of a week later to J. D. DeHuff to clarify some details also provided some specifics regarding his activities: "I am doing fine and like my new life very well. I am employed by the Penna R. R. Co. and also under the Mishler Theater Co. here as an orchestra member."

So, Bill got the money to buy his trombone. But what exactly was his bad attitude?

A letter dated July 30, 1915 from the Acting Superintendent to William Winneshiek contains all the known information to support that claim:

> There seems to be no doubt that you are one of the boys who, on the evening of the twenty-seventh of this month, took a bee hive from the premises of Mr. Lackey, just beyond the Indian School oats field, and destroyed the contents in the oats field nearby.
>
> It is my intention to take from the bank account of each of you boys the sum of $3.00 to be turned over to Mr. Lackey in payment of damages which he suffered in the loss of this bee hive.

No records exist of Winneshiek participating in sports at Carlisle, but he must have played on the band's football team if nothing else. If that experience didn't qualify him to play semi-pro football for the Altoona Indians, that he was friends with many of the team's players and coaches may have. He mostly played center but did play a little at left end for Altoona 1915–17. It's doubtful that he was a starter given that Joe Bergie was also on that team.

William enrolled in the Lebanon Valley College Prep School in the fall of 1916 and—surprise—he played center and guard on the school football team. His yearbook entry unveiled things about him that weren't previously known:

> Bill, this smiling Indian entered Lebanon Valley this fall after graduating from Carlisle. He had a fine reputation, but Coach had to be shown so Bill decorated the center of the scrub line for the first few games. He showed such ability and aggression here that he was given a position on the varsity eleven, being used mostly as a utility man. He played both guard and center and both positions were filled most ably by the Red-Skin warrior. Bill was a cartoonist of note before he came to us and consequently left Lebanon Valley this Winter to pursue that line of work. L. V. wishes him well and regrets the loss of his services.

Although a utility player, Bill played enough to letter. One wonders how someone who didn't previously play football at the varsity level could slip so easily into a semi-pro or college varsity squad. Assuming that he played on the band team at Carlisle and knowing that some band members, including his friend Joel Wheelock played on the varsity, it is logical to assume that the band team was taught the Warner system. That knowledge would have prepared him to play for Lebanon Valley and Altoona—along with some talent.

William Winneshiek returned to Altoona. That is, if he ever really left, what with playing football there on Sundays. Like many others, he kept Carlisle abreast of his activities and spent Christmas Day there along with Joel Wheelock and Charles Pratt. While working for the Pennsylvania R. R., he learned some metallurgy and may have done some painting, as did at least one other Carlislian employed there.

The details of his life get murky after this. He was still living in Altoona when he registered for the WWI draft in 1917. About that time, he married Marie Marguerite Zerbe, a white elementary school teacher of about his age from Schaefferstown, Lebanon County, Pennsylvania. Their daughter, Doris Winona, was born on October 1, 1917 and their son, William Sherwood, was born on May 10, 1919. It isn't clear whether they set up housekeeping in Altoona or moved immediately to Lebanon to be closer to Marie's family. Regardless, they were living in Lebanon when Leon Boutwell came to visit in 1923.

A reasonable guess is that William became a full-time musician at his earliest opportunity. Tyrrell's Military Band continued to perform for at least two years after the founder's untimely death in 1917. In the early years of their marriage, band work may not have provided all the income the family needed. In the fall of 1922, Bill put on the moleskins again to line up alongside friends from Carlisle for an NFL club, the Oorang Indians of LaRue, Ohio. Pro football paid well, but he wasn't happy. Hazel Haynes, assistant postmistress at the post office where the players received their mail, described him thusly: "He was grouchy. He wasn't much of a mixer, but not the loner Hill was." He didn't have time to be grouchy long because that gig didn't last. However, he did get something for his troubles. The October 15, 1922 game against the Canton Bulldogs was, to quote *The Evening Standard* of Massillon, Ohio and they should know, "In one of the most bitterly fought professional games ever staged here, Canton's Bulldogs defeated Jim Thorpe's Indians of Marion, O., by a score of 14 to 0 ...." Fisticuffs and bloody faces were standard fare for the day, but Bill restrained himself from any rough stuff. After the game, Bulldogs and their supporters showed their appreciation by giving him the game ball and a gold watch. He was a crowd favorite after playing in Canton over the years, generally for Altoona.

William and Marie lived in Schaefferstown for a period and then moved to nearby Lebanon, Pennsylvania. He worked in the chemical lab at the Lebanon Steel Foundry and played in local bands and participated in other musical organizations, possibly in Joel Wheelock's band. At times he worked as a painter. He continued to be involved in athletics, transitioning from playing to coaching with some overlap of the two. He assisted or was head coach for Lebanon Valley College, the Reading Professionals, the Ephrata Green Jackets and Lebanon High School. The Winneshieks became rooted in the Lebanon community. Their children attended public schools and participated in extra-curricular activities alongside their Pennsylvania German neighbors. But then, they were half Pennsylvania German themselves through their mother. Bill sometimes even spoke to groups at local churches.

The September 5, 1933 edition of the *Lebanon Daily News* reported that Richard Byrd had selected Bill for his Second Antarctic Expedition at the suggestion of Columbia University. "Winneshiek's qualities, achievements and ideals made him one of the first and most eagerly welcomed selections...[His] hobby and life work is his Boy Scout activities." Perhaps his Scout work was the reason he was chosen. Relatives remember clearly his involvement with the scouts. Budgetary constraints that required the participants on the Antarctic Expedition to forego pay for the trip might have made it impossible for a family man to participate at the height of the Great Depression. It is not clear that he actually went.

At some point, his musical talent caught the attention of a traveling show. He reputedly played with Rudy Vallee's orchestra. Somewhere along the way, he formed Chief Winneshiek's All-Indian Band and traveled around the U. S. and Canada. So acclaimed was the band that Conn Band Instrument Company included a photo of the band and a testimonial on their advertising literature along with a quotation:

> Chief W. P. Winneshiek's All-Indian Band is indeed a unique institution since it is headed by a real chief and

Conn Instruments flyer featuring Winneshiek's Band
Cumberland County Historical Society, Carlisle, PA

is composed exclusively of American Indians who appear in native costumes. On tour throughout the United States and Canada they have attracted much attention for their fine performances. Chief Winneshiek, who is shown at the right above, writes January 13, 1936: "Our band is 100% Conn. They give satisfaction always."

In late 1936 when in Philadelphia, Winneshiek visited Hugh Miller, former press agent for the Carlisle Indian School, and wrote him after the visit:

> I came to Carlisle purposely to visit the "Old School Grounds" as well as to call on the Hundreds of Remaining White Friends.
> Mr. Miller, I know that you are one of the few White men living that will realize fully the great injustice that was brought upon the Indian Race when Our Great Democratic Government decided to: "Take Away From The Redman The Last Remaining Treasure (Carlisle Indian School) He Had in U. S. A."
> Buildings had been burned down; complete destruction of the tall smokestack, which once answered the purpose of a monument; the Campus, which was once the pride of all who saw it for it was kept always in its natural beauty by the Indian students had faded into an unkept meadow; Our school mates who had been called by the Great Spirit and laid at rest near the Athletic Field, had been disturbed and moved to a more lonelier spot by the soldiers who now inhabit the Grounds where the American Indian made his last stand. No Government, no Race of People could have been more Cruel, No Christians, whether they be White, Yellow, Brown, Black or Red, could forget Providence long enough to commit that one last barbarous act as when Carlisle Indian School was taken from the Red Man. The saddest thing that has yet befallen the Indian.

I simply could not stand the pangs of torture at sight of what remained of Old Carlisle. I departed from there as quick as I could.

I suppose that the politicians were responsible for the abolishment of Carlisle as an Institution of Learning for Indians will go down in our American History as: "An Act For The Good Of Humanity" or "An Act Willed By Providence." Whatever be the cause for the abolishment of Carlisle and voicing my sentiment: I have lost faith in the White Man's ideals of American Democracy & Christianity. I shall remain forever—An American Indian.

In 1939, the year after Marie died, possibly after contracting a disease from the rabbits she kept, he remarried. A newspaper article announcing the upcoming wedding stated that Chief Winneshiek, best man Rolling Thunder, and the rest of the wedding party would be wearing Indian regalia for the

Joseph Poodry, William Winneshiek & Joel Wheelock reliving old times *Cumberland County Historical Society, Carlisle, PA*

Lutheran service. He and his new bride, Estella E. Winters, formerly of Reading, Pennsylvania, were to set up housekeeping in Hartford, Connecticut, the site of the wedding. That site was selected because it was the location of the headquarters of the National American Indian Defense Committee, of which Rolling Thunder was president and Winneshiek was connected. Little is known about Winneshiek's life after that. He reputedly died in a fire in Elkton, Maryland in 1951. Responsibility for his burial fell onto his daughter, Doris, due to his being estranged from his son. Making her task more difficult was that the local cemeteries were unwilling to accept Indians.

His son, William Sherman Winneshiek, was commissioned as a 2nd Lieutenant in the United States Army Air Force in 1942. He flew 42 combat missions in a B-17 from England to Germany and made the Air Force his career from which he retired in 1971. Col. Winneshiek died in 1995. His grandson, William S. Winneshiek II, maintains a web site on the family.

Winneshiek's Band at J. Riley Crippled
Children's Hospital, Indianapolis, IN
Cumberland County Historical Society, Carlisle, PA

Appendices

Carlisle Indians Inducted into the College Football Hall of Fame

Player*	Position	Year Inducted
Albert Exendine	End	1970
Joe Guyon	Halfback/Tackle	1971
James Johnson	Quarterback	1969
Ed Rogers	End	1968
Jim Thorpe	Halfback	1951†
Gus Welch	Quarterback	1975
Glenn S. "Pop" Warner	Coach	1951†
Lone Star Dietz	Coach	2012

Carlisle Indians Inducted into the Professional Football Hall of Fame

Player	Position	Year Inducted
Jim Thorpe	Halfback	1963†
Joe Guyon	Halfback	1966

Carlisle Indians inducted into Citizens Savings (originally Helms) Athletic Foundation Hall of Fame

Player	Position	Year Inducted
Jim Thorpe	Halfback	1950†
Glenn S. Pop" Warner	Coach	1951
Lone Star Dietz	Coach	1976

†Charter member.

Bibliography

Benjey, T. (2006). *Keep A-goin': the life of Lone Star Dietz.* Tuxedo Press, Carlisle, Pennsylvania.

Braunwart, B. and Carroll, B. (1997). *The Journey to Camp: the origins of American football.* P. F. R. A., Huntingdon, Pennsylvania.

Bynum, M. (1993). *Pop Warner Football's Greatest Teacher: the epic autobiography of major college football's winningest coach, Glenn S. (Pop) Warner.* Football Gridiron Properties Corp..

Carroll, B. (1990). *The Tigers Roar: professional football in Ohio: 1903-1909.* P. F. R. A., Huntingdon, Pennsylvania.

Carroll, B. and Braunwart, B. (1991). *Pro Football: From AAA to '03: the origin and development of professional football in Western Pennsylvania, 1890-1903.* P. F. R. A., Huntingdon, Pennsylvania.

Carroll, B. and Gill, B. (1991). *Bulldogs on Sunday 1919: twilight of the Ohio League.* P. F. R. A., Huntingdon, Pennsylvania.

Carroll, B. and Research, P. (1997). *The Ohio League: 1910-1919.* P. F. R. A., Huntingdon, Pennsylvania.

Curran, B. (1964). *Pro Football's Rag Days.* Bonanza Books, New York.

Danzig, A. (1971). *Oh, How They Played the Game: the early days of football and the heroes who made it great.* The Macmillan Company, New York.

Finoli, D. and Aikens, T. (2004). *The Birthplace of Professional Football: Southwestern Pennsylvania.* Arcadia Publishing, Charleston, South Carolina.

Fry, R. B. (1989). *The Crimson and the Gray: 100 years with the WSU Cougars.* Washington State University Press, Pullman.

Gridley, M. E. (1936). *Indians of Today.* Lakeside Press, Crawfordsville, Indiana.

Gridley, M. E. (1947). *Indians of Today.* Millar Publishing Company, Chicago.

Gridley, M. E. (1960). *Indians of Today. 3rd ed.* Towertown Press, Chicago.

Groshans, L. (1981). *The Complete Borzoi.* Howell Book House, New York.

Lester, R. (1995). *Stagg's University: the rise, decline, and fall of big-time football at Chicago.* University of Illinois Press, Urbana and Chicago.

McCallum, J. D. and Pearson, C. H. (1971). *College Football U. S. A. 1869-1971: official book of the National Football Foundation*. Hall of Fame Publishing, Inc., Greenwich, Connecticut.

McClellan, K. (1998). *The Sunday Game: at the dawn of professional football*. The University of Akron Press, Akron.

Newcomb, J. (1975). *The Best of the Athletic Boys: the white man's impact on Jim Thorpe*. Doubleday & Company, Garden City.

Ohio, S. o. (1926). *The Official Roster of Ohio Soldiers, Sailors and Marines in the World War 1917-1918*. The F. J. Herr Printing Co., Columbus.

Oriard, M..*King Football: sport & spectacle in the golden age of radio & newsreels, movies & magazines, the weekly & the daily press*.Chapel Hill.

Pratt, R. H. (1964). *Battlefield and Classroom: four decades with the American Indian, 1867-1904*. Yale University Press, New Haven & London.

Samuelsen, R. (1951). *The Rose Bowl Game*. Doubleday & Company, Garden City.

Smith, R. A. (1988). *Sports and Freedom: the rise of big-time college athletics*. Oxford Press, New York.

Steckbeck, J. S. (1951). *Fabulous Redmen: the Carlisle Indians and their famous football teams*. J. Horace McFarland Company, Harrisburg, Pennsylvania.

Thisted, M. N. (1982). *Pershing's Pioneer Infantry of World War I*. Alphabet Printers, Hemet, California.

U. S. Army, S. S. (1931). *Order of Battle of the United States Land Forces in the World War (1917-19): Zone of the Interior*. U. S. Government Printing Office, Washington.

Warner, G. S. (1912). *A Course in Football for Players and Coaches*. Warner, Carlisle, Pennsylvania.

Warner, G. S. (1927). *Football for Coaches and Players*. Warner, Stanford University.

Weyand, A. M. (1955). *The Saga of American Football*. The Macmillan Company, New York.

Wheeler, R. W. (1975). *Jim Thorpe: world's greatest athlete*. University of Oklahoma Press, Norman.

Whitman, R. L. (1984). *Jim Thorpe and the Oorang Indians: N. F. L.'s most colorful franchise*. The Marion County Historical Society, Defiance, Ohio.

Whittingham, R. (1987). *Sunday Mayhem: a celebration of pro football in America*. Taylor Publishing Company, Dallas.

Witmer, L. F. (1993). *The Indian Industrial School: Carlisle, Pennsylvania 1879-1918*. Cumberland County Historical Society, Carlisle, Pennsylvania.

Becker, C. M. (2003). Jim Thorpe and the Oorang Tribe. *Timeline*, 20(5):2-17.

Braunwart, B. (1981). Going to the Dogs. *The Coffin Corner*, 3.

Prescott, A. (1990). Time Tunnel. *College Football Historical Society Newsletter*, 3(3):11-12.

Scott, H. (1972). The Oklahoma Athletic Hall of Fame. *Oklahoma Today*, 22(2):13-17.

Shoemaker, A. (1967). Hominy Indians. *Oklahoma Today*, 17(4):7-9.

Ephemera

Minnesota, University of, Souvenir Program, *Minnesota vs. Wisconsin*, November 15, 1902.

Minnesota, University of, *Dedication of Northrop Field*, September 19, 1903.

Minnesota, University of, Souvenir Program, *Michigan vs. Minnesota*, October 31, 1903.

Southern Methodist University, *Texas Aggies –6 vs. S. M. U. –17 Official Program*, November 11, 1922.

Carlisle Indian Industrial School Publications

The Indian Helper, weekly newspaper, 1985-1900.

The Red Man, weekly magazine, 1988-1900.

The Red Man and Helper, weekly combined newspaper and magazine, 1900-1904.

The Arrow, weekly newspaper, 1904-1908.

The Carlisle Arrow, weekly magazine, 1908-1917.

The Indian Craftsman, monthly literary journal, 1909-1910.

The Red Man, monthly literary journal, 1910-1917.

The Carlisle Arrow and Red Man, monthly combined newspaper and magazine, 1917-1918.

Other Schools' Publications

Alumni Record. Dickinson College, Carlisle, Pennsylvania.
Anadarko Yearbook. Anadarko High School, Anadarko, Oklahoma.
Aucola, American University, Washington, DC.
The Badger, University of Wisconsin, Madison, Wisconsin.
Bizarre, Lebanon Valley College, Annville, Pennsylvania.
The Calendar, Hutchinson Central High School, Buffalo, New York.
Catalog, Dickinson College, Carlisle, Pennsylvania.
The Dickinsonian, Dickinson College, Carlisle, Pennsylvania.
College News, Lebanon Valley College, Annville, Pennsylvania.
The Evergreen, Washington State University, Pullman, Washington.
The Franklin and Marshall Weekly, Franklin and Marshall College, Lancaster, Pennsylvania.
Georgetown College Journal, Georgetown University, Washington, DC.
HailtoPurple.com, Northwestern University, Evanston, Illinois.
The Hoya, Georgetown University, Washington, DC.
The Indiana Daily Student, Indiana University, Bloomington, Indiana.
Instano, Indiana University of Pennsylvania, Indiana, Pennsylvania.
The Microcosm, Dickinson College, Carlisle, Pennsylvania.
Murmurmonte, West Virginia Wesleyan College, Buckhannon, West Virginia.
The Pharos, West Virginia Wesleyan College, Buckhannon, West Virginia.
Oriflamme, Franklin and Marshall College, Lancaster, Pennsylvania.
The Pow Wow, Washington State University, Pullman, Washington.
The Quittapahilla, Lebanon Valley College, Annville, Pennsylvania.
The Sophist, Indiana University of Pennsylvania, Indiana, Pennsylvania.
Ye Doomesday Booke, Georgetown University, Washington, DC.
The Rotunda, Southern Methodist University, Dallas, Texas.
The Tiger, Clemson University, Clemson, South Carolina.
Taps, Clemson University, Clemson, South Carolina.

Index

a

Altoona Indians   44, 52, 63, 209, 239, 278, 313, 314
Arcasa, Alex   22, 52, 246, 275
Archiquette, Chauncey   5, 86–101, 112
Archiquette, Rhoda Sweeney   101
Armstrong, Samuel   8

b

Baird, Phoebe   206–210
Balenti, Mike   50, 167
Beaver, Frank   16
Bender, Albert "Chief"   51, 76
Bergie, Joseph   52, 313
Bird, Sampson   235, 247, 274
Black, Jeanette, see also St. Germain, Thomas   215, 216
Blumenthal, Mose   17, 27, 30, 42, 180
Bohler, J. Fred "Doc"   259, 262
Boutwell, Leon   64, 65, 67, 69, 311, 315
Bowen, Nicholas   16, 181
Broker, Fred   65, 250
Broker, Henry   65, 250, 252
Busch, Elmer   64, 65, 69, 250

c

Calac, Pete   29, 34, 54, 56, 57, 61, 63–68, 84, 248, 250, 257
Camp, Walter   12, 15, 17, 21, 22, 40, 41, 78, 177–182, 284–287, 297, 300

Carter, Charles David   263
Carter, Julia   263
Cayou, Frank   12, 28, 31, 50, 200, 204, 221, 282
Charles, Wilson   16, 28, 100, 102–115, 119, 125, 180, 181, 301
Charles, Wilson "Buster"   115
Clark, Asa "Ace"   42, 149
Cornelius, Joel   16, 105, 119, 226
Curtis, Charles   37
Cusack, Jack   51–55, 61, 254

d

Daniel, Susan G.   102
DeCora, Angel   27, 28, 145–148, 156, 193
Denny, Wallace   5, 26, 104–106, 112, 116–143, 180, 231
Dickson, Charles H.   191
Dietz, William H. Lone Star   2, 5, 22, 24, 28, 31–33, 37, 61, 84, 144–163, 193, 196, 244, 258–265
Dillon, Charles   16, 17, 124, 180, 181, 285
Dobie, "Gloomy" Gil   151, 155
Downwind, Xavier   65
Drexel, Mother Catherine   249

e

Eichenlaub, Ray "Iron Eich"   251
Exendine, Albert   16, 28, 31, 32,

79, 80, 84, 122, 181, 259, 289, 290, 293, 295, 301

f
Farnum, Mark 154
Flanders, Carl 121
Flores, Louis 181
Francis, John 35, 36, 137, 254, 256, 257
Friedman, Moses 4, 22, 25–28, 38, 135, 136, 186, 191, 195, 208, 213, 214, 220, 228–231, 237, 238, 249

g
Gardner, William 28, 52, 53, 61, 80, 84, 112
Garlow, William 28, 54, 61, 132
Garvie, James 279, 280, 309–311
Goesback, Bruce 248
Guyon, Charles, aka Wahoo 28, 30, 31, 38, 87, 97, 100
Guyon, Joe 3, 35, 50, 54–57, 60, 61, 63–69, 84, 237, 238, 248

h
Halas, George 56, 58, 60, 156, 160
Hampton Institute 7, 87
Hankey, Nina 232
Harsh, Phoebe 173
Haskell Institute 18, 35, 37, 65, 89–97, 103, 109, 113, 115, 167, 254, 265
Hauser, Emil, aka Wauseka 28, 79, 84, 96, 212, 288
Hauser, Pete 28, 68, 80, 84, 96, 101, 212, 273
Haynes, Hazel 216

Hendricks, Fritz 28, 79, 109, 110, 181
Hominy Indians 68, 101
Hudson, Frank 19–21, 31, 78, 84, 207, 221, 282, 284

i
Island, Louis 164–174

j
Jamison, Jake 12
Johnson, James 5, 16, 17, 28, 50, 79, 84, 106, 119, 175, 181–188, 207, 231, 285–297
Jordan, Peter 236, 252
Jude, Frank 181

k
Kelley, Victor M. 31–34, 152, 252, 253
Kerr, Andy 141
Kinney, Ralph 19, 97
Knudsen, Elizabeth 110, 111, 114, 125

l
LaFlesch, Rosa B. 26
Large, Roy 193
La Roque, Paul 108, 109
Lassaw, Nick, aka Long Time Sleep 64, 65, 67, 69
Lassaw, Nick Mrs. 69
Lebanon Valley College 169, 276–279, 310, 313, 314
Levi, John 68
Libby, Archie 108
Lingo, Walter 63–68
Lipps, Oscar 27, 30, 34, 42, 139, 215, 251–253, 277, 311, 312
Lone Star, Frank 162, 189–196

Lone Star, John *189, 190, 192,* 196
Lone Wolf, Delos *200, 204*
Longstreth, Mary *8*
Longstreth, Susan *8, 9, 110, 137, 212, 270*
Lubo, Antonio *16, 28, 79, 84, 181, 289–297, 299, 301*
Lyon, Isaac *37*

m

Mare Island Marines *156–157, 258, 260*
Marshall, George Preston *160*
Martin, E. L. *27, 28*
Mathews, Walter *16, 181*
McClellan, Keith *44, 53, 257*
Mercer, William A. *4, 9, 18, 21, 22, 38, 78, 112, 136, 184, 186, 190, 191, 228*
Metoxen, Emily Doxtator King *210*
Metoxen, Jonas *84, 101, 197–210, 221*
Miller, Artie *46, 207*
Miller, Hugh *27, 28, 318*
Miller, Iva *133, 248*
Moran, Charles *137*
Mt. Pleasant, Frank *21, 22, 28, 31, 44, 50, 79, 84, 99, 106, 112, 119, 120, 166, 167, 180, 244*

n

Naismith, James *91, 99*
Newashe, William *169, 274, 275*
Nori, Siceni *19, 27, 100, 186, 223*

o

Oorang Indians *57, 63–68, 101, 216, 315*
Outland, John *90, 91*

p

Peairs, Hervey B. *35, 254*
Phillips, James *16, 178, 182, 299*
Pierce, Bemus *18–21, 28, 31, 45–47, 64, 69, 77, 78, 84, 97, 109, 121, 183, 199, 200, 202, 221, 282*
Pierce, Hawley *46, 47, 77, 84, 109, 200, 207, 221, 285*
Platt, Joel *162*
Pollard, Fritz *33, 152–154*
Porter, Scott, aka Little Boy *21, 79, 84, 97*
Pottlitzer, Doris, O. *159*
Pratt, Richard Henry *1, 4, 7–18, 26, 38, 42, 73, 75, 77, 127, 129, 131, 133, 136, 137, 140, 224, 292*

r

Robertson, Nellie *124–142, 231*
Rockne, Knute *53, 57*
Rogers, Edward *18, 38, 50, 84, 108–109, 207, 221, 285*
Rose Bowl *42, 149, 155, 156, 161, 258, 260*
Roy, Charles *87*
Russeau, John aka Roussian, Russian *83*

s

Saunooke, Stilwell *52, 64, 65, 69*
Schmidt, Ray *159*
Schouchuk, Nikifer *16, 181, 291*
Schoulder, Joseph *28, 207*
Sells, Cato *24–27, 32, 139*

Index 329

Seneca, Isaac   16, 46, 84, 200, 207
Sheldon, Arthur   16, 108, 109, 181, 301
Sherman Institute   183, 301, 302
Sickles, Caleb   5, 38, 176, 207, 218–233
Smith, Ed   28, 207
Stagg, Amos Alonzo   21, 31, 41, 57, 80
Stauffer, Claude M.   27, 310
Steckbeck, John S.   1, 20, 24, 148, 221
St. Germain, Thomas   28, 50, 64, 65, 69, 211–217

t

Teachnor, Mabel   227, 231
Thompson, W. G.   207
Thorpe, Jim   2–3, 21–23, 37, 38, 43–61, 63–68, 79, 84, 97, 115, 132, 142, 159, 235, 237, 245, 248, 249, 256, 257, 262, 264, 267, 268, 274, 276
Tyrrell, George F.   277, 310–312, 315

v

Vedernack, George   52, 234–240
Venne, Alfred   99, 105, 110

w

Wardecker, Fred   17, 27
War Eagle   30
Warner, Glenn S. "Pop"   2–3, 15, 16–38, 42–50, 70–85, 89, 98, 105, 117, 119, 121, 125, 137–143, 145, 148–149, 159, 160, 162, 177, 181–183, 185, 205, 207, 223, 235, 244–246, 249, 250, 252, 258, 284, 287–297, 299–301
Washington State College   42, 148–157, 161, 258–263
Webster, Lena   271, 288
Welch, Florence   184, 186
Welch, Gus   5, 22, 26–29, 44, 54, 84, 159, 162, 196, 237, 242–268, 275
Weyand, Alexander M.   78
Wheeler, Robert W.   97, 324
Wheelock, Dennison   14, 103, 113, 129, 269–271, 281, 285
Wheelock, Hugh   52, 269–280, 309
Wheelock, James   103, 221, 258, 269, 270
Wheelock, Joel   35, 52, 269–280, 309, 310, 316
Wheelock, Martin   15, 84, 177, 199, 207, 221, 270, 271, 281–297, 299, 300
Whitecloud, see also St. Germain   211–217
White, William   16, 181
Whitman, Robert L.   69
Wilkins, Janet, see also St. Germain, Thomas   69, 216, 217
Williams, Charles   16, 181, 289, 295, 296, 298–303
Winneshiek, Estella E. Winters   320
Winneshiek, Marie Marguerite Zerbe   314, 315, 319
Winneshiek, William   5, 35, 52, 64, 65, 69, 280, 304–321
Woodruff, George   19, 97

Other Books by Tom Benjey

Keep A-goin': the life of Lone Star Dietz
Biography of football's most colorful coach—ever. Dietz is as controversial 40 years after his death as when alive.
ISBN 978-0-9774486-0-9 softcover
ISBN 978-0-9774486-1-6 hardback

Doctors, Lawyers, Indian Chiefs: Jim Thorpe & Pop Warner's Carlisle Indian School football immortals tackle socialites, bootleggers, students, moguls, prejudice, the government, ghouls, tooth decay and rum
Learn who was one of Eliot Ness's Untouchables. Find out whose life story served as the basis for the William C. DeMille play, *Strongheart*, which was adapted into a movie by D. W. Griffith and later remade as *Braveheart* by Cecil B. DeMille. Discover who had a school named in his honor and wonder why these men are no longer famous.

ISBN 978-0-9774486-7-8 softcover

Oklahoma's Carlisle Indian School Immortals
Other than for Jim Thorpe and Pop Warner, the accomplishments of the Carlisle Indian School football teams are largely forgotten. Although these teams were legendary in their own time, they are now virtually unknown except to the most ardent football historians. Their contributions to the game were substantial and deserve to be remembered. Seven Carlisle Indians are in the College Football Hall of Fame (not bad for a program that played its last game in 1917) and helped get Pop Warner, their coach, inducted.
ISBN 978-0-9774486-8-5 hardback
ISBN 978-1-936161-20-1 softcover

Gridiron Gypsies: How the Carlisle Indians Shaped Modern Football
After pleading with Superintendent Pratt to be allowed to play football against other schools, the small complement of students old enough competed against college men from coast to coast. Some had never seen a real football before and most were learning English. Located in a small town in Southcentral Pennsylvania, they traveled considerable distances to play all their important games on the road, but still won most of them. Learn why the Carlisle Indians are still talked about today.
ISBN 978-1-936161-06-5 softcover

www.ingramcontent.com/pod-product-compliance
Lightning Source LLC
Chambersburg PA
CBHW030303080526
44584CB00012B/422